Sachar Paulus
Norbert Pohlmann
Helmut Reimer

Securing Electronic Business Processes

T0233035

vieweg-it

www.vieweg-it.de

Sachar Paulus
Norbert Pohlmann
Helmut Reimer

Securing Electronic Business Processes

Highlights of the Information Security Solutions Europe 2003 Conference

vieweg

Bibliographic information published by Die Deutsche Bibliothek
Die Deutsche Bibliothek lists this publication in the Deutsche Nationalbibliographie;
detailed bibliographic data is available in the Internet at <http://dnb.ddb.de>.

Many of designations used by manufacturers and sellers to distinguish their
products are claimed as trademarks.

1st edition January 2004

Vieweg is a company of Springer Science+Business Media.
www.vieweg.de

Cover design: Ulrike Weigel, www.CorporateDesignGroup.de
Printing and binding: Lengericher Handelsdruckerei, Lengerich
Printed on acid-free paper.
Printed in Germany

ISBN 3-528-05887-0

Preface

The Information Security Solutions Europe Conference (ISSE) was started in 1999 by EEMA and TeleTrusT with the support of the European Commission and the German Federal Ministry of Technology and Economics. Today the annual conference is a fixed event in every IT security professional's calendar. The aim of ISSE is to support the development of a European information security culture and especially a cross-border framework for trustworthy IT applications for citizens, industry and administration. Therefore, it is important to take into consideration both international developments and European regulations and to allow for the interdisciplinary character of the information security field. In the five years of its existence ISSE has thus helped shape the profile of this specialist area.

The integration of security in IT applications was initially driven only by the actual security issues considered important by experts in the field; currently, however, the economic aspects of the corresponding solutions are the most important factor in deciding their success. ISSE offers a suitable podium for the discussion of the relationship between these considerations and for the presentation of the practical implementation of concepts with their technical, organisational and economic parameters.

An international programme committee is responsible for the selection of the conference contributions and the composition of the programme:

- Jan Bartelen, ABN AMRO (The Netherlands)
- Ronny Bjones, Microsoft (Belgium)
- Alfred Buellesbach, DaimlerChrysler (Germany)
- Simon Corell, Corell Consulting (Sweden)
- Marijke De Soete, Mastercard (Belgium)
- Danny de Temmermann, CEC DG INFSO
- Jos Dumortier, KU Leuven (Belgium)
- John Hermans, KPMG (Netherlands)
- Jeremy Hilton, EEMA (UK)
- Dave Hobart, EEMA (UK)
- Patrick Horster, University of Klagenfurt (Austria)
- Dimitris Karagiannis, University of Vienna (Austria)
- Matt Landrock, Cryptomathic (Denmark)
- Gabriel Neagu, National Institute for R&D in Informatics - I.C.I. (Romania)
- Karel Neuwirt, The Office for Personal Data Protection (Czech Republic)
- Sachar Paulus, SAP (Germany)
- Norbert Pohlmann, University of Applied Sciences Gelsenkirchen/TeleTrusT (Germany)
- Reinhard Posch, TU Graz, (Austria)
- Bart Preneel, KU Leuven (Belgium)
- Helmut Reimer, TeleTrusT (Germany)
- Paolo Rossini, TELSY, Telecom Italia Group (Italy)
- Ulrich Sandl, BMWA (Germany)
- Wolfgang Schneider, Fraunhofer Institute SIT (Germany)
- Robert Temple, BT (United Kingdom)

Many of the presentations at the conference are of use as reference material for the future, hence this publication. The contributions are based on the presentations of the authors and thus not only document the key issues of the conference but make this information accessible for further interested parties.

The editors have endeavoured to allocate the contributions in these proceedings – which differ from the structure of the conference programme – to topic areas which cover the interests of the readers.

Sachar Paulus   *Norbert Pohlmann*   *Helmut Reimer*

EEMA (www.eema.org):

For 16 years, EEMA has been Europe's leading independent, non-profit e-Business association, working with its European members, governmental bodies, standards organisations and e-Business initiatives throughout Europe to further e-Business technology and legislation.

EEMA's remit is to educate and inform around 200 Member organisations on the latest developments and technologies, at the same time enabling Members of the association to compare views and ideas. The work produced by the association with its Members (projects, papers, seminars, tutorials and re-ports etc) is funded by both membership subscriptions and revenue generated through fee-paying events. All of the information generated by EEMA and its Members is available to other members free of charge.

Examples of papers produced in recent months are:- Role Based Access Control – a User's Guide, Wireless Deployment Guidelines, Secure e-Mail within the Organisation, The impact of XML on existing Business Processes, PKI Usage within User Organisations. EEMA Members, based on a requirement from the rest of the Membership, contributed all of these papers. Some are the result of many months' work, and form part of a larger project on the subject.

TeleTrusT (www.teletrust.de):

TeleTrusT was founded in 1989 to promote the security of information and communication technology in an open systems environment.

The non-profit organization was constituted with the aim of:

- achieving acceptance of the digital signature as an instrument conferring legal validity on electronic transactions;
- supporting research into methods of safeguarding electronic data interchange (EDI), application of its results, and development of standards in this field;
- collaborating with institutes and organizations in other countries with the aim of harmonizing objectives and standards within the European Union.

TeleTrusT supports the incorporation of trusted services in planned or existing IT applications of public administration, organisations and industry. Special attention is being paid to secure services and their management for trustworthy electronic communication.

Table of Contents

Strategy

Technology

Application

Practice

Strategy

A Quantitative Decision Support Model for Security and Business Continuity Management

Rolf von Roessing

Ernst & Young Austria
rolf.von-roessing@at.ey.com, rvr@scmltd.com

Abstract

Risks and the business impact of a critical event are often difficult to quantify. In many cases, the strategic decisions with regard to mitigating risk and minimising financial damage must be taken on the basis of qualitative estimates and expert opinion. However, formulating a continuity and security strategy requires quantitative support across several dimensions: temporal, financial and systemic thresholds must be defined to ensure the optimum level of investment. The paper outlines a strategic decision support model for quantifying risk and business impact. It is further shown how the resulting risk management decisions of the firm can be optimised, and how typical problems of event (disaster) frequency and severity can be resolved. The paper builds on earlier research in audit, insurance and business continuity management to present an innovative approach towards this well-known problem.

1 Introduction

Modern information security and business continuity significantly depend upon an initial risk and business impact assessment. Adverse events as well as critical situations represent risks to an organisation, and they strongly influence the subsequent investment decision in security, disaster recovery, emergency planning and business continuity programmes. The term "risk" as such has been subject to various definitions, often including the notion of "event" and "consequence" as well as risk in the proper sense of the word. Traditional risk analysis and evaluation relies on quantitative and qualitative methods. While the former attempt a reasonable degree of quantitative accuracy by including probabilistic estimates and frequency distributions, the latter seek to leverage the experience of experts and other subjective input to form an overall picture of the risks identified in the process. Existing business impact assessment techniques, on the other hand, are a means of estimating the damage resulting from the fact that one or more risks have materialised, causing some sort of disruption to the organisation.

Traditional literature on risk appears to be preoccupied with managing risk rather than analysing it, usually in a portfolio-type approach. The insurance perspective on risk [Brüh94, Dohe00, GaGM97, Poll01] – one specific risk is shared among many entities – is less useful for the organisation or company having to identify and analyse risks to its own assets and processes, quite simply because the existing risks cannot be "shared" across many business entities, in a manner often suggested by risk management models [Imbo83, Roes01]. Indeed, the managerial aspect of reducing or transferring risk may not be valid if no clear data exists on how frequent the risk-related events are and what their significance is to the organisation or company being reviewed. Similarly, formalised risk transfer may fail [Lind86] where the entity transferring (company, government or other) is perceived as having ultimate responsibility for an event and its consequences [UK02]. This is often the case where stakeholders or the public at large focus on international companies or governments in terms of moral obligation and reputational damage [SmIr84].

Business impact, on the other hand, is seen as an ex post tool that determines the actual damage caused by an adverse event or disruption. While it can be used in an ex ante sense, it is rarely implemented to serve its original purpose: forward-looking risk management.

Both risks and business impacts impinge on investment strategy and budgeting [Neub89, Schl98, YoKo01], inasmuch as they influence resource allocation to certain risk reduction or impact reduction measures. Given that the financial resources available are limited, risk reduction and impact reduction form part of the strategic planning process within the organisation. In this sense, they can no longer be seen as low-priority projects that are implemented by choice rather than necessity: if a risk emerges as a going concern issue, meaning that it may threaten the existence of the company as a whole, its immediate reduction, transfer or elimination is in the interest of the firm and therefore essential. Recent developments suggest that the notion of good corporate governance [CodG02, CodÖ02] includes the ongoing analysis of such risks and business impacts that may endanger the company [WoRu00] or its sound financial background and viability. Furthermore, the discussion of "operational risk" [BIS03, BIS03b, DEGK01, EmKS02] has broadened the perspective on risk in general and given specific examples of what may constitute a risk to day-to-day business, at least in the financial sector. Regulatory pressure and formalisation of "risk" as a technical term are therefore progressing, and any current and future analytical or empirical models will have to consider the new, wider sphere of business risk instead of restricting themselves to the field of information technology.

2 Problems

2.1 Risk, Events, Consequences

Both risk evaluation and business impact assessment are subject to known problems that are, at first sight, difficult to resolve. The initial problem arises from the technical term "risk" as such, as this is often erroneously interpreted as "event" or "consequence". The term as used in this paper denotes the probability of something (an event) happening, regardless of the immediate consequences. A risk manifests itself as an event, and the immediate consequences of this event will determine the impact. Again, the word "risk" often encompasses the notion of adverse consequences and negative impacts. Conversely, the word "opportunity" will be used where the very same event will lead to positive consequences as perceived by the firm. Practically speaking, an event is often experienced as a risk by one or more firms, whereas other companies (their competitors) make the most of it by turning the event into an opportunity.

"Risk" is therefore often used subjectively and as a collective term that includes:

- the (estimated) probability of an event happening
- the fact that this event will have negative consequences for the firm
- the fact that there is a causal relationship between event and impact

This empirical use of the term appears impractical. It requires a more differentiated and more objective treatment prior to applying formal methods to it. It will be shown that reversing the deductive chain of "risk – event – consequence" yields a more objective and impartial basis for quantification when seen from within the company.

2.2 High-Impact, Low-Frequency Events

When analysing extraneous events and their likelihood in a quantitative manner, the typical "high impact, low frequency" (HILF) events often encountered in real life are difficult to predict in the absence of meaningful statistics. However, it is the HILF event – a scenario of widespread disruption, catastrophic events, and massive damage to the environment – that is invoked much more often than the smaller event, due to psychological reasons [Linn01]. Likewise, a constant trickle of small but costly events is seen as less threatening than a single HILF event [KaTv79].

Hence, techniques have been developed to estimate rather than calculate such risks. However, this inevitably reduces the accuracy of the end result, and it has become popular wisdom that, since some events cannot be anticipated, the quantitative risk analysis approach in itself is rejected for corporate use. It has also been argued that an event that may occur once in a hundred years cannot be considered within the scope of "normal" risk analysis due to cost restrictions and the overall level of plausibility. Hence, the qualitative approach towards risk identification and evaluation has been favoured both in literature and corporate management [Krei97, Küpp97, Pepe94].

This subjective approach pre-empts reality by excluding a whole class of events, although they might still happen at any moment in time, albeit with a limited probability. It is nevertheless characteristic of current management practices that risks and impacts will be "defined out" of the model when they appear to be unmanageable. In other words: if you cannot swim, you will deny the existence of water in order not to be too scared. The "bounded rationality" problem has been known at least since 1957 [Simo57], and has received extensive theoretical attention since then [Turn76]. In order to define the problem for the purposes of this paper, it is subdivided into the following steps or stages:

- Adverse events of a HILF nature exist; by definition, these events are big or damaging enough to potentially endanger the existence of the business, but their probability is low

- Low probability is conducive to "taking a gamble"

- High impact (often catastrophic) induces simplification and "bounded rationality"

- Risk analysis and management activities are restricted to manageable risks

- Correlated HILF events are ignored

- Reality is – in the final stages of this process – adapted to the wishes and prerogatives of senior corporate management: risk-related thinking is subject to "tunnel view" narrowing

Conversely, if HILF events are being recognised as inevitable, their likelihood and the consequences for organisations or firms are often misunderstood. As a result of limited empirical data, high-impact events rarely lend themselves to quantitative analysis. Hence, qualitative estimates are applied to such events, and subjective perception of an event will often dictate its subsequent managerial treatment. An extreme example is the round table discussion where events will be considered qualitatively and as a function of hierarchy: the most important risks are those that the CEO is most afraid of. While this is a deliberately controversial example, it nevertheless demonstrates the fallacies of subjective (qualitative) risk analysis [BaCo96, Neub89]. Qualitative assessments have been further challenged on grounds of misperception [Renn01, Renn84, SBCC00]: regardless of experience, it is likely that people will overestimate the impact and severity of HILF events whilst underestimating high-frequency, low-impact events such as day-to-day accidents.

Both empirically and theoretically, risk analysis has suffered from the fact that in the absence of sufficient amounts of quantitative data, the estimation of probabilities is, at best, educated guesswork. From the corporate point of view, the quantification of HILF events, or indeed any extraneous event, remains a hazy area that cannot be approached in practice. The (very few) publications addressing risk analysis under conditions of sparse data, for instance on extreme value theory (EVT) [EmRS98, Embr99] do not provide practical guidance that might be used at operational levels within the firm.

2.2.1 Event-oriented Thinking

Likewise, earlier research has shown that a strong bias exists towards event-oriented planning. Both from a practical and from a psychological point of view, the process of identifying and listing potentially threatening events appears to be more attractive than facing the unknown, although the popular "list of risks" approach leaves the possibility of events or threats not on the list, with disastrous consequences. The "external event" that has not been foreseen within the given system of reference is often equal or similar to the above-mentioned HILF events. In this context, it is immaterial whether the omission of such an external event is the actual result of a conscious decision (bounded rationality) or a genuine oversight.

In the light of resulting damage, it is less than helpful to argue that such events could not have been foreseen, although this "hindsight dilemma" is often observed in the aftermath of major disasters or crises [SmSi93, Turn76]. The underlying difficulty with identifying any event is that the resulting list of risks or events is finite, regardless of their quantitative or qualitative identification. At any corporate level, it cannot be said with certainty that a risk list or events list will contain all pertinent items that might endanger the business or part of it. In practice, this is often illustrated by heated discussions about whether to include or exclude a specific event. Considerations of likelihood and impact are implicit to these discussions, although the underlying assumptions may not be objective. Empirically, there seems to be a very strong preference indeed for identifying any number of events and talking about them, in order to contribute personal opinion rather than quantitative consideration. As a result, it may be argued that the final list of risks and events represents all that is "humanly possible", including the potential for human error. It is shown below how the event-oriented risk identification and information gathering process must be replaced with a more objective approach.

2.2.2 Impact Estimates

A similar situation persists where the overall business impact of an event or crisis is to be determined. In practice, organisations encounter difficulties when attempting to identify the cost of a disrupted or dysfunctional department, process, system or application. The question "how much will we lose per day if this process is down?" gives rise to qualitative estimates and even wild guesses, whereas quantitative methods are rarely applied [Lind86]. The logical inversion "how long can we live without this process?" is strongly biased by psychological factors, such as the sense of self-importance felt by organisational units [Myat99, Wrob98]. However, earlier research on assessing the business impact of an adverse event has been unable to identify any definitive quantitative models.

Using traditional models of impact analysis, it is even more difficult to determine the long-term effects of an adverse event. While primary, material damage is apparent, the immediate period following the disruption is likely to cause significant secondary (material, medium and long term) and tertiary (immaterial) damage leading to serious consequences for the firm. The oft-quoted statistic claiming that more than 75% of companies affected by a disaster will cease to exist over a period of five years [Gart00] is indicative of this problem. Leaving aside such empirically correct observations, the theoretical foundations of this "extinction" pattern require further research.

In conjunction with the limited ability to quantify risk, these deficiencies found in impact assessment are a significant threat to companies and whole industry sectors [Hall86]. It is obvious that a "pick and choose" approach towards risk management, coupled with a somewhat vague idea of potential financial impact, does not satisfy the criteria of prudent business management.

2.3 Investment Decisions

Risk analysis and business impact assessment provide essential decision support for managerial investment decisions. Regardless of the actual treatment of recognised risks (reduction, transfer, acceptance), some form of investment will be needed to move from an existing risk position to a more favourable position [Runz99]. The anticipated level of damage, the potential risks and threats, and the mitigation possibilities as a whole present a range of options: the risk management mix [WoRu00]. Reducing, transferring or mitigating risks thus identified usually requires a substantial investment. Such investment decisions are taken on the basis of initial risk, reductions achieved, and residual risk; in other words, they are an expression of the entrepreneurial risk that management is willing to accept "before" and "after" introducing a security and continuity programme. However, the existing tendency towards qualitative estimates represents a considerable danger, as investments may be made on the basis of inaccurate or misleading data.

Hence, risk identification, quantitative estimates and proper business impact assessment are prerequisites to informed decisions on investments. The problem encountered with current techniques is that the investment optimum – maximise risk reduction at minimised cost – cannot be determined with sufficient accuracy. An expensive risk reduction strategy may cover all perceived risks and threats, but it may prove ineffective when tested against reality. Only where risk and impact are quantified can the investment problem be formalised and solved.

3 Strategic Decision Support Model

3.1 Assumptions

It has been shown that traditional risk analysis and business impact assessment do not lend themselves to sufficiently accurate quantification. In day-to-day business, a more pragmatic approach is needed to reach an acceptable risk level for the overall entity. Hence, the strategic decision support model presented in this paper rests on three assumptions:

- Risky events matter only inasmuch as they impact the business. The nature of an event is less important than the resulting damage.

- External data are scarce, but data internal to the business are readily available (well-known data sets).

- The business itself is well-defined in terms of processes and external interfaces.

In sharp contrast to traditional risk analysis, the model takes an internal perspective towards risks and related events. As a simplified example, consider a situation in which a data centre is threatened by fire. The fire brigade duly arrives and floods the building. While the fire has been extinguished successfully, the data centre is ruined. Had the fire brigade not arrived in time, the data centre would have been destroyed by fire. From an internal point of view, both scenarios are identical, as they lead to an unusable data centre and massive financial damage. This simple example suggests that an impact-based view – rather than an event-based view – is required to understand the priorities of the business itself. The main interest of the business is survival, which is in turn measured by damage sustained and the ability to compensate this damage financially. In an insolvency case, the root cause is negligible: the actual fact that the business cannot continue tends to dominate the discussions.

Environmental data and statistics are often unavailable or very costly to obtain. Where business decisions about natural catastrophes are based on statistics and probabilities, the initiative passes from a decision-oriented management style to a reaction-oriented management. The question "is this event likely enough to plan against it" is best answered by "if in doubt, play safe and prepare a plan". For the prudent business manager, the likelihood of the event is less important than ensuring the survival of the firm – better safe than sorry. Internal data, on the other hand, should be readily available from various sources. From the balance sheet and the profit and loss account downward, controlling and financial information are generated as a matter of course, and these may be utilised for risk and business impact decision support.

Finally, the business itself requires some degree of formalisation in terms of processes and interactions with third parties [Schu89, Smit03]. Core business, supporting functions and infrastructure should be well-defined or thoroughly analysed where uncertainties exist. In practice, this may require some research, as hidden dependencies often exist between internal processes, or between the company and suppliers or customers. Similarly, the supply chain is often defined at a high level without recognising the full significance of infrastructural processes such as information technology.

3.2 Quantifying Business Impact

More often than not, firms find themselves unable to determine with any degree of precision the impact that an external event might have on their ability to continue operations. This is mainly due to the event-based perspective: when considering a specific event such as fire or flooding, it is very difficult indeed to predict the parts of the business that may be affected. The reverse approach is comparatively straightforward: assets, process output and sales do have a defined value. The loss of an asset or the loss of a day of production can be quantified using traditional financial data.

Table 1 illustrates the direct or indirect internal impact at the business process level and its deductive estimate using known financial figures. The more immediate damage observed, for instance to an individual fixed asset, is easily expressed as a balance sheet loss, whereas damage at a level far removed from profit-generating processes, say information technology, requires a step-by-step calculation. As a rule, the dependencies between business processes will determine the cascading effect that eventually causes tangible (balance sheet or profit and loss account) damage. Note that the well-known financial data sets are used in a predictive manner rather than using traditional retrospective analysis.

Table 1: Selected impacts and internal information sources

Loss	Information Source	Manifestation of Impact
Fixed Asset	Asset Register	Balance Sheet
Current Asset	Financial Accounting	Balance Sheet
Disrupted Output (productive)	Sales / turnover figures	Profit and Loss Account
Disrupted Output (services)	Sales / turnover figures	Profit and Loss Account
Disrupted Output (market share)	Market share as a function of turnover (in terms of total market size)	Strategic
Disrupted support processes	Delayed output reduction or disruption, indirect impact	Profit and Loss Account
Disrupted infrastructure processes	"Ripple-through" effect, temporary bottlenecks, cascading effects impacting support and core processes	Profit and Loss Account

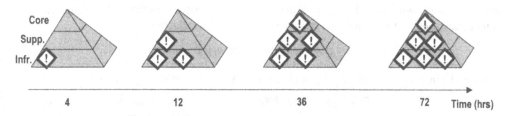

Figure 1: Cascading damage as a function of time

While these primary causes of financial damage are easily obtained, the "ripple-through" effects of widespread damage along the supply chain should be expressed as a function of time. Figure 1 illustrates this typical development process. The onset of delays or disruptions occurs with a distinct time lag, although initially small impacts are (potentially) sufficient to create damage at the highest level. Figure 2 provides the next level of abstraction, where individual components of damage are aggregated as a function of time. Table 2 shows how the individual components are linked to well-known financial data sets, in a simplified example. Further research is desirable to identify a definitive mapping between the set of financial data usually found in a firm, and the impacts observed in practice.

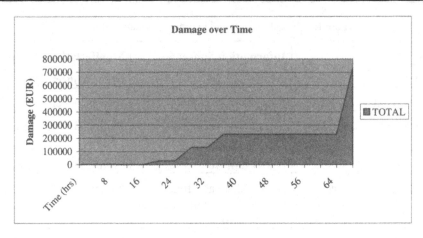

Figure 2: Financial damage as a function of time

Even if absolute and objective impact figures have been determined, their relative significance to the business requires further qualification. In order to assess the inherent danger of any single or multiple loss, the concepts of materiality and going concern must be introduced to the model. The oft-quoted "appetite for risk" – the calculated risk accepted by management – must be commensurate with the probability of insolvency (ruin), should any event or cluster of events be severe enough to endanger the existence of the firm. The prudent yet entrepreneurial manager will undoubtedly seek the optimum position where the de facto financial risk is less than or equal to the investment in prevention or risk reduction.

Table 2: Linking damaging impacts to well-known financial sets

Elapsed Time (hrs)	Description and Amount (€)	Well-known Set
4	IT hardware loss 2000,- IT SLA callout fee 400,-	Asset register, service level agreement
12	Bottleneck finance 1000,- Bill of Lading / Bill of Materials down 500,-	Personnel / internal hourly rate
24	Logistics slowdown 10%, 25000,- Invoicing down 500,-	Internal / external logistics calculated daily rate; materialised cost of logistics; personnel rates (invoicing)
32	Logistics slowdown 50%, additional 75000,- Order processing down 2000,-	as above
40	Logistics slowdown 80%, additional 100000,-	as above
72	Sales down 10%, 500000,-	Controlling / sales monitoring data, PoS terminals etc.

3.3 Definition of Financial Boundaries

As shown in table 2, it is straightforward to record and substantiate financial damage under adverse conditions. Similarly, the "what if" estimate of what might happen if an adverse event occurred at any time, can be mapped against well-known financial data sets. In other words, this is an exercise in linking what is already known about the firm (financially) to a time-dependent function. In practice, it is often found that controlling or strategic planning departments have introduced such mappings without necessarily applying them to the field of damage assessment or damage estimating.

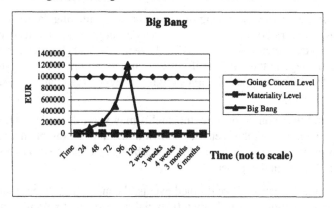

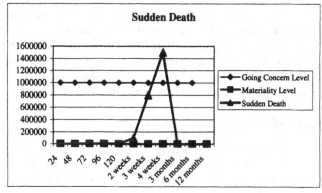

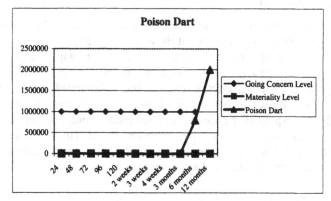

Figure 3: Financial impact, boundaries and time-dependent characteristics

Financial impact in itself requires a defined set of boundaries in order to quantify the severity. On the one hand, the question of survival is best expressed by the maximum damage sustainable under the "going concern" assumption. On the other hand, damage as a function of time must be assessed in terms of when and in what manner this "danger zone" will be reached. In some cases, the immediate financial impact may be high and stabilise after some time. In other cases, the initial impact may be low and exhibit subsequent "jumps" to higher levels of damage. Figure 3 illustrates these scenarios. The upper boundary of business impact assessment is complemented by the lower boundary of "materiality", meaning the amount of money deemed significant enough to influence balance sheet and / or profit and loss account.

It is advisable to select a sufficiently long time horizon for estimating damage against the materiality and going concern boundaries, so as to include long-term consequences of an event. Figure 3 further depicts a scenario where a critical event causes negligible damage in the short run, but terminal damage in the long run if not recognised and mitigated. To suggest a working terminology, the different types of curves might be called "big bang", "sudden death" and "poison dart" respectively.

Both materiality and the "going concern" thresholds may vary, depending upon a number of factors[1]. Hence, it is likely that the scenarios shown in the above example may have to be approximated. This is due to the definitions of the thresholds that are commonly used, and therefore not discussed further in this paper.

It has been shown that, irrespective of defined events, the amount of damage sustainable by a corporate entity is a function of well-known financial data sets that require no external information. It is reiterated here that, for reasons of clarity, extraneous parameters like service level agreements, payment delay, credit lines and others are assumed to be well-defined and known beforehand. Where the maximum tolerable impact has thus been identified, management will be able to make informed investment decisions on the basis of known facts. When compared with the traditional "risk list" approach, this presents some decisive advantages, as managers can begin their strategic reasoning from a quantitatively reliable point.

3.4 Risk Quantification

Given that the question of survival is decided by internal impact, the overall risk represented by a variety of events can be quantified and formalised. In sharp contrast to the qualitative – intuitive – identification of events and consequences, the quantitative decision support model proposes the reverse approach.

Consider a random event that may or may not happen at any time in the future. For decision support purposes, the interesting properties of the event are expressed by the business process model: what parts of the supply chain are affected, when and to what degree. From the point of view of a single corporate entity, it is less important what other consequences the event might have, for instance for third parties. Events can thus be assigned certain parameters, such as maximum financial impact, maximum downtime, and exposures of any given business process that might be "exploited" by the event. The existing impact quantification provides a "corporate radar screen", and events will be visible or filtered. This is particularly important for the HILF type of event where frequencies and probabilities are difficult or impossible to determine. Hence, any risk may be tested as shown below:

---

[1] The reader is referred to the comprehensive body of literature on financial audit that explains both the threshold levels and the assumptions made by audit and finance, as additional references would be outside the scope of this paper.

- if the risk manifests itself (i. e. an event occurs), will the quantified business impact reach the going concern boundary at any time ?

- if the going concern condition is satisfied, does the damage follow a distinct pattern (big bang, sudden death, poison dart) ?

Simultaneously, business processes are tested in a similar manner:

- how does an impact on the process manifest itself: direct damage (destruction, disruption, strategic), indirect damage (e. g. bottlenecks in supporting processes)

- can this impact be neutralised (prevention, transfer etc.) with a sufficient degree of certainty ?

When mapping the process-related view against the event-related view as shown in table 3, the actual number of "vulnerable" business processes and the corresponding number of pertinent risks are surprisingly small. Very few events indeed – whatever their nature – will be severe enough to affect all business processes. Conversely, most business processes will be robust enough to withstand most events. Table 3 further shows that in a process mode of thinking, the actual impact will fall into one of a few categories, regardless of the event causing the impact. The "probability" column shows how the process might be vulnerable in one or more ways, for instance in terms of location, physical security, dependencies on other processes etc. The internal vulnerabilities are taken from the quantified business impact assessment.

Table 3: Generic risk matrix at process level

Business process P = prevention T = transfer **R** = residual risk	Direct damage (destruction, lengthy disruption, strategic)	"Starving", disruption by failure of another process	"Stuffed", disruption by additional workload	Probability
Sales	P	**R**	P	unlikely
Finance	**R**	P	**R**	moderate
Operations	**R**	P	P	moderate
IT	P	P	P	unlikely
Electricity	P	P	P	unlikely

Even the simple example in table 3 highlights the fact that the number of significant exposures is limited. In practice, the generic risk matrix often identifies single vulnerabilities or single points of failure that can be resolved by prevention, or enhanced robustness of the process itself.

Quantification of a risk therefore results from two criteria. Firstly, the expected consequences must be such that business processes are vulnerable; secondly, the expected impact must be equal to or higher than the going concern threshold. Given this second criterion, it is self-evident that probabilities based on frequency of occurrence should be avoided. Anything that is even remotely able to endanger the existence of the firm must be addressed as a matter of prudent management and legal compliance [Brüh94, Camp98, Hall86, Kles98, Prit97].

The strategic decision support model thus categorises and "clusters" events in terms of their relevance for the process, rather than using traditional probabilities and frequency distributions. In other words: the overall risk position "from within the business process" may be a conglomerate of a large number of external events that would effectively have the same consequences – remember the data centre example as described above. Figure 4 illustrates the traditional probability-based approach as opposed to the clustering and categorising method used in this decision support model.

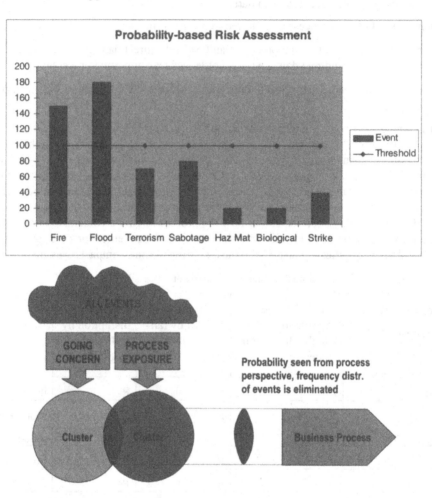

Figure 4: Process-oriented vs. probability-oriented risk quantification

4 Investment Decisions

In an environment where both risk and potential business impact are known with certainty – or at least with a limited degree of uncertainty – investment decisions for reducing the overall risk position may be formalised as shown below. Common investment strategies optimise for the intersection (P_0) of risk-reducing investment with potential damage, depicted in figure 5. The curves denoting damage over time (D) and the cost of securing against risk (C) usually follow shapes as shown. The distance to the left or to the right of P_0 denotes the relative risk taking or conservatism of the decision maker, as a function of time and money. Pure risk as expressed in the diagram does not change and is assumed to be constant.

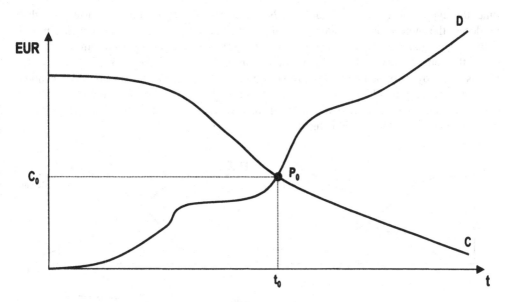

Figure 5: Traditional damage / cost curves

As a first step, the going concern boundary (GC line) is introduced (figure 6). The going concern criterion thus denotes the maximum tolerable damage, P_1. At this point, the damage arising over time is a purely process-driven issue and independent of root causes and events. While the optimum solution is still represented by P_0, the distance to P_1 becomes an important factor (the "safety margin"). If materialised damage approximates the going concern line, the company may just survive, but with near-disastrous consequences. Hence, the formal investment problem is to find P_0 as well as a reasonable distance to P_1.

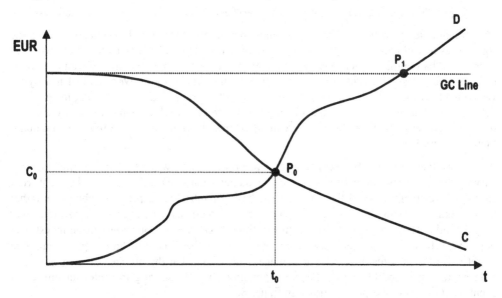

Figure 6: Maximum tolerable damage and optimum investment

The traditional approach favours a shift in the cost curve, thus reducing the investment needed to reach P_0. However, the increasing optimisation of business processes (i. e. revenue over time, throughput over time) inevitably leads to a steeper damage curve: the faster something produces, the more money at stake. It is therefore likely that – given an optimised process with a steeper damage curve – the cost curve will shift to the right together with a shift to the left of the damage curve. The initial investment in achieving a certain recovery time objective is thus offset by increased cost of recovery (figure 7). Little research exists on this phenomenon, but it is suggested here that as optimisation converges towards maximum efficiency, the cost of recovery will increase in a non-linear manner and beyond the going concern threshold, thus invalidating the traditional investment paradigm.

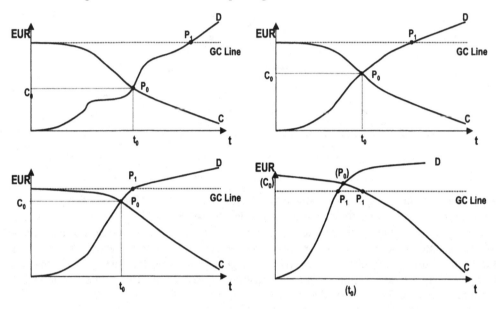

Figure 7: Increasing and prohibitive cost of recovery with growing process vulnerabilities

The strategic decision support model presented here aims at shifting the damage curve to the right, so as to yield an optimum point P_0 at a lower investment. This is achieved by investing in process "hardening" rather than accomplishing a recovery time objective. Given the event-independence of such process-related investments, the efficiency of every unit of money invested is likely to be much higher. In other words: while traditional risk-reducing investments defend a number of processes against a single risk, the proposed investment strategy here defends one process against a cluster of prequalified risks insofar as they are relevant and quantitatively significant.

It is likely that this largely event-independent process view will assist in keeping the cost curve C within reasonable limits, while the damage curve D will shift to the right very sharply. Investments should be made on the basis of introducing process robustness rather than spending large amounts of money on optimised processes that are becoming increasingly volatile and unstable as a result of just this optimisation. Process robustness as an investment objective offers the additional advantage of narrowing the cluster of "relevant" events that might still present a residual risk for management. Given that the number of risky events is reduced to a manageable level, the corresponding cost of securing the relevant cluster of events will decrease sharply, as shown in figure 8.

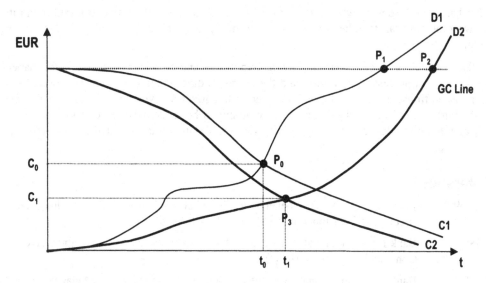

Figure 8: Introduction of process robustness and decreasing cost of recovery

5 Conclusions

The event-oriented ("risk list") approach towards identifying and evaluating risk may be substituted with a process-oriented view that eliminates the difficulties connected with probabilities and high-impact, low-frequency effects. From a corporate perspective, this obviates the need for portfolio-type methods that are awkward to apply or simply inapplicable. Instead, the situation where one firm faces multiple risks is resolved by using internal data (well-known financial data sets) to determine damage over time.

The business impact assessment thus obtained is matched against defined thresholds, namely materiality and going concern lines easily identified from balance sheet and profit and loss account. Known problems with impact estimating and impact significance are therefore eliminated.

It has been shown that, by clustering risks in terms of relevance and process vulnerabilities, the probabilistic approach may be replaced with a more direct, company-specific view on risky events. Not every event is relevant, and not every process is vulnerable to all events that might possibly happen (including the unknown). It is further suggested that by applying appropriate filters (going concern, materiality) to individual events, their significance can be quantified with sufficient certainty.

The strategic decision support model presented in this paper offers several constants that have not been used in traditional models. These well-known financial constants serve as qualifiers for – otherwise subjective – impact and risk assessments. Furthermore, the model formalises business processes by linking their cost / damage and profit / damage expectations to well-known internal data sets that are easily obtained from controlling departments or other analytical instances. Both the risk side and the process side are therefore quantifiable with sufficient reliability.

In introducing the concept of "hardening" processes by adding robustness rather than protecting the existing – fragile – processes, the resulting investment decisions take into account two dimensions: on the one hand, the traditional approach of "protect what is there", and on the other hand, the "redesign what is there to reduce risk" strategy. Process optimisation and its known problems can thus be controlled and formally analysed in terms of optimum investment.

Further research is needed regarding several hypotheses and problems presented in this paper, particularly on process optimisation and the corresponding increase in recovery cost. Moreover, the optimisation for multiple investment alternatives (prevention / recovery / process hardening) merits further discussion. Finally, it should be tested whether existing theory on risk may be reintroduced to the model to better describe the process-related risk clusters and categorisations.

References

[BaCo96]   Bamberg, G., A. G. Coenenberg. Betriebswirtschaftliche Entscheidungslehre. [Economic Decision Theory] 9th ed., Munich 1996.

[BIS03]   Bank for International Settlements. Overview of The New Basel Capital Accord. Consultative Paper, April 2003.

[BIS03b]   Bank for International Settlements. Sound Practices for the Management and Supervision of Operational Risk. February 2003.

[Brüh94]   Brühwiler, B. Internationale Industrieversicherung: Risk-Management, Unternehmensführung, Erfolgsstrategien. [International Industrial Insurance: Risk Management, Corporate Leadership, Success Strategies] Karlsruhe, 1994.

[DEGK01]   Danielsson, J., P. et. al. An Academic Response to Basel II. Special Paper 130, LSE Financial Markets Group and ESRC Research Centre, May 2001.

[Embr99]   Embrechts, P. Extreme Value Theory in Finance and Insurance. Zurich, 1999.

[EmKS02]   Embrechts, P., R. Kaufmann, G. Samorodnitsky. Ruin theory revisited: stochastic models for operational risk. Zurich, 2002.

[EmRS98]   Embrechts, P., S. I. Resnick, G. Samorodnitsky. Extreme value theory as a risk management tool. Zurich, 1998.

[GaGM97]   Garz, H. S. Günther, C. Moriabadi. Portfolio-Management: Theorie und Anwendung [Portfolio Management: Theory and Applications]. Frankfurt: Bankakademie e. V., 1997.

[Gart00]   Gartner Group. Business Continuity Benchmarking Program, 2000.

[Hall86]   Haller, M. Risiko-Management – Eckpunkte eines integrierten Konzepts [Risk Management – Boundaries of an Integrated Concept], in Jacob, H. (ed.): Risiko-Management, vol. 33, Wiesbaden, 1986.

[Imbo83]   Imboden, C. Risikohandhabung: Ein entscheidungsbezogenes Verfahren. [Risk Handling: A Decision-oriented Method] Stuttgart / Bern, 1983

[KaTv79]   Kahneman, D., A. Tversky. Prospect Theory: An Analysis of Decision Under Risk. Econometrica, 47, 1979.

[Kles98]   Kless, T. Beherrschung der Unternehmensrisiken: Aufgaben und Prozesse des Risikomanagements [Control of Corporate Risks: Tasks and Processes in Risk Management]. DStR, vol. 3, 1998.

[Krei97]   Kreikebaum, H. Strategische Unternehmensplanung. [Corporate Strategic Planning] 6th ed., Stuttgart, 1997.

[Küpp97]   Küpper, H.-U. Controlling: Konzeption, Aufgaben und Instrumente. [Controlling: Concepts, Tasks and Instruments] 2nd ed., Stuttgart 1997.

[Lind86]   Lindeiner-Wildau, K. v. Risiken und Risikomanagement im Anlagenbau [Risks and Risk Management in Plant Engineering], in Funk, J., G. Laßmann. Langfristiges Anlagengeschäft – Risiko-Management und Controlling. ZfbF, Sonderheft Nr. 20, Düsseldorf 1986.

[Linn01]   Linneweber, V. Zur veränderten Sozialpsychologie der Katastrophenprävention [On the Changed Social Psychology of Catastrophe Prevention], in Linneweber (Hrsg.), Zukünftige Bedrohungen durch (anthropogene) Naturkatastrophen. Deutsches Komitee für Katastrophenvorsorge e.V., 2001.

[Myat99]   Myatt, P. B. Business Continuity: Going in for Analysis. Huntington Beach: Comdisco, 1999.

[Neub89]   Neubürger, K. W. Chancen- und Risikobeurteilung im strategischen Management: die informatorische Lücke. [Evaluation of Opportunities and Risks in Strategic Management: The Information Gap] Stuttgart, 1989.

[Poll01]   Pollner, J. D. Catastrophe Risk Management: Using Alternative Risk Financing and Insurance Pooling Mechanisms. World Bank Policy Research Paper 2560, 2001.

[HoPr97]   Hommel, U., G. Pritsch. Notwendigkeit des unternehmerischen Risikomanagements aus Shareholder-Value-Sicht [Corporate Risk Management Requirements from a Shareholder Value Perspective], in Achleitner, A.-K., G. Thoma (eds.). Handbuch Corporate Finance, Cologne 1997.

[Renn84]   Renn, O. Risikowahrnehmung der Kernenergie [Risk Perception of Nuclear Power], Frankfurt: Campus, 1984.

[Renn01]   Renn, O. Zur Soziologie von Katastrophen: Bewusstsein, Organisation und soziale Verarbeitung [On the Sociology of Catastrophes: Awareness, Organisation and Social Process], in Proceedings of the 2nd DKKV Forum on Catastrophe Prevention, September 2001.

[Roes01]   Roessing, R. v. Robustheit und Kontinuität elektronischer Geschäftsprozesse [Robustness and Continuity in Electronic Business Processes]. Arbeitskonferenz Elektronische Geschäftsprozesse, St. Leon-Rot, 2002.

[Runz99]   Runzheimer, B. Operations Research: Lineare Planungsrechnung, Netzplantechnik, Simulation und Warteschlangentheorie. [Operations Research: Linear Programming, Critical Path Analysis, Simulation and Queuing Theory] 7th ed., Wiesbaden 1999.

[SBCC00]   Streffer, C. et. al. Umweltstandards. Kombinierte Expositionen und ihre Auswirkungen auf den Menschen und seine Umwelt [Environmental Standards. Combined Exposures and their Impact on Man and Environment]. Wissenschaftsethik und Technikfolgenbeurteilung vol. 5. Berlin etc.: Springer, 2000.

[Schl98]   Schlienkamp, C. Grundlagen der Asset Allocation [Fundamentals of Asset Allocation], in Eller, R. (ed.). Handbuch des Risikomanagements: Analyse, Quantifizierung und Steuerung von Marktrisiken in Banken und Sparkassen. Stuttgart, 1998.

[Schu99]   Schuy, A. Risiko-Management: eine theoretische Analyse zum Risiko und Risi-kowirkungsprozeß unter besonderer Berücksichtigung des Marketing. Frankfurt, 1989.

[Simo57]   Simon, H. Administrative Behavior. New York: Free Press, 1957.

[SmIr84]   Smith, D., A. Irwin. Public attitudes to technological risk: the contribution of survey data to public policy-making. Trans. Inst. Br. Geogr. N. S. 9: 419-26, 1984.

[Smit03]   Smith, D. Business Continuity Management Good Practice Guide. Worcester: The Business Continuity Institute, 2003.

[SmSi93]   Smith, D., C. Sipika. Back from the Brink – Post-Crisis Management. Long Range Planning, vol. 26 no. 1, 1993.

[Turn76]   Turner, B. A. The Organizational and Interorganizational Development of Disasters. Administrative Science Quarterly, vol. 21, September 1976.

[UK02]   Strategy Unit. Risk: Improving government's capability to handle risk and un-certainty. United Kingdom Cabinet Office, November 2002.

[WoRu00]   Wolf, K. B. Runzheimer. Risikomanagement und KonTraG. [Risk Management and the Business Control and Transparency Act 1998] 2nd ed., Stuttgart: Gabler, 2000.

[Wrob98]   Wrobel, L. A. Conduct a Hard-Hitting Business Impact Analysis: Proven Tips for Success! Disaster Recovery Journal, 1998.

[YoKo01]   Yokomatsu, M., K. Kobayashi. Physical Asset Loss and Economic Benefits of Disaster Risk Mitigation. IIASA Laxenburg, 2001.

IT Risk Assessment

P.J.M. Poos RA RE[1]

SNS Reaal Groep
The Netherlands
piet.poos@home.nl

Abstract

Based on an earlier version of a risk assessment tool, the case shows an approach to achieve an overview of the IT risk of a large financial institution (a bank and an insurance company). In this approach we assess the potential damage (based on IT dependence) and the likelihood of the occurrence of adverse events. We first get an overview of the various business units and of the business processes in the business units. These lower level assessments are later consolidated in an organization wide IT risk profile. The tool is effective in the planning of IT audit activities. The tool is also useful in complying with Dutch regulatory requirements for financial institutions.

1 Introduction

Today's business and IT environments are fast becoming more complex. Large corporations are faced with a double challenge. They do not only have to develop new systems to keep up with the ever increasing speed of change. They also need to maintain and change their old legacy systems in order to stay ahead of competition.

For financial institutions[2] this is well known territory. Most have grown considerably over the last decade; taking over and merging smaller institutions. At the same time supervisory authorities have, justly, demanded improved risk management policies and procedures. In the new Basel Capital Agreement there is a direct link between the bank's funding capacity and the quality of its risk management. In the 'old' agreement only a bank's traditional risk areas were taken into consideration (e.g. credit risk and interest rate risk). In the new agreement however, operational risk management has become part of a bank's risk management. It should be understood that the use of IT is just a part of operational risk (albeit a significant part).

In the Netherlands, as in most other countries, supervising authorities have anticipated international agreements and have issued regulations regarding operational risk.

---

[1] Piet Poos is since two years head of IT Audit at SNS Reaal Groep in the Netherlands. Before holding this position he has been a senior manager with Ernst & Young EDP Audit for 15 years. He is both a CPA and CISA. Most of his work has been in the area of management control and IT control. Piet is a member of the AIS faculty at Nyenrode University and he is a member of the IT Audit examination board at the Tilburg Institute of Academic Studies (University of Tilburg).

[2] Financial institutions are conglomerates that compromise not only banks but also insurance companies, lease companies, investment institutions and other organizations that offer financial services. Most of these institutions have to deal with supervisory authorities. Usually the bank's supervisors have the most stringent regulations on operational and IT risk.

S. Paulus, N. Pohlmann, H. Reimer (Editors): Securing Electronic Business Processes, Vieweg (2004), 21-30

The Regulation on Organisation and Control (in Dutch Regeling Organisatie en Beheersing, or in short ROB) has become effective from 1 April 2001. It gives a comprehensive overview of all a bank's risk areas: Credit risk, Market risk, Liquidity risk, Operational risk, Information technology (IT), Outsourcing of (components of) business processes, Integrity risk.

For the purpose of this paper we will focus only at the IT risk. In the ROB IT risk has been defined as: "the current or prospective threat to an institution's earnings and capital as a result of an inadequate strategy or policy or shortcomings in the technology applied and/or use with regard to information processing and communication, which translate into strategic, manageability, exclusivity, information integrity, controllability, continuity and user operations risk".

This definition is explained in several articles:
54. An institution shall have clearly formulated policies for controlling IT risks. The policies shall be documented and communicated to all the relevant personnel of an institution.
55. An institution shall systematically perform an analysis of IT risks. The analysis shall be performed both on an institution-wide basis and at the level of the various business divisions.
56. An institution shall ensure that the policies for controlling IT risks are translated into in visible organizational and administrative procedures and measures that are integrated into the IT processes and the day-to-day activities of all relevant personnel. There shall also be systematic monitoring of compliance therewith.
57. An institution shall implement specific measures to ensure the adequate security of information and the continuity of the IT. The legal security and the privacy of clients shall be adequately safeguarded where use is made of IT applications.

Taken in all, these are not unreasonable demands for IT operations. Article 55 however demands that the IT risks will have to be analyzed. In order to address the rapid change of IT risk analysis needs to be a continuous process.

Performing organization wide risk analysis is an enormous task. Traditional risk analysis is a labor intensive job that needs to be done by highly paid specialists. The cost of such an exercise, even on a two or three years' cycle, is prohibitive. Moreover, by the time they have finished the results of the first analysis will be outdated. Adding to that, putting a large team on the job is not really a solution. It needs a large coordination effort in order to get consistent result across all professionals involved.

The question is simple. How can we perform a cost efficient systematic risk analysis across a large organization? By preference this should be a repeatable process that results in consistent results.

In the rest of this paper we will explain such an approach. First we will describe the organization. Following that we will show the approach we have followed.

2 SNS Reaal Groep

2.1 Profile

SNS Reaal Group is an innovative Dutch financial services provider with total assets of more than € 46 billion and over 5,400 employees at the end of 2002. The Group's head office is in Utrecht. SNS Reaal Group serves its private and business clients mainly through SNS Bank

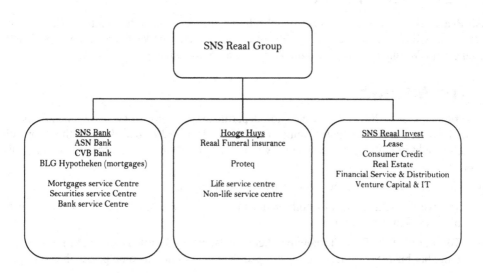

and Hooge Huys. SNS Bank reaches customers directly through its branch offices and financial advisors, by telephone and via the internet. Hooge Huys markets its products and services through independent intermediaries. The third group subsidiary, SNS Reaal Invest, focuses on supporting the financial activities within SNS Reaal Group. Strong social commitment is a traditional characteristic of SNS Reaal Group, as expressed in its specialized research into sustainable investments, sustainable products, and donations and sponsoring activities.

2.2 SNS Bank

With 3,500 employees, SNS Bank is one of the top five banks in the Netherlands. It has a national network of approximately two hundred branches. The bank wants to expand its network of branches, particularly in the Randstad conurbation. The branch offices serve mainly as sales units for the more complex products. Most of the 'normal' banking transactions (e.g. payments and brokerage) are processed through extensive real-time internet services. All back office activities are concentrated in three 'service centers': mortgages, securities and banking (foreign and domestic payments, debit and credit cards transactions).

In all there are about 25 business units.

2.3 Hooge Huys

Hooge Huys provides financial products through independent intermediaries. The range includes a wide variety of insurance products and a related range of life insurances, mortgages, investment and additional banking services, which allows the intermediary to offer services in 'personal financial planning'. For business customers, Hooge Huys has an Employee Benefits package, which includes flexible employer and employees products.

All back office activities are concentrated in two main service centers: the Life service centre for all life insurance products and claims and the Property service centre for all other products and claims.

In all there are about 15 business units.

2.4 SNS Reaal Invest

SNS Reaal Invest contains a number of subsidiaries that are outside the main banking and insurance activities. For that reason these subsidiaries are only under financial control of SNS Reaal Group. We have not assessed the IT risk of these subsidiaries.

3 The Method

In the first quarter of 2003 the internal audit department has performed an assessment if the IT risk in the most important business units of both SNS Bank and Hooge Huys. In this approach we gain insight in the major IT risk areas within the various business units in the group. This allows us:

- To make a comparison between disparate business units;
- To give the management of both the business units and of the group in the areas where improvement is necessary;
- To improve the IT Audit planning. Actually the method started as an aid in audit planning, but business value soon outstripped the audit value. In some places the audit perspective is still visible.

When developing the method, we used a much simpler definition of 'risk' than has been shown in the ROB. We defined risk as the chance that at an unexpected moment an adverse event occurs. IT risk is than the chance that these events occur in the IT domain. In the method we use the word 'assessment' on purpose. We do not use an approach in which we carefully judge the probability of adverse events, we consider the measures that have been taken and calculate the potential damage. As stated in the introduction, this is an approach that takes far too much time. Instead we consider the IT dependence in order to assess the potential damage. We then consider the organization of IT and business processes and assess the likelihood of things going wrong.

We must emphasize that the method we have used is in itself insufficient detailed to advise concrete measures. This is not the purpose of the method. It is also not realistic to expect startling new notions about the risks we run in the business units. What we can do is to explicitate the feelings that already exist into a model that we can compare to other business units. To do all that we examine the causes of risk. Based on extensive literature search and on empirical research we have come up with a number of such causes.

In order to get the overview we need, we follow a three layered approach:
1. we determine the risk profile of the business unit
2. we assess the risk profile of the processes within the business unit
3. we consolidate the business unit risk profiles into an organization wide profile.

To gather the information we need, we have developed two sets of questions: one set of 34 questions for the business unit profile and one set of 30 questions for each process in the business unit. The answer to each question is scored (from 1 to 6). The approach we used was based on an earlier developed tool for a general IT audit practice spanning multiple industries (mostly smaller and midsized companies). This tool was adapted to fit a large bank.

An IT Auditor and the information manager of the business unit together score each question. It is very important that de motivation for each score is carefully discussed and recorded. This discussion is necessary to determine the validity of the score. It is also the IT auditor's role to ascertain that each business unit uses the same interpretation of the scoring table.

4 Business Unit Risk Profile

Rather than to give a simple figure we show the risk profile as a series of graphs that illustrate the various risk areas and the interdependence of these areas. We show here the profile of the call centre.

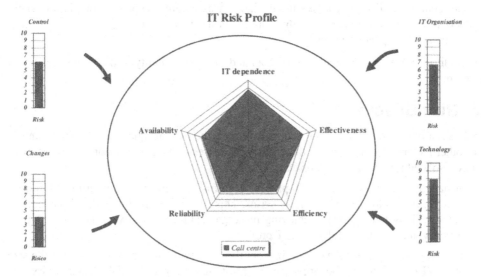

The business unit risk profile comes in two parts:

- Dependence and quality;
- Risk drivers

4.1 Dependence and Quality

It risk is shown as a combination of IT dependence and quality. Quality is separated into four aspects: effectiveness, efficiency, reliability and availability. In order to make a correct interpretation of the risk it is important to explicitly distinguish between dependence and quality. It dependence shows the degree to which an organization is dependent on IT. High IT dependence will lead to large damages in the case of adverse events. Large damages are an indication of a high risk. The scores of the quality aspects are always related to the IT dependence.

In the quality aspect the following elements will come up:

- Effectiveness: the questions are about the need for manual intervention is processing and the usefulness of the generated management information. We also ask for the adequatecy the technical infrastructure (mainly the network).
- Efficiency: user friendliness, the probability of mistakes, the effort of maintaining the systems and the flexibility of the systems;
- Reliability: in the end the only question is whether or not the systems show a sufficiently true view of reality. This core question is operationalised by further questions regarding logical access control, access to the systems by third parties (both the internet and EDI) and the need for manual intervention.
  To be absolutely clear: a low score does not mean that the systems and processes are unreliable; it means a high risk of unreliability.

- Availability: this is the degree in which processing is clear of disruptions (mean time between failures) and the time necessary to clear interruptions (mean time to repair). The scope is larger than contingency planning;
  Ideally the graph is in balance. In the example IT dependence is higher than effectiveness, efficiency, reliability and availability. In discussions with the management of the call centre was determined that the deviation was within acceptable boundaries. There was some concern about availability, but the issues there ware addressed in an ongoing business contingency project

As IT auditors however, we decided to plan an audit of the reliability of the IT systems in the call centre.

4.2 Risk Drivers

IT risk is not only determined by IT dependence and (the lack of) quality, but also of a number of other factors. Risk drivers are the underlying causes of risk, but are not risk themselves. We have isolated four areas of risk drivers:

- management control over the IT-process (control): has management sufficient control over IT. As control lessens, risk increases. This risk is specified by enquiries about the support IT systems give in achieving the organization's objectives, the ownership of systems and the successfulness of IT projects;
- the nature and size of the IT organization: there are two issues here. The first is the size of the IT organization. The larger the organization, the higher the risk. The other issue is the knowledge and experience of the IT organization. The broader the knowledge and larger the experience, the lower the risk;
- the nature and complexity of technology. The more complex the IT infrastructure, the higher the risk.
- the number and scope of changes in the environment (changes). Changes in themselves are a cause of risks. That is the reason we ask about the scope of the changes for the coming year;

With the complexity of IT systems of the call centre, there was nothing out of the ordinary. We saw no need to plan an audit into any of these areas.

4.3 Interpretation of the Model

Given the interdependence of the various areas it is very difficult to provide hard rules about the interpretation of the outcome. We can give some indication about desirable and undesirable combinations.

IT dependence and quality are supposed to be in balance. High IT dependence and lower quality indicates a possible higher risk. Either we need to perform a more detailed risk analysis or there is room for improvement. This will have to be decided in discussion with the responsible management. A much higher score on a one of the quality aspects could indicate past over expenditure on this topic.

A well controlled organization will have a relatively low score on the 'Control' risk driver. Many of the questions establish the organization's past track record on this subject. The other risk drivers are more an indication of inherent risk. A combination of high control risk and high change risk must be seen as a clear warning.

5 Process Risk Profile

The process risk profile too, is shown as a number of graphs. Many of the subjects in the organization profile return, but there are some other topics as well.

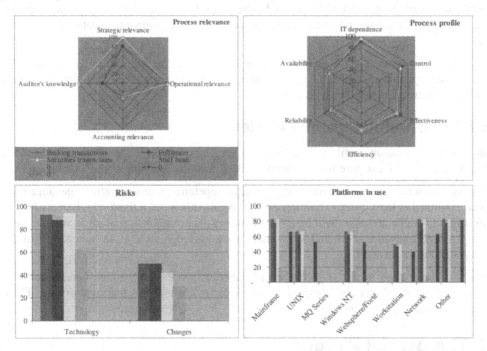

We start by determining the relevance of the processes within the business unit. Process relevance is not only measured for the business unit, but also for the organization as a whole. There are three kinds of relevance:

- Strategic relevance: how important is the process to realize the business unit's and the organization's objectives
- Operational relevance: how important is the process for the day to day running of the business;
- Accounting relevance: how important is the process for the generation of management information and the financial statements.

We end by asking ourselves what the audit department knows about the process; what has been the degree of change over last years and when was the last time we did a thorough audit of the process.

In the example we have discussed with management the place of the staff bank (a bank branch whose only customers are SNS Reaal Group staff). This process does not fit with the other processes. It costs disproportionately much management attention and lowers the overall averages.

The questions in the process profile are for the most part the same questions as in the organization profile. However, we have added some questions about the level of control that is exercised over the process. These are questions about identifying, measuring and following up on process key performance indicators. The core question here is the degree to which process objectives are realized.

Risks are the same as the technology and change questions in the organization profile. The technology risks are adjusted for the number of platforms that are in use; the higher the number, the higher the risk. The graph about platforms in use allows the IT Audit department to match the necessary technical knowledge with the technical infrastructure. It also allows us to decide which platforms should be audited. The black bar is the average importance of the platform adjusted for the relevance of the process In this adjustment operational relevance counts for 50%.

In the example we have an 'other' platform. In this case it is the platform to connect the telephone exchange with the other IT systems. Based on the importance of this platform it was decided to outsource an audit to this platform.

5.1 Interpretation of the Model

As in the organization profile it is difficult to give hard rules for the interpretation of the model. Here too, we can give some indication about desirable and undesirable combinations.

Process with a high relevance score either strategic, operational or accounting relevance need to be examined at least every two to three years. Again this is not a fixed rule. Exhaustive examination of stable processes will be farther between than examination of more volatile processes. A high relevance score and a low auditor's knowledge score is an indication that the process is due for an audit.

Here too, the process profile ought to be in balance. A process with a high operational relevance and low reliability and control is a very clear indication of a high risk profile. These situations need to be avoided.

6 The overall Picture

Because of the number of business units, the overall picture is a bit of a mess. Fortunately, we have the individual models to zoom in on details. The thickish black line is the average for the whole organization. In this case we have chosen for a simple average, a more advanced method where the relevance of each business unit is weighted is also possible.

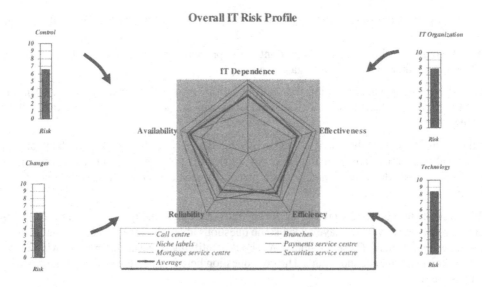

Overall IT Risk Profile

The risk drivers have not been averaged out. Instead we have answered the questions for the organization as a whole. Had we shown the individual scores or the risk drivers for the individual business units we could have seen that these scores are actually much higher than the average of the business units. This is obvious because the organization as a whole is much larger and much more complex than the individual units.

7 Conclusion

After having gained experience with the model for a year, we can draw a tentative conclusion that the outcome of the model helps us in assessing and comparing IT risks in the various business units. In the present version the model is still far from perfect. There are some areas that need improvement.

* Correlate the risk profile and the occurrence of actual adverse events.
  The risk profile indicates a probability of occurrence of adverse events. In order to validate this probability we need to gather information about the actual occurrence of adverse events, e.g. IT projects that fail, serious outages of IT systems, occurrences of fraud etc. At this moment we do not have enough statistical data to generate the correlation;

* Fine tune the scores
  The model has started as a tool for a general IT audit practice, to be used in a wide variety of industries. As a consequence the use in financial institutions may lead to little discriminating scores. A slightly different method of assigning scores (especially in the areas with very overlapping scores) may lead to an improved understanding of risk profiles across the organization

* Improve the consolidation mechanism
  In the overall picture we show the profile of some business units. In order to understand the profile of the bank we need a mechanism to add all of these profiles together. How do we weight the profile of e.g. the branch offices as opposed to the profile of e.g. the mortgage back office?

* Integrate with Operational Risk Management
  To comply with the Basel II Capital Agreements, the bank has started a project to assess the Operational Risk. The IT risk is a part of the operational risk. In the near future we need to integrate both risks.

References

Advies- en coördinatiepunt informatiebeveiliging (ACIB), *Handboek A&K-analyse*, August 1998

D. Bladergroen, B. Maas (et al.), *Planning en beheersing van IT-dienstverlening*, Deventer: Kluwer Bedrijfswetenschappen, 1995

J.F. Bautz RI RE, J.C. de Deugd, dr. G.F. Mes en drs. Ing. C.S. van der Zwan RE, *Contingency Management*, Handboek EDP Auditing, afl. 10, 1995

Drs. A. van den Berg, N.J.C. Schouten, drs. R. Toppen, *Automatisering onder controle; EDP auditing als volwassen beroep*, Deventer: Kluwer Bedrijfswetenschappen/Moret EDP Audit,

R. Berg en R. van Bruggen, *Effectiviteitsmeting en risico-analyse van informatisering*, Schoonoven: Academic Service, 1991

Drs. C.J. Coumou, Drs. J.W.R. Schoemaker, Het managen van ICT-risico's; over de onderhandelbaarheid van risico's en maatregelen, Compact Jubileumuitgave, 1996

Ir. Th.J.G. Derksen, Drs. H.W. Crins, *Automatisering van de informatieverzorging*, Schoonhoven: Academic Service, 4^e druk 1992

Ir. J.A.M. Donkers, M. Groesz RE, ir. J.A. Verstelle RE, *Informatie-technologie, Management control van de geautomatiseerde informatievoorziening*, Deventer: Kluwer Bedrijfswetenschappen (Controlling in de praktijk; 11)

European Security Forum, *SARA: Simple to Apply Risk Analysis*, mei 1993

European Security Forum, SPRINT: Risk Analysis for Information Systems, januari 1197

Prof. W. Hartman RA, *De kwaliteit van informatie*, Handboek EDP Auditing, afl. 14, 1998

J. E. Hunton Ph.D. CPA, C. Frowfelter-Lohrke Ph.D. CPA, G.L. Holstrum Ph.D. CPA, *New Assurance Opportunities for Information Systems Auditors*, IS Audit & Control Journal, Volume IV, 1999;

Information Systems Audit and Control Foundation, *CobiT*, 2nd edition, april 1998

Information Security Forum, FIRM: Fundamental Information Risk Management. Implementation Guide, 2000

Information Security Forum, FIRM: Fundamental Information Risk Management. Supporting. Supporting Material, 2000

R.A. Jonker RA, *ISO 9000*, Handboek EDP Auditing, afl. 14, 1998

Drs. L.J.J. Kordel CISA RE, *CobiT, een referentiemodel voor de controle van IT*, Informatie, november 1997.

K. de Laet, D. Deschoolmeester, *Informatievoorziening in (middel)grote organisaties*, Informatie, november 1997.

Ing. K. Meijer, *Apparatuurbeheer*, Handboek EDP Auditing, afl. 11, 1995

Ir. B.M. Middel, *Security-plan*, Handboek EDP Auditing, afl. 14. 1998

T.O. Mos CISA RE RE, Het (accountants?) audit risk voor IT-auditing beschouwd, De EDP Auditor, nummer 3, 1998

Prof. A.W. Neisingh RE RA, Informatie- en communicatietechnologie en accountants: een verstandshuwelijk?, Compact 1998/3.

Nederlands Genootschap voor Informatica, Studierapport toepassing van risico-analyse bij geautomatiseerde gegevensverwerking, 1991

Dr. Ir. Paul L. Overbeek, Ir. Gerben N. Nelemans, Common Criteria voor evaluatie van beveiliging van informatietechnologie, afl. 14, 1998

Drs. G.J. van der Pijl, *Kwaliteit van informatie in theorie en praktijk*, Deventer: Kluwer Bedrijsinformatie, Amsterdam: Limpberg instituut, 1994.

Drs. G.J. van der Pijl, Risico-analyse en beveiliging van informatiesystemen: noodzaak en probleem, BIKmag, april 1996.

Drs. Ing. G.J.P. Swinkels RE RA, ing. L.J.M.W. Gielen RE, *Knelpuntenanalyse projectmanagement*, Handboek EDP Auditing, afl. 9, 1994

H.T.M. van der Zee, Kwantitatieve kwaliteitsbeheersing en benchmarking van IT, Informatie, mei 1998.

H.T.M. van der Zee, Invoering van kwaliteitsbeheersing in de IT-organisatie, Handboek EDP Auditing, afl. 14, 1998

Cybercrime and Cyber Terrorism

Carolyn Nisbet

QinetiQ
Trusted Information Management
cnisbet@QinetiQ.com

Abstract

The view of cybercrime and cyber terrorism as bringers of mass disruption and destruction has been in existence for almost as long as the medium through which these attacks are perpetrated. While there is no doubt that there is a credible threat from cybercrime, as shown by the increasing numbers of incidents that are reported, the current threat from cyber terrorism is perhaps not as high as it has been made out to be on occasion.

There is often a degree of confusion between cybercrime and cyber terrorism. While one is becoming more widespread and better understood, the other is still seen as a major cause for concern and even panic in some quarters. This paper aims to explore the current risks posed by both cybercrime and cyber terrorism and to develop a position on where things actually stand with regard to the level of threat.

1 Introduction

Barely a week goes by without a new 'cyber-exploit' being reported in the media. This may consist of a new virus, the exploitation of a security flaw, a scam or even the announcement of a new file sharing service. These are all becoming fairly commonplace, and while they are by no means welcomed, they are unlikely to be the cause of mass outbreaks of panic among the population. Cybercrimes, as these types of activities are most commonly known, are on the increase. They have the potential to cause a nuisance, financial loss and some disruption, but they are not generally thought capable of causing destruction on a grand scale.

While it is clear that the theft of information is at the very least an irritation and can have financial consequences, it is not something that is likely to provoke a feeling of fear or terror. There is however a new threat on the horizon – cyber terrorism. The question is, should we be in genuine fear for our lives or our critical infrastructures as a result of cyber terrorism, or is the current risk more concentrated around activities more easily associated with cybercrime?

2 Defining the Problem

In order to establish the nature of the problem, it is necessary to define exactly what is meant by 'cybercrime' and 'cyber terrorism'.

Cybercrime is given a straightforward and wide-ranging definition:

- Crime committed using computers or the Internet[1]

---

[1] Source: Oxford English Dictionary Online

S. Paulus, N. Pohlmann, H. Reimer (Editors): Securing Electronic Business Processes, Vieweg (2004), 31-37

Cyber terrorism is much harder to quantify. The most common understanding of 'terrorism' is that of the unlawful use of force or violence against people or property to intimidate or coerce a government or a civilian population in pursuit of political objectives.

This definition clearly relates to the physical world. It may not be sufficient to simply prefix 'terrorism' with 'cyber' and expect the definition to have equal merit, as the physical and terror-inducing elements of terrorism are not easily replicated in the online world.

It has therefore become necessary to develop a separate definition of cyber terrorism. There have been a number of attempts to define this threat, two of which are reproduced below:

- Cyber terrorism is the use of computer network tools to shut down critical national infrastructures (such as energy, transportation, government operations) for the purpose of coercing or intimidating a government or civilian population.[2]

- 'Cyber terrorism' means intentional use or threat of use, without legally recognized authority, of violence, disruption, or interference against cyber systems, when it is likely that such use would result in death or injury of a person or persons, substantial damage to property, civil disorder, or significant economic harm.[3]

If either of these definitions become accepted as the norm, it will be necessary to examine i) how likely it is that death and injury can or will result from attacks on cyber systems and ii) how cyber terrorism in its current form differs from cybercrime, if at all.

3 Cyber Terrorism

At present, a cyber attack alone is not capable of causing terror in the same way that a car bomb does. It may however, be a means by which the effects of a physical attack are magnified, or it may be capable of causing significant economic damage. As we begin to place more reliance on computers, particularly mobile, multi-function systems, cyber attacks may begin to play a more significant role in augmenting physical terror attacks. The fact that they have not done so yet does not mean that this will be the case in the future.

Currently, an isolated cyber attack is not going to have the same impact as a more traditional terrorist attack. It may however, be used as a force multiplier to a physical attack, or it may result in the wasteful and unnecessary use of resources on a grand scale. Although a cyber attack may not cause loss of life, it has the potential to cause economic damage, either through direct attacks on financial institutions or through the indirect method of reducing trust in a particular organisation.

3.1 Separating Fact from Fiction

There have been many examples of possible cyber terrorism attacks discussed in recent years. These include, among others, disrupting water or power supplies, disabling air traffic control systems, attacking banking systems and altering additive levels in food so as to cause illness or death.

To determine whether these represent a significant threat, it is worth examining the arguments for and against these types of attack that have been put forward.

---

[2] www.fbi.gov/congress/congress00/cyber032800.htm at 15/08/2003

[3] Article 1.2 of the 'Proposal for an International Convention on Cyber Crime and Terrorism' by the Center for International Security and Co-operation.Located at www.iwar.org.uk/cyberterror at 15/08/2003

3.2 Utilities

The disruption of power or water supplies may not be possible unless a person is physically present at the site or has intimate knowledge of the system and its controls. An attack of this type was carried out in Australia in 2000[4] by a consultant who was involved in setting up the system in question and therefore had intimate knowledge of the processes required to launch the attack. The attacker released millions of gallons of raw sewage into the area around the processing plant after being refused a job by the local council. Although this was a disruptive act that caused environmental damage and inconvenience, it was not an act of terror. The fact that the attacker needed 46 attempts before he managed to penetrate the system, even with stolen control software, should be an adequate indication of the level of threat faced.

3.3 Air Traffic Control

As with many critical infrastructure components (such as utilities), the air traffic control systems (ATC) of any given country are invariably not connected to the Internet and are also not completely reliant on computers. While there is always a faint possibility that software may have been tampered with, the human element should help to counteract a lot of potential mistakes in may cases. The likelihood of vast numbers of planes falling out of the sky due to a breakdown of ATC systems brought on by cyber terrorism is slim. An attack was carried out on an ATC system in Massachusetts in 1997. Services were disrupted but there was no loss of life. Both ATC staff and pilots are fully trained to cope with problems relating to instrument and ATC failures. It is perhaps for this reason that terrorist attacks on aircraft tend to be of a physical nature, as they have a much greater effect.

3.4 Food

The possibility of food being contaminated through computer based alterations to a production line is not considered to be very likely. In the first place, food is generally tested fairly regularly and any contaminants would be picked up. If the contaminant in question were a very high dose of iron (as has been previously suggested) supplies on the production line would soon run low and the error would quickly be noticed[5].

3.5 Finance

Perhaps the most likely and easily brought about scenario relates to the financial world. It is not difficult to imagine a situation where a bank or other financial institution is the victim of a cyber attack. This is largely because the idea has already been accepted and proven to be possible by the numbers of incidents involving credit card numbers being stolen from databases by hackers.

Nevertheless, it would take a massive amount of time and resources to bring about the types of catastrophic stock market crashes and economic breakdowns that are very often forecast in conjunction with cyber terrorism.

---

[4] See www.theregister.co.uk/content/4/22579.html at 15/08/2003

[5] See www.cs.georgetown.edu/~denning/infosec/pollitt.html at 15/08/2003

3.6 Is there a Future for Cyber Terrorism?

The reason that 'traditional' terrorist acts succeed is because they are generally unexpected, difficult to stop and rely on tried and tested techniques such as the use of high explosives. To produce the same effect with an electronic attack would be a much more difficult feat.

The typical examples of cyber terrorism attacks that have been discussed are generally related to components of the critical infrastructure. These traditional targets, such as utility providers, have contingency plans for most situations. If a power station is taken off line, or even if an entire area is subject to continual blackouts as has been shown in August 2003 in the United States and Canada, the companies and users will cope. Although the events in August 2003 were by no means a minor occurrence, they did not result in a high loss of life or even a high panic rating once the population were made aware of the cause of the incident.

For any attack, physical or cyber based, to succeed, there must be a high degree of planning and information gathering. In a physical attack, there is generally only one opportunity to get things right; with a cyber attack, it may take numerous attempts before a successful attack is carried out. With every attempt, the risk of detection grows.

The mere fact that cyber terrorism is not as easily accomplished as physical terrorism means that it will be some time before computers take over from bombs, knives and guns as the terrorists' weapon of choice. This is not to say that computers do not have a part to play in terrorist campaigns. The Internet provides a great source of information on potential targets and is an effective method of communication between terrorist group members.

Terrorist groups are in essence, criminal organisations, and as such, they will use the Internet to raise money, collect intelligence and carry out acts (such as defacing web sites) that may not cause a great deal of destruction but that will get their message across. There is no doubt that cyber terrorists are also cyber criminals, although they are by no means alone in their desire to use the Internet for criminal purposes.

4 Cybercrime

It is generally accepted that cybercrime is on the increase. This does not necessarily mean that there are in fact any new crimes, more that there are new methods of committing existing crimes and better ways of detecting them. This increase in cybercrime is partly due to the fact that the authorities are more adept at spotting electronic crime than they were ten years ago. Confidence in sophisticated monitoring systems, increased use of computer forensics and the creation of organisations such as the UK National High Tech Crime Unit (NHTCU) have all contributed to the increase in visibility of cybercrime.

Although it is clear that the instances of reported crime are on the rise, the true state of cybercrime is less obvious. Companies are still reluctant to report attacks, fearing negative publicity. The legislative system is in need of greater cross-border strength. A recent Interpol conference calling for international regulation of cybercrime states that over 100 countries still do not have any laws relating to computer crime on their statute books.

4.1 Old Wine in New Bottles

With cybercrime on the increase, the implication is that there are in fact new crimes being committed. This is generally not the case. The majority of offences on the statute books have not required additional clarification in relation to the use of computers in their commission.

The changes in the way that cybercrime is being committed has meant that authorities and Internet users need to become more aware of potential scams and security issues. Criminals are finding new and often ingenious ways of carrying out offences that are proving harder to manage and are stretching resources to the limit in some cases.

4.2 The Oldest Trick in the Book?

A criminal group has been discovered spoofing a bank's website in order to collect revenue from an email scam. The spoofed site used logos and details from the genuine website, therefore giving it an air of legitimacy. This is the future of cybercrime – exploiting existing tactics in an innovative way. There is nothing new about a confidence trick; the difference is that the criminals have found a new way of running it.

4.3 Exploiting Security Concerns...

A virus alert was released in September 2003 relating to an email with the subject 'Internet security update'. The 'Microsoft security patch' enclosed in the email was in fact a virus. Unsuspecting users were downloading the 'patch' in the mistaken belief that they were securing their systems when in actual fact they were opening them up to greater vulnerabilities.

4.4 Changing the Target...

It was reported in October 2002 that a Denial of Service attack was attempted against 13 key Internet root servers. The attack failed, as it was not sufficiently powerful to overwhelm the servers; it did cause a minor slowdown that would have gone unnoticed by the majority of Internet users.

These examples illustrate the fact that cybercrime is developing along new lines, some more successful than others. Although all of the cases above have been discovered and dealt with, there are many more crimes that are going undetected.

This is due to a number of factors. Cyber criminals are getting sharper, 'polymorphic' viruses, i.e. viruses that can change their characteristics from infected machine to infected machine are on the increase, automated tools are taking a lot of the grief out of developing new cyber attacks. A programmer was recently charged under the Computer Misuse Act for writing and distributing a hacker toolkit thereby reducing the need for any of his 'customers' to have more than a basic understanding of computers.

4.5 Crimes Haven't Changed, Criminals Have...

It is estimated that almost 4000 Denial of Service attacks take place every week[6]. The majority do not make the headlines as they do not cause sufficient amounts of damage or disruption. The question is who is responsible for initiating these attacks?
Having said that the advent of the Internet is generally not creating new crimes, it may be creating new criminals. Today, a criminal could be anyone with access to the Internet and a vague idea of how to use it. Go to any search engine, type in 'hacker tools' and receive approximately 1,140,000 links to sites that will enable you to download a toolkit that will among other things, crack passwords, create a Trojan virus, sniff out weak network connections and so on.

---

[6] See www.internetnews.com/bus-news/article.php/773341 at 15/08/2003

These toolkits have enabled criminals to become increasingly confident. It is much easier to rob someone when you don't actually have to go into the bank with a gun, but can instead switch on your PC and get the computer to do the dirty work for you. The difficult part is hiding it.

In 1998, an attack was launched against US Department of Defense (DoD) computers. Known as 'Solar Sunrise' it was originally thought that the attacks were originating from, among other places, Israel, Taiwan and the United Arab Emirates. As the US was preparing for a bombing campaign against Iraq at the time, the attack was seen as a serious threat to US security. The attackers obtained hundreds of passwords to US defence networks. Although these were unclassified, many critical systems could have been affected including the finance and health databases.

Was this an attack by a sophisticated group with a political motive for harming US defence interests? No. The attack was eventually found to have originated from one teenager in Israel and two in California. The lesson from Solar Sunrise is twofold:

1. US defence systems were not adequately protected against what was essentially an unsophisticated attack,

2. The attack was carried out using tools downloaded from the Internet.

4.6 Are there New Victims of Crime?

As the range and ease of commission of cybercrime increases, so does the range of criminals. This in turn means that the range of potential victims is also increased. If you have ever bought anything from a website, or submitted your details to a website to receive information then you may be on a list of potential victims.

The acts committed against you may be as trivial as ending up on a spam email distribution list. At the moment this is an annoyance, however, sending unsolicited email is due to become regulated by law in Europe in 2003.

There is a risk that consumers may end up getting more than they had bargained for when using the Internet. It has already been shown that the potential for corporate identity theft is growing with the recent spoofing of a bank's website; the risk to individuals is also on the increase.

Identity theft is generally related to financial crimes, with credit card number theft being the most common occurrence. However, once your details have been stolen, they could be used to create a new virtual identity. If your address and other details such as your mother's maiden name are taken and used by a criminal, then there is a whole range of activities open to them, including taking out loans, re-directing mail, opening new bank accounts, applying for credit and so on. Identity theft is on the rise in the UK at the moment, with a growth rate of approximately 500% per annum.

There is also a more sinister side to identity related crimes. Criminals have been targeting Japanese users of Internet dating sites. Local police dealt with 888 crimes with links to dating sites in 2001, these included rapes and murders. If you do not protect your identity online, it could cost you your life.

5 Defending Against the New Threats

While there have been a number of consultations and recommendations on the subject of high tech crime and cyber terrorism, the situation is largely unchanged. This is due in part to a seemingly global reluctance of victims to admit to being affected by cybercrime, and also to a lack of understanding of the implications that may arise from the continued growth of high tech crime. This must change if the current problems surrounding crimes of this nature are to be effectively managed and if cyber terrorism is to be maintained as a low-level threat.

There are two main methods that can be used to manage the growth of cybercrime. The first is to ensure that the law is sufficient, it must be strong enough to act as a deterrent to potential criminals. However, the law cannot prevent crimes taking place; it can only deal with what has already happened. The second is to ensure that network security and general security awareness are as effective as possible.

5.1   How Can this be Achieved?

- Strong authentication techniques
  Using public key cryptography, reliable biometric authentication, smartcards and other secure identity tokens can prevent unauthorised access to personal data and provide assurance of identity.

- Forensic readiness
  Monitoring network facilities to maintain awareness of potential misuse, maintaining rigorous access control procedures, keeping audit logs and responding to incidents in an appropriate manner. Forensic readiness ensures that any attacks that do take place are dealt with quickly and in the most appropriate manner.

- Network security
  Correctly configured firewalls, Intrusion Detection Systems (IDS), privacy policies and regularly patched systems will all play a part in making a criminal's life more difficult. If information is not available to steal, then cybercrime will be reduced.

These will all contribute to a more secure environment in which cyber criminals have fewer opportunities to act. However, securing a network is only part of the solution.

The other vital part of the equation is to ensure that the law is moving in the right direction. It has already been noted that the law does not often require updating to cope with new crimes, however, there may be areas of liability that have yet to be fully addressed. Some legislation that was drafted with protecting information in mind is now being updated as the technologies and methods for exploiting user data become more sophisticated. This is most strongly embodied in the EU Directive 2002/58/EC – on Privacy and Electronic Communications.

6   Conclusion

There must be a coherent approach taken by lawmakers, companies and consumers alike if cybercrime is ever going to become a manageable problem. While there is a great deal of discussion in the media about the problem of cyber terrorism, and while most of it is discounted as hyperbole, there is still a threat. The fact that the threat is currently considered to be fairly low does not mean that this will remain the case.

Cybercrime is not going to go away, it is on the increase. Unless steps are taken to improve awareness of the types of attacks that a typical Internet user could be subject to the situation is not going to improve. Security is not just about protecting systems from attack; it must be a total awareness of the environment in which increasing numbers of people spend their time. You wouldn't walk down a dark and deserted street in the 'wrong area' of town carrying your life savings, why would you do the equivalent on the Internet?

Providing Cost-effective Security Functionality into Applications

Jeremy Hilton

Viviale Ltd, 1 Hunters Meadow
Chippenham, Wilts, SN14 7JF, UK
jhilton@viviale.com

Abstract

This paper asserts that the current approach to the use of asymmetric cryptography and the provision of digital certificates is overly cumbersome, expensive and forces unreasonable requirements on standard business users and consumers; so they ignore or resist their use. In addition, many web-based applications are emerging without appropriate security functionality built-in. It proposes the management of digital certificates within an enhanced commercial environment using best practice personnel recruiting and management procedures and best practice information security management combined with enhanced cryptographic services within the installed base of the corporate IT infrastructure. This, combined with a security middle layer based on the XML Key Management Specification will suffice. The benefit is commercially "fit-for-purpose" identity management, and security functionality, provided at a corporate level, which meets the requirements of applicable law whether it is the EU Directive, or other legislation such as the US HIPAA and Sarbanes-Oxley law.

1 Background

With the OECD Guidelines for the Security of Information Systems and Networks, the EU proposal for a European policy approach on Network and Information Security as well as the increasing emphasis on corporate governance, it can be argued that we need security and confidence in IT systems more than ever, but the current commercial climate is depressed and unsure. Therefore investment in IT infrastructures is low, and greater risks are being taken by businesses. There is a paradox that whilst the EU is requiring more use of electronic signatures (and for those, read digital signatures – X.509-style) for business use and e-invoicing, many businesses are continuing to follow what the experts believe are insecure practices involving open communications across the Internet. It can be argued that it is their business and they manage the risks that they identify – some insure, some ignore, some apply controls. However, some of that information is personal such as pay details and terms of employment etc.

In addition, many companies have invested heavily in the development and marketing of Public Key Infrastructure software and services, but their current success is limited at best and failure for many. The hype surrounding PKI during the technology boom has died away, and reality has set in causing a valuable reconsideration of the real needs.

2 Introduction

PKI has been seen to be to complex, too expensive and too much for a business to use effectively. It is often perceived (if understood) to be more of a technician's "game" than a real

S. Paulus, N. Pohlmann, H. Reimer (Editors): Securing Electronic Business Processes, Vieweg (2004), 38-48

business tool and problem solving technology. To date, much of this is true and this has to change.

We need to reconsider the whole approach to implementing security functionality into applications. The view must begin with what applications are desired to provide a "business service" either within an organisation, between organisations in a community and to an organisation's customers, combined with what are the appropriate functions required to mitigate risk to an acceptable level.

One of the significant enablers of information security is the use of asymmetric encryption underpinned by a Public Key Infrastructure, but in many areas the practical implementation of Public Key Infrastructures has failed.

3 Current Environment

Some of the apparent reluctance to change IT systems to embrace security controls is a non-acceptance of the risks as perceived by IT specialists, as there may be greater business risks that have a higher priority for corporate management. In other situations, the size of the organisation (number of employees and number of sites) means that producing a consistent and manageable solution across the organisation is extremely difficult – even to introduce a PCMCIA or USB-based token solution for identity management will be very expensive and time-consuming for an organisation – not least to provide a solution easy enough for the majority of employees to use and have confidence in.

Therefore, we make a number of assertions. Use of third party services can be expensive. Though there is generally a benefit of scale through using third party services, this is not the case in identifying one's own employees and registering them for digital certificates. In addition, the acclaimed high secure infrastructure of third party service providers may be more than is required by your organisation and certificate fees are (naturally) priced to produce a revenue stream for the provider and are high due to the (current) low utilisation of their services.

Use of proprietary software is expensive and implementations have been overly complex. Public Key Infrastructure solutions are driven by the certificate software vendors. They have developed the software based on their perspective of what is right for the end user. The standards have been developed in parallel to support the products and (hopefully) provide a common structure. However, implementations differ and interoperability can easily be lost through selecting different options. Complexity remains as once a vendor has laid down a product base, they will maintain that approach to support their investment, even if it is too complex for the end user.

It should be born in mind that the use of Public Key Infrastructure functionality must be "fit for purpose" to reduce risk to an acceptable level. Also with the investment in IT infrastructure already in place, an organisation should make the best use of it and not duplicate the functionality it contains. So, if your infrastructure includes the ability to manage digital certificates then use it and only add the necessary functionality to mitigate any outstanding risks, and to ease administration.

Most organisations operate within a community – a loosely self-defined closed use group, according to trade, sector etc. Therefore there is no need to invest in a huge directory infrastructure. There will generally be trading agreements in place, or prior negotiations of some form before business transactions begin. Therefore there is not the need for lengthy Certification Practice Statements, or Certificate Policies. The substance of these will be included in Terms and Conditions, Service Level Agreements and other existing contracts. A consumer will never read a Certificate Policy or Certification Practice Statement, so any obligations placed on them must be expressed simply.

There is no perfect or absolutely foolproof solution; things will still go wrong as in real life. Therefore, the process of transacting must recognise this and not expect (unreasonably) that using encryption and digital certificates will remove all risks. Other checks and balances must be built into applications.

4 Areas of Trust

The principal areas of trust that need to be considered in providing security functionality are identity verification, security administration, key and certificate management and security/privacy. In assessing the risk in your business information systems, controls in these areas must be adequate ("fit for purpose").

Therefore in operating a Public Key Infrastructure, you must also consider the operational issues which include:

1. Strong authentication of PKI system administrator and operator functions;
2. Registration of the subjects;
3. The confusion that surrounds the Certificate Policy and the Certification Practice Statement;
4. Certificate validation (checking the chain);
5. Trust Anchors;
6. Application Integration.

If you are using your existing IT infrastructure, you must ensure the controls are adequate in these areas; i.e., using hardware cryptographic devices to underpin the CA functionality in either open source or Microsoft certification authorities, proper validation of identity of administrators and end users, and dual person log-in with two factor authentication for critical administrative functions.

5 Integration of Security Functionality

There has to be a valid reason for investing in the protection of critical business applications. However, the decision to invest will generally be a financially-based one. The more expensive the life-time cost of security measures, the more likely it is that an organisation will "take the risk" and remain exposed.

Once a decision has been taken, then the appropriate controls must be properly integrated into the application, otherwise the cost of administration (and, therefore, ownership) is increased. As Grinter and Smetters state [GrSm03], security cannot be considered in the abstract away form a particular application and context of use. They state that purely considering a threat model doesn't consider the user as part of the equation. The work of Sasse and others [AdSa99] [SaBW01] has argued that to be effective, security has to be designed in terms of 1) the user, 2) the task they are using the technology to accomplish, and 3) the context of that task activity (for example, whether it is in the office or at home).

Security functionality, if properly designed, is invisible. People working the way they are supposed to will not be hindered in any way; in fact, properly design and implemented security functionality can be an enabler. It is only when people attempt to work against the security policy that the controls become visible.

Effective integration will depend on your IT infrastructure. In a Microsoft environment, it helps to use Microsoft provided security functionality (suitably enhanced where required); likewise in an open source environment. In a web services environment, the same applies. Indeed, web services introduce significant opportunities for properly integrating security functionality.

5.1 Business

Many references cite the need to understand the user model, often captured using business process modelling techniques. Grinter and Smetters [GrSm03] propose that even if the tasks can be identified, the user expectation is often missed. Hagel [Hage02] uses the term process networks to reflect the new set of business relationships that are emerging. Understanding these process networks will enable the related businesses to identify their critical security issues. These can be modelled using a number of methods including Soft Systems Methodology [Wils90] and Business Process Management [SmFi03] as well as the Unified Modelling Language. Other research [HiMc95] proposes an approach to relate security functional requirements to business processes. This is summarised below.

5.1.1 Analysing the Threats and Vulnerabilities

Once the business processes have been captured and endorsed by senior management, a further analysis may be made of each one in order to identify the threats and vulnerabilities.

Done Now		Reach	
By Whom		Volumes	
How		Frequency	
With Whom		Location	
Success		Mode	
Threats		Reliability	
Vulnerabilities		Single/shared	

Figure 1 - Tabular analysis of the process activity

This can be confirmed with the business area and provides the link between the business process and the requirement for a countermeasure.

The advantage of this is that the countermeasure is seen in the context of the business process, and the cost of implementing the countermeasure can be directly related to the value generated by the business process or the loss incurred through unavailability of a resource.

5.1.2 Relationship to Core Business Processes

The impact of one business process on any other one can be identified, which will ensure that threats are not seen in isolation and that the countermeasures are seamless and cost-effective. By taking a systemic view of the enterprise and understanding the relationship between processes, business processes throughout the enterprise can be related to the core business activities. Therefore, senior management can better understand the threats to their core business processes and concentrate their efforts accordingly.

5.1.3 Management Buy-in

Development of business models necessarily involves input from many parts of the enterprise. Our experience has been that the use of workshops and other group activities to develop business models results in a wide ownership of the models, making them both more robust and facilitating a consensus. Senior management is thus better placed to understand the risks to their area and collectively understand the risks that their enterprise faces. Any individual perspectives can be brought out and a consensus obtained.

With this understanding, the roles of staff can be better defined to alleviate the inherent risks and to ensure that any countermeasures are implemented in an acceptable fashion. More importantly, the modelling approach will ensure that all staff can understand the threats and vulnerabilities within their area of operation, as well as understand and accept the need for any countermeasures.

5.2 Architecture

SSL and S/MIME are standard implementations that use digital certificates. Even though there are a few outstanding issues in the interoperation between different vendor's applications.

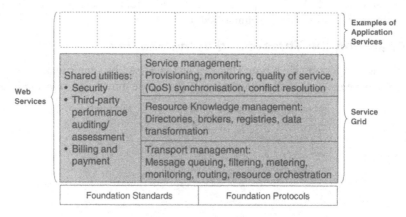

Figure 2 - Web Service architecture

Within the emerging Web Services architecture, there is a Service Grid which comprises a set of specialized utilities which provide a broad range of enabling services to both users and providers of applications. At its broadest level, the Service Grid performs four roles: deliver mission-critical functionality; create, discover, refine and disseminate shared meaning; support the capture of monetary value from Web Services; and find and access appropriate resources.

5.3 Key Enabler

The key enable in this is Web Services Security (WS-Security) [WS-Sec]. Web services can be accessed by sending SOAP messages to service endpoints identified by URIs, requesting specific actions, and receiving SOAP message responses (including fault indications). Within this context, the broad goal of securing Web services breaks into the subsidiary goals of providing facilities for securing the integrity and confidentiality of the messages and for ensuring that the service acts only on requests in messages that express the claims required by policies.

Today the Secure Socket Layer (SSL) along with the de facto Transport Layer Security (TLS) is used to provide transport level security for web services applications. SSL/TLS offers several security features including authentication, data integrity and data confidentiality. SSL/TLS enables point-to-point secure sessions.

IPSec is another network layer standard for transport security that may become important for Web services. Like SSL/TLS, IPSec also provides secure sessions with host authentication, data integrity and data confidentiality.

A joint IBM/Microsoft white paper [DDF+02] proposes the following architecture which is aimed to ensure that:

- A Web service can require that an incoming message prove a set of *claims* (e.g., name, key, permission, capability, etc.). If a message arrives without having the required claims, the service may ignore or reject the message. We refer to the set of required claims and related information as *policy*.

- A requester can send messages with proof of the required claims by associating *security tokens* with the messages. Thus, messages both demand a specific action and prove that their sender has the claim to demand the action.

- When a requester does not have the required claims, the requester or someone on its behalf can try to obtain the necessary claims by contacting other Web services. These other Web services, which we refer to as *security token services*, may in turn require their own set of claims. Security token services broker trust between different trust domains by issuing security tokens.

This model is illustrated in the figure below, showing that any requester may also be a service, and that the Security Token Service may also fully be a Web service, including expressing policy and requiring security tokens.

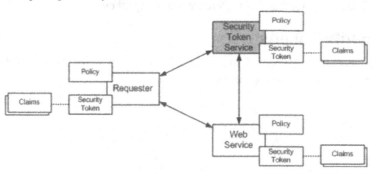

Figure 3 - Web Services Security Model

The WS-Security specification is a message security model that provides the basis for other trust security specifications. WS-Security is flexible and is designed to be used as the basis for the construction of a wide variety of security models including PKI, Kerberos, and SSL. Specifically WS-Security provides support for multiple security tokens, multiple trust domains, multiple signature formats, and multiple encryption technologies.

The specification provides three main mechanisms: security token propagation, message integrity, and message confidentiality. These mechanisms by themselves do not provide a complete security solution. Instead, WS-Security is a building block that can be used in conjunction with other Web service extensions and higher-level application-specific protocols to accommodate a wide variety of security models and encryption technologies. This is illustrated below:

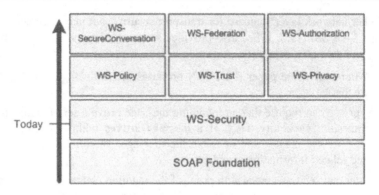

Figure 4 - Proposed Web Services Security Architecture

Message integrity is provided by leveraging XML Signature in conjunction with security tokens (which may contain or imply key data) to ensure that messages are transmitted without modifications. The integrity mechanisms are designed to support multiple signatures, potentially by multiple actors, and to be extensible to support additional signature formats. The signatures may reference (i.e. point to) a security token.

Similarly, message confidentiality is provided by leveraging XML Encryption in conjunction with security tokens to keep portions of SOAP messages confidential. The encryption mechanisms are designed to support additional encryption technologies, processes, and operations by multiple actors. The encryption may also reference a security token.

5.4 Security Tokens

The common and absolutely key element within WS-Security is the Security Token. A *security token* [WS-Sec] represents a collection of claims.

Figure 5 - Security Tokens

A *signed security token* [WS-Sec] is a security token that is asserted and cryptographically endorsed by a specific authority (e.g. an X.509 certificate or a Kerberos ticket).

Management of these tokens is one of the key areas of trust. The correct identification, authentication and authorisation of the users (and systems) within business processes should enable risk mitigation appropriate to the threats identified.

Within the Web Services environment, XML Key Management Specification (XKMS) provides a modern XML/SOAP-based protocol for key management. It includes functions for key information, registration, verification, reissue, recovery and revocation [XKMS01].

XKMS is intended to provide key management support to technologies such as XML Signature and Encryption, but it is equally suited for use with other technologies such as S/MIME and SSL. Also, XKMS hides most of the complexity of Public Key Infrastructure in the service, rendering clients thinner and less complex.

6 Cost Effective Security

Remember the principal areas of trust that need to be considered in providing security functionality are identity verification, security administration, key and certificate management and security/privacy. From an operational view, points that need addressing are application Integration, registration of the subjects, strong authentication of PKI system administrator and operator functions, the confusion that surrounds the Certificate Policy and the Certification Practice Statements, certificate validation (checking the chain), and trust anchors.

6.1 XKMS and WS-Security

The first cost area is the cost of integrating security into applications. Invariably it is not included at the design stage, but has to be added on. Recognising this, the most cost effective way of integrating security into applications is to use the main standards such as SSL (TLS), S/MIME and WS-Security. Token (key management) for all of these can be provided through an XKMS interface. This means standardised functions for key information, registration, verification, reissue, recovery and revocation thus enabling a consistent interface for security services. These are utilised directly by business applications as well as Public Key Infrastructure management applications. The additional benefit in using XKMS is that it both connects to legacy applications and future-proofs you for future requirements as well as shields the client from the complexity of Public Key management.

6.2 Manage your Own Keys

Another major cost area is the registration and identity validation of the users – whether they are employees accessing applications as a part of doing their job, consumers or those in sensitive posts such as system administrators and security officers.

But, putting things in context and being pragmatic, the risks are to your business systems. You make the choice of the level of security you require if you own the application. Within process networks, the organisations involved will define the requirements for the systems, but essentially it is still to secure systems where the users are acting on behalf of the companies in question. Consumers are a different issue, but rarely do you need to consistently identify a consumer. Generally you are interested in their ability to pay (credit Card number), or in a delivery address. Any more than that is because you wish them to enrol in "something". At that point, identity verification can occur to the level required by the business, within the constraints of applicable laws.

Therefore, why shouldn't the organisation issue its own certificates?

Certificates should be issued as part of registering for a service, and often will be hidden from the user. For example, registering a new customer/supplier is often done by an organisation as a standard business function for financial management, or contractual agreements. Why does the customer need to undergo more than this.

Yes, the individual may collect a number of certificates, but those issued by some organisations, especially if they are known to meet slightly more strict requirements (such as the "Directive" [DIR99/93] and be known as Qualified Certificates) may be accepted by other organisations. Indeed this could be a benefit provided by some organisations that could issue company ID cards which comply with the Directive. This already happens in Sweden where many Company ID cards comply with the Swedish SIS standard for National Identity Cards.

6.3 Utilise the Existing IT Infrastructure

Another significant benefit of XKMS is the ability to access more than one Certification Authority. Therefore you may wish to use more than one Certification Authority. You may operate all of these, but you may choose to use a third party service for some certificates, and your own for others. This is one way of future-proofing applications as changing or adding Certification Authorities is (technically) very straightforward.

However, many organisations have a Microsoft or (increasingly) an Open Source infrastructure. By having a registration application built on XKMS (with suitable user and application interfaces), the Microsoft Server 2000 or 2003 Certification Authority, or Open Source CA can provide the necessary certificate signing capability. Therefore, why pay additional unnecessary and expensive license or service fees for functionality you do not need.

Considering that incorporating the security functionality provided by a Public Key Infrastructure is to secure your critical business applications, it is unlikely that you will need significantly greater physical or environmental security controls for your Certification Authority than your business servers. Certainly, if you comply with standards such as [ISO 17799] the additional controls required will be minimal. Hardware cryptographic devices for key generation, storage and singing will be necessary, as well as a rack-mountable security container for the CA server. However, it is likely that these can reside alongside the critical business systems.

6.4 Token-based Authentication

Simultaneous strong authentication of multiple administrators will probably be required. This should utilise hardware cryptographic tokens with integrated smartcard reader or USB token interfaces. The same devices should be used for identification and authentication of registration agents.

6.5 Integrated Procedures

Securing the infrastructure with appropriate cryptography and administrative capabilities, and operating the infrastructure in a secure way (which may include the use of security containers for servers rather than hugely expensive vaults) will probably be adequate and fit-for-purpose operation of the corporate Certification Authority. Operating an open-source CA in this environment will probably achieve the aim if users are not happy with the functionality provided by their existing platforms.

This would not need to be an expensive option for an organisation. When they recruit, they already (should) conduct some background checks (references etc) of employees. Companies such as healthcare providers, financial services firms and airlines already have to screen all employees and costs between $25 and $35 in the US. Corporate servers are often in relatively secure environments (for their own business continuity purposes) and may only need some hardware security modules incorporated. Specific operating procedures and some additional audit checks during their existing audit programme would be required.

6.6 CP/CPS

Within the business environment the Certificate Policy and Certification Practice Statement are not strictly necessary. Businesses will agree specific terms and conditions for process networks, and these are likely to be incorporated into contracts. End user obligations should be built into the application interfaces and business logic. Any specific employee end-user obligations should be incorporated into either an employment contract, or specific agreement signed when the employee is issued with a security token.

Outside the business environment, individuals choose to join clubs and organisations etc. According to the club/organisation's function (football supporters club, library, frequent flyer, university etc) the identification needs vary. So be it, but it is up to the club in order to meet their needs. The Certificate Policy and Certification Practice Statement are not an issue as it is up to the organisation and they generally have their own rules which include membership requirements and privileges etc.

6.7 Trust Anchors

Businesses generally operate within a community of suppliers, distributors and trade associations. Within a community or application, the Trust Anchor may not be an issue, but without one in the browser, there are usage issues. It is proposed that instead of the expensive Root Update programme provided by the browser manufacturers, there are organisations that provide Root Chaining services and Bridging functionality such as the European Bridge CA. The European Bridge CA already provides services for one self regulated community, but they would be happy to host other self-regulated communities. In this fashion, Certificate Policy and Certification Practice Statements are not required – there would be a community membership contract in place. Relying party agreements are replaced by membership rules or contracts such as exist already.

7 Summary

Integrating the security functionality into applications has often been a challenge even when required. Too often, security functions have been added by "bolt-on" products, not through being designed in. With the emergence of web-based applications and XML, this is now much easier with WS Security.

- Take a standard windows server
- Add a hardware cryptographic card with integrated Card reader & PIN pad
- Include an integrated card reader and PIN pad for strong administrator(s) authentication
- Provide security functionality for applications based on XKMS
- Add an open source CA hosted on the cryptographic card if MS CA is not acceptable
- Operate in a secure manner

Figure 6 - Cost Effective Security

A combination of WS Security, open source CA operated on a hardware cryptographic card with integrated card reader and PIN-pad/biometric device for strong authentication of administrators, proper procedures and appropriately enhanced commercial Information Security Management will provide a pragmatic solution to identity management and security functionality in business applications.

References

[AdSa99]   Adams, A and Sasse, M.A. Users are not the enemy. Communications of the ACM, 42 (12). 1999. 41-46.

[DDF+02]   A Joint White Paper from IBM and Microsoft. Security in a Web Service World: a Proposed Architecture and Roadmap, 2002. (available from: http://msdn.microsoft.com/library/default.asp?url=/library/en-us/dnwssecur/html/securitywhitepaper.asp)

[DIR99/93] Directive 1999/93/EC of the European Parliament and of the Council of 13 December 1999 on a Community framework for electronic signatures

[GrSm03]   Grinter, R and Smetters D, Three challenges for embedding security into appliacations. In Workshop on Human-Computer Interaction and Security Systems, CHI2003, April 5-10, 2003, Fort Lauderdale, Florida.

[Hage02]   Hagel III, John.: Out of the Box; Strategies for achieving profits today and growth tomorrow through web services. Harvard Business School Press, 2002.

[HiMc95]   Hilton, J., McIntosh, S, Business Assurance - a Business Modelling Approach to Information Systems Security, 1995 (available from jeremy.hilton@cs.cf.ac.uk or S.B.McIntosh@cs.cf.ac.uk)

[ISO17799] ISO/IEC 17799:2000. Information Technology - Code of Practice for Information Security Management.

[SaBW01]   Sasse, M.A., Brostoff, S. and Weirich, D. Transforming the "Weakest Link" – a human/computer interaction approach to usable and effective security. B.T. Technology Journal, 19 (3). 2001. 122-131.

[SmFi03]   Smith, H. and Fingar, P. Business Process Management; the Third Wave. Mehgan-Kiffer Press. 2003

[Wils90]   Wilson, B. Systems: Concepts Methodologies and Applications, 2nd Edition. John Wiley & Sons. 1990.

[WS-Sec]   Web Services Security (WS-Security). Version 1.0 2002.

[XKMS01] XML Key Management Specification (XKMS), W3C Note 30 March 2001. This version: http://www.w3.org/TR/2001/NOTE-xkms-20010330/ . Latest version: http://www.w3.org/TR/xkms/

Technology

Trends in Cryptology Research

Bart Preneel

Katholieke Univ. Leuven, Dept. Electrical Engineering-ESAT/COSIC,
Kasteelpark Arenberg 10, B-3001 Leuven-Heverlee, Belgium
bart.preneel@esat.kuleuven.ac.be

Abstract

Cryptology is an essential building block for any IT security solution. In the past decades, cryptology has evolved from a secret art to a modern science. Political controls of cryptography have diminished substantially, crippled algorithms are disappearing, and secure and efficient cryptography is becoming more and more a commodity. This may lead us to believe that the cryptography problem is "solved." However, this article will show that there are still many challenging problems ahead of us in the area of cryptographic algorithms. We will discuss the increasingly powerful attacks on implementations that are based on side channels, faults and errors (the recent SSL problem), but also the more fundamental problems such as the conjectured difficulty of factoring and the progress of quantum computers. Part of the work discussed in this paper is based on the STORK (http://www.stork.eu.org) and NESSIE (http://www.cryptonessie.org) projects.

1 Introduction

While cryptology is getting increasingly important in the information society, it is also becoming less and less visible. Cryptology has been integrated into smart cards for financial transactions, web browsers, operating systems, mobile phones and electronic identity cards. This may give the false impression that cryptography is a research discipline that has ran out of practical problems and that should be left over to theoreticians who can keep trying to solve the question whether or not one-way functions exist. While our intuition seems to suggest that it is very straightforward to design a function that is "easy" to compute but "hard" to invert, so far the best theoretical result can prove that there exist functions that are twice as hard to invert as to compute [Hilt92]; it is clear that such functions would be completely useless to cryptology.

Most of the applications are covered by the block ciphers DES and triple-DES [FI46], the hash function SHA-1 [FI180-2] (in some applications RIPEMD-160 [DoBP95]) and RSA [RiSA78]. In addition there are a number of proprietary algorithms in GSM (A3/A8, A5/1 and A5/2 [BiSW00,Vedd91]) and the stream cipher (`alleged') RC4[1] which is widely deployed for SSL/TLS; recent results cast some doubts on the security of the key setup of RC4 [FlMS01,MaSh02].

What we will try to explain in this article is that there remain many challenging problems in practical cryptography.

---

[1] RC4 is claimed to be a trade secret of RSA Security Inc.

S. Paulus, N. Pohlmann, H. Reimer (Editors): Securing Electronic Business Processes, Vieweg (2004), 51-58

2 New Algorithms and Standards

This section will briefly discuss the recent algorithms proposed by NIST (National Institutes for Standards and Technology), ETSI (European Telecommunications Standardisation Institute) and the research project NESSIE (New European Schemes for Signature, Integrity and Encryption).

2.1 NIST

Even if triple-DES offers a security level of 80 bits (which means that even a well-funded opponent would take more than 10 years to recover a key by exhaustive search), this will not be sufficient for long term security (15 years or more). Moreover, the performance of triple-DES is not very good (115 cycles/byte on a Pentium III) and the block length of 64 bits implies that at most 2^{32} blocks can be encrypted under a single key in the common modes due to the birthday paradox.

In 2001, NIST has published the AES (Advanced Encryption Standard) [DaRi01,FI197], which offers a high security level (key lengths of 128, 192 and 256 bits and block length of 128 bits) and a much better performance (15 cycles/byte).

The security level of SHA-1 against collisions is also limited to 80 bits. In 2002, NIST has published new hash functions SHA-256, SHA-384 and SH-512 [FI180-2] which offer a security level of 128, 192 and 256 bits, matching the AES key sizes. In contrast to AES, these new hash functions are substantially slower (21-40 cycles/byte) compared to SHA-1 (8 cycles/byte).

2.2 ETSI

In 2000 ETSI has published the block cipher KASUMI that will be used in 3GPP/UMTS, which was a substantial change of policy. KASUMI is a 64-bit block cipher with a 128-bit key, that is a slightly simplified version of the block cipher MISTY1 (published in 1996). In July 2002 ETSI has also announced A5/3, a variant of KASUMI, that will replace A5/1 and A5/2. Weaknesses of A5/1 and A5/2 have been reported for example in [BiSW00] and [BaBK03] respectively.

2.3 NESSIE

NESSIE (New European Schemes for Signature, Integrity, and Encryption) [NESSIE] is a research project within the Information Societies Technology (IST) Programme of the European Commission. NESSIE is a 40-month project, which started in January 2000. The goal of the NESSIE project is to put forward a portfolio of strong cryptographic primitives that has been obtained after an open call and been evaluated using a transparent and open evaluation process. In February 2000, the NESSIE project has launched an open call for a broad set of primitives providing confidentiality, data integrity, and authentication. These primitives include block ciphers (not restricted to 128-bit block ciphers), stream ciphers, hash functions, MAC algorithms, digital signature schemes, and public-key encryption schemes. In September 2000, more than 40 primitives have been received from major players in response to the NESSIE call. Two-thirds of the submissions came from industry, and there was some industry involvement in every 5 out of 6 algorithms. During 12 months, a first security and performance evaluation phase took place, which was supported by contributions from more than 50 external researchers. In September 2001, the selection of a subset of 26 primitives for the second phase has been published. In February 2003, the portfolio of recommended NESSIE primitives has been announced. It contains the following 17 algorithms (twelve of these are NESSIE submissions and five have been selected from existing standards):

- block ciphers: the 64-bit block cipher MISTY1, the 128-bit block ciphers Camellia and AES, and the 256-bit block cipher Shacal-2;
- MAC algorithms TTMAC and UMAC, and the standardized algorithms EMAC, HMAC from [IS9797];
- hash functions Whirlpool and SHA-256, -384, -512;
- asymmetric encryption algorithms: PSEC-KEM, RSA-KEM, ACE Encrypt;
- digital signatures schemes RSA-PSS, ECDSA, SFLASH;
- asymmetric identification scheme: GPS.

The goal of NESSIE is to publish the recommended primitives and to submit these primitives to standardization bodies.

Some of the important conclusions from the NESSIE project are:

- The submitted stream ciphers were designed by experienced researchers and offer a very good performance, but none of them seems to meet the very stringent security requirements;
- In 2002, a new class of attacks (algebraic attacks, e.g., [CoPi02,MuRo02] has been introduced. They seem to form a very powerful tool to cryptanalyse stream ciphers, but they may also be apply to certain classes of block ciphers. One year after their announcement, it is still unclear how effective these attacks are on block ciphers; further research is clearly needed.
- Most asymmetric primitives needed small modifications and corrections between the 1st and 2nd phase, which shows that many subtle issues are involved in the specification of these primitives;
- The NESSIE project has influenced many designers to make their algorithms less expensive to use. Thirteen algorithms (out of 17) are in the public domain and the conditions for PSEC-KEM are very mild. Only one algorithm was eliminated due to IPR problems.

3 Cryptographic Algorithms for New Environments

While the algorithms discussed in Sect. 2 present a substantial improvement in the state of the art, we will argue in this section why further cryptographic research is needed.

3.1 Highly Secure Cryptographic Algorithms

All of the new symmetric algorithms discussed above have only *heuristic* security. This implies that for the time being we are now aware of any attack which can break these schemes. However, it may well be that tomorrow or next year a new clever attack is discovered which demonstrates that the scheme is much weaker than anticipated.

For the asymmetric primitives, the situation is slightly better: the seven primitives listed in Sect. 2.3 have a "proof of security"; this means in practice that if the primitive can be broken, then a problem believed to be hard (such as factoring, computing a discrete logarithm in an elliptic curve group) can be solved. However, in most cases the proof uses some additional assumptions. A more serious problem is that a problem widely believed to be hard (such as the factoring an integer that is the product of two large primes) may not be hard at all. For example, if large quantum computers can be built, factoring may be very easy (a result by Shor [Shor94]). While early experiments are promising [VSB+01], experts are divided on the question whether sufficiently powerful quantum computers can be built in the next 15-20 years.

This clearly shows the need to develop new algorithms: for symmetric algorithms, we need better heuristics and proofs of resistance against a larger class of known attacks; it would be even better if we could reduce their security to well known problems. For asymmetric algorithms, there is a need for algorithms based on a wider range of problems believed to be hard, and more in particular for algorithms which would be secure even if large quantum computers can be built.

3.2 Low Cost Algorithms

While symmetric cryptographic algorithms are inexpensive on modern PCs with 2 GHz clocks, there is a clear need for highly efficient algorithms that would be suitable for environments where the gate count and power consumption is absolutely critical; one can think for example of distributed sensor networks (piconets [RASP+00]) or ubiquitous computing models. For the time being we don't know how to build a stream cipher or a block cipher that offers a security level of 80 bits or more, that offers a reasonable performance, and that fits in less than 1000 gates.

For asymmetric cryptographic algorithms, this is clearly way beyond reach. However, here we would like to have algorithms that require less than one second for a public or private key operation on an 8-bit processor with a few hundred bytes of RAM (currently this is only feasible with a co-processor). Another challenge is the design of secure public key algorithms that have short block lengths (160-bit for encryption and 80 or 160-bit digital signatures).

3.3 High Performance Cryptography

At the other end of the application spectrum, there are requirements for hard disk encryption, bus encryption and high speed connections (Gigabit/s to Terabit/s). For such applications, the main requirements would be high performance and a high degree of parallelism. As the NESSIE project has demonstrated, for the time being there does not exist a highly secure stream cipher that runs at a few cycles/byte, that is, 5 to 10 times faster than the AES block cipher.

4 Cryptography Against New Attack Models

Even if the cryptographic algorithms are more secure, the way they are used and implemented has to change substantially. In the last decade, we have learned that weaknesses in modes and in implementations are even more of a problem than most mathematical attacks on the underlying algorithm.

4.1 Blockwise Adaptive Attackers

A first type of new attacks are attacks on modes where the attacker does not submit the complete plaintext to the encryption device, but rather block by block [JoMV02]. This may have as implication that a provably secure way of using a block cipher becomes highly insecure. New modes of block ciphers are being developed that take into account this problem. A similar attack on stream ciphers exploits the resynchronization mechanism of synchronous stream ciphers (a typical example is the attack on the use of RC4 in the IEEE 802.11 WLAN standard WEP, which has been exploited in [FIMS01] and demonstrated in [StIR02]).

4.2   Chosen Ciphertext Attacks or Reaction Attacks

The secure encryption of a plaintext requires some additional formatting, which includes for example the padding of the plaintext to a fixed length or to a multiple of 8 or 16 bytes and the conversion of a string to an integer. The decryption algorithms perform the reverse conversion; if something goes wrong, they may produce an error message. It has been demonstrated that these error message can allow an attacker to trick a server to decrypt a given ciphertext (examples include the Bleichenbacher attack [Blei98] and the Manger attack [Mang01] for RSA and the Vaudenay attack for the CBC-mode of a block cipher [Vaud02]); some of these attacks apply to certain SSL implementations [CHV+03]. What is also remarkable is that even implementations that have been fixed for such a reaction attacks, may become vulnerable to new similar reaction attacks, such as the one by [KlPR03] based on the version number of the SSL protocol. Also remarkable is the slow spread of cryptographic patches, or general security patches for that matter.

4.3   Side Channel Attacks

Side channel attacks have been known for a long time in the classified community; these attacks exploit information on the time to perform a computation [Koch96], on the power consumption [KoJJ99], or on the electromagnetic radiation [GaMO01,QuSa01] to extract information on the plaintext or even the secrets used in the computation.

Protecting implementations against side channel attacks is notoriously difficult: it requires typically a combination of countermeasures at the hardware level (adding noise, special logic, decoupling power source), at the algorithmic level (e.g., blinding and randomization) and at the protocol level (e.g., frequent key updates) (see [BoPR01] for a brief overview). While many countermeasures have been published, many fielded systems (even new ones) are still very vulnerable. This is in part due to cost reasons, delays in upgrades, but also due to the development of ever more sophisticated attacks.

4.4   Fault Attacks

The most powerful attacks induce errors in the computations, by varying clock frequency or power level, by applying light flashes, etc. Such attacks are typically devastating: small changes in inputs during a cryptographic calculation typically reveal the secret key material [BoDL97]. Protecting against these attacks is non-trivial, as it requires continuous verification of all calculations, which should also include a check on the verifications. And even that may not be enough, as has been pointed out in [YeJo00]. It is also clear that pure cryptographic measures will never be sufficient to protect against such attacks.

5   Conclusions

The basic theoretic research questions in cryptology (which problems are hard?) are in fact very hard problems, and researchers have only scratched the surface in this area. In this article, we have argued that even in practical cryptography, there are many interesting questions on algorithm design and implementations that require further study and research.

References

[BaBK03]   E. Barkan, E. Biham, N. Keller, "Instant Ciphertext-Only Cryptanalysis of GSM Encrypted Communication," *Advances in Cryptology, Proceedings Crypto'03, Lecture Notes in Computer Science 2729*, D. Boneh, Ed., Springer-Verlag, 2003.

[BiSW00]   A. Biryukov, A. Shamir, D. Wagner, "Real Time Cryptanalysis of A5/1 on a PC," *Fast Software Encryption, Lecture Notes in Computer Science 1978*, B. Schneier, Ed., Springer-Verlag, 2002, pp. 1-18.

[BoDL97]   D. Boneh, R. DeMillo, R. Lipton, ``On the Importance of Checking Cryptographic Protocols for Faults," *Advances in Cryptology, Proc. Eurocrypt'97, Lecture Notes in Computer Science 1233*, W. Fumy, Ed., Springer-Verlag, 1997, pp. 37-51.

[Blei98]   D. Bleichenbacher, "Chosen Ciphertext Attacks Against Protocols Based on the RSA Encryption Standard PKCS #1," *Advances in Cryptology, Proceedings Crypto'98, Lecture Notes in Computer Science 1462*, H. Krawczyk, Ed., Springer-Verlag, 1998, pp. 1-12.

[CHV+03]   B. Canvel, A. Hiltgen, S. Vaudenay, M. Vuagnoux, "Password Interception in a SSL/TLS Channel," *Advances in Cryptology, Proceedings Crypto'03, Lecture Notes in Computer Science 2729*, D. Boneh, Ed., Springer-Verlag, 2003.

[CoPi02]   N. Courtois, J. Pieprzyk, "Cryptanalysis of Block Ciphers with Overdefined Systems of Equations," *Advances in Cryptology, Proceedings Asiacrypt'02, LNCS 2501*, Y. Zheng, Ed., Springer-Verlag, 2002, pp. 267-287.

[DaRi01]   J. Daemen, V. Rijmen, *"The Design of Rijndael. AES - The Advanced Encryption Standard,"* Springer-Verlag, 2001.

[DoBP95]   H. Dobbertin, A. Bosselaers, B. Preneel, "RIPEMD-160: a Strengthened Version of RIPEMD," *Fast Software Encryption, LNCS 1039*, D. Gollmann, Ed. Springer-Verlag, 1996, pp. 71-82. See also http://www.esat.kuleuven.ac.be/~bosselae/ripemd160.

[FI46]   FIPS 46, *"Data Encryption Standard,"* Federal Information Processing Standard, National Bureau of Standards, U.S. Department of Commerce, January 1977 (revised as FIPS 46-1:1988; FIPS 46-2:1993).

[FI180-2]   FIPS 180-2, *"Secure Hash Standard,"* National Institute of Standards and Technologies, U.S. Department of Commerce, Draft, May 30, 2001.

[FI197]   FIPS 197, *"Advanced Encryption Standard (AES),"* Federal Information Processing Standard, National Institute of Standards and Technologies, U.S. Department of Commerce, December 6, 2001.

[FlMS01]   S.R. Fluhrer, I. Mantin, A. Shamir, "Weaknesses in the Key Scheduling Algorithm of RC4," *Proceedings Selected Areas in Cryptography 2001, Lecture Notes in Computer Science 2259*, S. Vaudenay and A.M. Youssef, Eds., Springer-Verlag, 2001, pp. 1-24.

[GaMO01]   K. Ganddolfi, C. Mourtel, F. Olivier, "Electromagnetic Analysis: Concrete Results", *Proc. Cryptographic Hardware and Embedded Systems - CHES 2001, Lecture Notes in Computer Science 2162*, C.K. Koc, D. Naccache and C. Paar, Eds., Springer Verlag, 2001, pp. 251-261.

[Hilt92]   Alain P. L. Hiltgen, "Constructions of Feebly-one-way Families of Permuta-
             tions," *Advances in Cryptology, Proc. Auscrypt '92, Lecture Notes in Computer
             Science 718*, J. Seberry and Y. Zheng, Eds., Springer-Verlag, 1992, pp. 422-434,

[ISOSC27]   ISO/IEC JTC1/SC27, *"Information technology - Security techniques,"*
             http://www.din.de/ni/sc27.

[IS9797]   ISO/IEC 9797-1, *Message authentication codes (MACs) - Part 1: Mechanisms
             using a block cipher, 1999, Part 2: Mechanisms using a dedicated hash-
             function, 2002.*

[JoMV02]   A. Joux, G. Martinet, F. Valette, "Blockwise-Adaptive Attackers: Revisiting the
             (In)Security of Some Provably Secure Encryption Modes: CBC, GEM, IACBC,"
             Advances in Cryptology, Proceedings Cryptot'02, LNCS 2442, M. Yung, Ed.,
             Springer-Verlag, 2002, pp. 17-30.

[KlPR03]   V. Klima, O. Pokorny, T. Rosa, "Attacking RSA-based Sessions in SSL/TLS,"
             *Proc. Cryptographic Hardware and Embedded Systems - CHES 2003, Lecture
             Notes in Computer Science 2779*, C. Walter, C.K. Koc, C. Paar, Eds., Springer
             Verlag, 2003, pp. 426-440.

[Koch96]   P. Kocher, "Timing Attacks on Implementations of Diffie-Hellman, RSA, DSS
             and Other Systems", *Advances in Cryptology: Proceedings of CRYPTO'96, Lec-
             ture Notes on Computer Science 1109*, N. Koblitz, Ed., Springer-Verlag, 1996,
             pp. 104-113.

[KoJJ99]   P. Kocher, J. Jaffe, B. Jun, "Differential Power Analysis", *Advances in Cryptol-
             ogy: Proceedings of CRYPTO'99, Lecture Notes on Computer Science 1666*, M.
             Wiener, Ed., Springer-Verlag, 1999, pp. 388-397.

[Mang01]   J. Manger, "A Chosen Ciphertext Attack on RSA Optimal Asymmetric Encryp-
             tion Padding (OAEP) as Standardized in PKCS #1 v2.0," *Advances in Cryptol-
             ogy, Proceedings Cryptot'01, LNCS 2442*, J. Kilian, Ed., Springer-Verlag, 2001,
             pp. 230-238.

[MaSh02]   I. Mantin, A. Shamir, "A Practical Attack on Broadcast RC4," *Fast Software
             Encryption 2001, Lecture Notes in Computer Science 2355*, M. Matsui, Ed.,
             Springer-Verlag, 2002, pp. 152-164

[MuRo02]   S. Murphy, M.J.B. Robshaw, "Essential Algebraic Structures within the AES,"
             Advances in Cryptology, Proceedings Crypto'02, LNCS 2442, M. Yung, Ed.,
             Springer-Verlag, 2002, pp. 1-16.

[NESSIE]   NESSIE, http://www.cryptonessie.org.

[NIST]   NIST, AES Initiative, http://www.nist.gov/aes.

[QuSa01]   J,-J. Quisquater, D. Samide, "ElectroMagnetic Analysis (EMA): Measures and
             Countermeasures for Smart Cards", Smart Card Programming and Security, In-
             ternational Conference on Research in Smart Cards, E-smart 2001, Lecture
             Notes in Computer Science 2140, I. Attali, T. Jensen, Eds., Springer-Verlag,
             2001, pp. 200-210.

[RASP+00]   J. Rabaey, J. Ammer, J. da Silva, D. Patel, S. Roundy, "Picoradio Supports Ad-
             hoc Ultra-low Power Wireless Networking, *IEEE Computer Magazine*, July
             2000.

[RiSA78]   R.L. Rivest, A. Shamir, L. Adleman, "A Method for Obtaining Digital Signatures and Public-Key Cryptosystems," *Communications ACM*, Vol. 21, February 1978, pp. 120-126.

[Shor94]   P.W. Shor, "Algorithms for Quantum Computation: Discrete Logarithms and Factoring," *Proc. 35nd Annual Symposium on Foundations of Computer Science*, S. Goldwasser, Ed., IEEE Computer Society Press, 1994, pp. 124-134.

[StIR02]   A. Stubblefield, J. Ionnidis, A. Rubin, "Using the Fluhrer, Mantin and Shamir attack to Break WEP," *Proceedings of the 2002 Network and Distributed Systems Security Symposium (NDSS)*, 2002, pp. 17-22.

[VSB+01]   L.M.K. Vandersypen, M. Steffen, G. Breyta, C.S. Yannoni, M.H. Sherwood, I.L. Chuang, "Experimental realization of Shor's quantum factoring algorithm using nuclear magnetic resonance," *Nature*, 414, 2001, pp. 883-887.

[Vaud02]   S. Vaudenay, "Security Flaws Induced by CBC Padding - Applications to SSL, IPSEC, WTLS .... ," *Advances in Cryptology, Proceedings Eurocrypt 2002, Lecture Notes in Computer Science 2332*, L. Knudsen, Ed., Springer-Verlag, 2002, pp. 534-546.

[Vedd91]   K. Vedder, "Security Aspects of Mobile Communications," *Computer Security and Industrial Cryptography, State of the Art and Evolution, Lecture Notes in Computer Science 741*, B. Preneel, R. Govaerts, and J. Vandewalle, Eds., Springer-Verlag, 1993, pp. 193-210.

[YeJo00]   S.-M. Yen, M. Joye, "Checking Before Output May Not Be Enough Against Fault-Based Cryptanalysis," *IEEE Transactions on Computers*, Vol. 49, No. 9, 2000, pp. 967-970.

Implementing AES

Joan Daemen[1] · Vincent Rijmen[2]

[1]STMicroelectronics – Proton Technology Division
Excelsiorlaan 44-46, B-1930 Zaventem, Belgium
Joan.Daemen@st.com

[2]Cryptomathic
Lei 8A, B-3000 Leuven, Belgium
Vincent.Rijmen@Cryptomathic.com

[2]IAIK
Inffeldgasse 16A, A-8010 Graz, Austria
Vincent.Rijmen@iaik.at

Abstract

In October 2000, the US National Institute of Standards and Technology (NIST) announced that the algorithm Rijndael was selected as Advanced Encryption Standard (AES). During the selection process and thereafter, significant progress has been made in making implementations of Rijndael faster and more secure. This paper presents an overview of the techniques that are used to optimise the performance of AES in practical implementations.

1 Introduction

Since the adoption of Rijndael as AES, many people have been implementing the algorithm in their favourite programming languages and on various platforms. One of the design principles behind Rijndael was to deliberately keep the design simple, in order to facilitate implementations adapted to the individual strengths and weaknesses of each platform. Because of the simple algebraic cipher structure, the programmer has many degrees of freedom. Consequently, there are many possible ways to optimise the performance of an implementation, depending on the platform and depending on the most critical constraint: code size, chip area, speed, throughput, ...

In this paper we don't try to present all possible optimisations for every individual platform. Instead, we explain the techniques that are of use on a wide range of platforms. We start with a short overview of the design of Rijndael.

2 AES in Brief

The input and output of AES are represented by 4-by-4 arrays, where each element of the arrays is a byte. Similarly, the key is represented by a two-dimensional byte array with 4 rows and a number of columns depending on the key length. Figure 1 illustrates this for a key length of 192 bits.

S. Paulus, N. Pohlmann, H. Reimer (Editors): Securing Electronic Business Processes, Vieweg (2004), 59-65

p_0	p_4	p_8	p_{12}
p_1	p_5	p_9	p_{13}
p_2	p_6	p_{10}	p_{14}
p_3	p_7	p_{11}	p_{15}

k_0	k_4	k_8	k_{12}	k_{16}	k_{20}
k_1	k_5	k_9	k_{13}	k_{17}	k_{21}
k_2	k_6	k_{10}	k_{14}	k_{18}	k_{22}
$k_{\backslash 3}$	k_7	k_{11}	k_{15}	k_{19}	k_{23}

Figure 1: Input and key representation for a key length of 192 bits.

AES is a key-iterated block cipher: it consists of the repeated application of a round transformation. The number of iterations, or rounds, depends on the key length.

The round transformation is a sequence of four different component transformations, called steps.

1. SubBytes: This is a non-linear substitution, operating on each byte of the input independently. The transformation acts the same on each byte in every round.

2. ShiftRows: This is a byte shuffle operation. The last three rows of the state are shifted cyclically over different offsets. Row 1 is shifted over 1 byte, row 2 over 2 bytes and row 3 over 3 bytes.

3. MixColumns: The 4 columns of the input are transformed independently. Each column is transformed by means of a multiplication with a fixed matrix. The operations are *not* the standard integer addition and multiplication, but are performed in the finite field with 256 elements (cf. Section 5).

4. AddRoundKey: The round key addition consists of a bit-wise addition with the round key. The round keys are derived from the key by means of the key schedule. The round key length is equal to the block length.

Before the first round, an initial AddRoundKey operation is performed. In the final round, only SubBytes, ShiftRows, and AddRoundKey are used.

The four transformations have been selected according to several design criteria, both involving security and ease of implementation. We will here however not dwell on the security of the cipher. For more details we refer to the standard [FIPS197] and to [DaRi02].

3 Platforms

The best way to implement AES is to consider the specific strengths of the target platform. We can distinguish 4 types of platforms.

1. `Big' software platforms: These platforms have 32-bit CPU's, typically a large block of RAM available and few restrictions on code size.

2. `Small' software platforms: These platforms are constrained in RAM, and typically have an 8-bit processor. Code size is sometimes a problem as well.

3. FPGA-like hardware platforms: These are the hardware platforms with predefined logic functions. There is usually a limited amount of RAM available.

4. ASIC hardware: The designer has full freedom, but also pays the price for every component. For instance, it is possible to include RAM on an ASIC, but this is usually avoided because it consumes a lot of chip area.

For each platform, there are some typical choices for the implementation of the different steps. They are summarized in Table 1. On big software platforms, the best performance can be achieved by using 4 tables of 1 kbyte each. Hand-optimised assembly implementations can then encrypt at 14 cycles/byte on a Pentium III platform. Small platforms typically don't have the RAM available for these tables. For this type of platforms, there are implementations using less than 50 bytes of memory. The code size can easily be kept below 1 kbyte; even as little as 460 bytes has been achieved.

Table 1: Typical implementation choices for the 4 main platform types.

	Big SW platform	Small SW platform	HW FPGA	HW ASIC
SubBytes		Table	Table/ logic	Logic
ShiftRows	Table	Register shuffle	Wiring	Wiring
MixColumns		Table/ explicit operations	Logic	Logic

4 The Key Schedule

AES uses a key of 128, 192 or 256 bits. This key is expanded by the key schedule into an array of round keys. There are 11, 13, or 15 round keys respectively and each round key has a length of 128 bits. Basically, there are two options to implement the key schedule.

1. Compute once – use many: When several blocks of text are encrypted under the same key, it is not necessary to recompute the key expansion for each text block. Instead, it is usually better to compute the key expansion once and store the array of round keys in RAM for future use. This option is used mainly on big software platforms and sometimes also on FPGA-like platforms.

2. Compute while you encrypt: Some platforms are heavily constrained in the RAM available to the decryption algorithm, and cannot afford the 176, 208, or 240 bytes to store the round keys. This is for instance the case in most small software platforms and custom-design hardware. The key schedule has been designed with this type of platforms in mind.

4.1 Compute while you Encrypt

The key schedule is defined as the repeated application of two transformations: the key update transformation and the round key extraction. The key schedule can be described most easily by describing the key and the round keys as a number of 32-bit columns. The round key array then consists of 44, 52 or 60 columns. The first 4, 6 or 8 columns are filled by simply copying the key.

The key update transformation is a non-linear invertible transformation that computes the next column of the round key array from the last computed column and the column 4, 6, or 8 positions before. The round key extraction produces round key i by concatenating columns $4i$, $4i+1$, $4i+2$ and $4i+3$.

In a memory-constrained application, only 4, 6 or 8 columns of the round key array are kept in memory at any time. Newly computed columns are stored over the older ones, which have already been used in a round key.

4.2 Compute while you Decrypt

The decryption operation needs the round keys in inverse order. Since the key update transformation is non-linear, there is no shortcut to compute the round key of the last round directly from the key. Hence, in a straightforward implementation, the decryption key schedule would start by computing successively all the round keys, only to overwrite them immediately with the next round key, until the last one is computed. Subsequently, the inverse operation of the round key update can be used to compute round key i-1 from round key i. This results however in a long key setup time before each decryption. A better strategy is to sacrifice some memory and store with each key also the output of the last iteration of the round key update transformation. This allows to start with the decryption operation immediately. In terms of memory, this means that 32, 48 or 64 bytes are needed to store a key of 16, 24 or 32 bytes. This still compares favourably to most other encryption algorithms.

5 Finite Field Operations in Hardware

AES has several features that favour hardware implementations. Firstly, the use of integer arithmetic operations was avoided, and hence no arithmetic units need to be incorporated in the logic. Secondly, the algorithm is highly parallel.

Except for some advanced FPGA boards, hardware platforms have no cheap large memory blocks available. Hence, the main challenge for compact or high-speed hardware implementations of AES seems to be the efficient implementation of the substitution. In software, the substitution can be implemented by means of a 256-byte lookup table. For compact hardware implementations, the table can't be implemented: instead a dedicated logical circuit has to be designed. In order to achieve maximal performance, 16 instances of the table would have to be hardwired (neglecting the key schedule). Since 16 256-byte tables would occupy too much area, also here a dedicated logical circuit is required. Commercially available optimisers are incapable of finding the optimal circuit fully automatically. Hence we have to look at the structure of the substitution and look for optimisations, but first we briefly introduce finite fields.

5.1 Finite Fields

A mathematical field consists of a set of elements and two operations on these elements, satisfying some conditions. An example is given by the set of real numbers with the operations "addition" and "multiplication". In a finite field, the set contains a finite number of elements. It can be shown that a finite field is defined uniquely by its number of elements. This means that two finite fields with the same number of elements are in fact two different representations of one and the same field.

The definition of the substitution uses the finite field with 256 elements. The elements are often represented as the set of polynomials of degree 7 or less, with binary coefficients. Another representation is formed by the strings of 2 hexadecimal characters: 0xA9, {B3}, ...

It is a well-known fact that the choice of representation influences the hardware gate complexity of the operations on these elements. For instance, the use of so-called normal bases in the representation allows for very efficient circuits to implement the squaring operation.

5.2 Definition of the Substitution

The substitution operates byte by byte. The transformation of one byte consists of the following steps.

1. The byte is interpreted as an element of the finite field.
2. The element is replaced by its multiplicative inverse (multiplication as defined in the finite field).
3. The field element is interpreted as a vector X with 8 binary coordinates.
4. The vector X is multiplied by a binary matrix and added with a constant vector to produce the output.

5.3 New Representations

Using a finite field representation different from the one adopted in the design will always at first introduce some additional complexity, as transformations to and from the new representation have to be included. But, this is more than compensated for by the increased efficiency of the multiplicative inversion. This idea is proposed and worked out in [Rijm00,SMTM01, WoOL02].

The resulting improvements are shown in Table 2. Several implementations using a different representation for the field elements are compared [SMTM01,WoOL02]. Besides the raw performance measures as throughput, clock frequency and gate count, the table also lists an efficiency indicator that is computed as follows:

$$\text{Indicator} = \text{Throughput} / (\text{Clock frequency} \times \text{Gate count})$$

Although one of the changes of representation can be merged with the matrix multiplication in the last step, the overhead is still considerable. The authors of [RDJ+01] propose to do the change of field element representation only once, at the beginning of the cipher. Subsequently, all steps of the cipher are redefined to work with the new representation. At the end of the encryption, the data is transformed back to the original representation. This eliminates the overhead in every round. The resulting improvements are also shown in Table 2.

Table 2: Performance of hardware Rijndael implementations (ASIC).

Reference	Throughput (Gb/s)	Clock frequency (MHz)	Number of gates (10^3 gate)	Indicator (10^{-3} b/gate)
Graz-impl	0.12	100	5.7	0.21
Satoh-impl	0.3	131	5.4	0.42
	2.6	224	21	0.55
	0.8	137	8.8	0.66
Ibm-impl	7.5	32	256	0.92

6 Decryption

AES is not a Feistel cipher. Encryption and decryption use in principle different components: decryption consists of applying the inverse components in the inverse order. On most hardware platforms and some software platforms, it is desirable to be able to reuse the encryption components for the decryption.

The reusability is different for each of the parts of the round transformation.

- AddRoundKey: This operation is its own inverse, hence completely reusable
- ShiftRows (byte shuffle): This simple operation is always easy to implement, but has to be re-implemented completely for the decryption operation
- SubBytes (substitution): This operation is discussed in more detail in Section 5. If the different steps of this operation are implemented separately, then the multiplicative inverse is the step that consumes the most resources. This step is its own inverse and can be shared between encryption and decryption.
- MixColumns: The inverse operation of this step can be implemented in such a way that it reuses the implementation of the forward operation. We explain below how this can be done.

The MixColumns transformation operates on the input column by column. Each column is considered as a vector with 4 coordinates, which is multiplied with a 4-by-4 matrix. Addition and multiplication are performed in the finite field.

$$MC(X) = \begin{bmatrix} 02 & 03 & 01 & 01 \\ 01 & 02 & 03 & 01 \\ 01 & 01 & 02 & 03 \\ 03 & 01 & 01 & 02 \end{bmatrix} \bullet X$$

The inverse transformation consists of multiplication with the inverse of the matrix. Since the inverse matrix has different coefficients, the multiplication requires a different hardware circuit. However, the inverse matrix can be written as the product of the original matrix and a very simple matrix.

$$MC^{-1}(X) = \begin{bmatrix} 0E & 0B & 0D & 09 \\ 09 & 0E & 0B & 0D \\ 0D & 09 & 0E & 0B \\ 0B & 0D & 09 & 0E \end{bmatrix} \bullet X$$

$$= \begin{bmatrix} 05 & 00 & 04 & 00 \\ 00 & 05 & 00 & 04 \\ 04 & 00 & 05 & 00 \\ 00 & 04 & 00 & 05 \end{bmatrix} \bullet \begin{bmatrix} 02 & 03 & 01 & 01 \\ 01 & 02 & 03 & 01 \\ 01 & 01 & 02 & 03 \\ 03 & 01 & 01 & 02 \end{bmatrix}$$

This means that the circuit for the inverse of MixColumns can reuse the circuit for MixColumns, preceded by a simple precomputation.

7 Conclusion

The simple mathematical definition of the AES allows for many different optimizations to the straightforward implementation. Depending on the options available on the practical target platform, different trade-offs can be made between code size, memory usage, speed, throughput, etc.

References

[DaRi02]   Daemen Joan, and Rijmen Vincent: The design of Rijndael, AES – the advanced
            encryption standard. Springer-Verlag, 2002.

[FIPS197]   Specification for the Advanced Encryption Standard (AES). In: Federal Informa-
            tion Processing Standards, Publication 197. 2001.

[Rijm00]   Rijmen Vincent: Efficient implementation of the Rijndael S-box.
            http://www.esat.kuleuven.ac.be/~rijmen/rijndael/sbox.pdf, 2000.

[RDJ+01]   Rudra Atri, Dubey Pradeep K., Jutla Charanjit~S., Kumar Vijay, Rao Jo-
            syula~R., and Rohatgi Pankaj: Efficient Rijndael encryption implementation
            with composite field arithmetic. In: CHES 2001, LNCS 2162. Editors: Naccache
            David et al. Springer-Verlag, 2001. p. 171-184.

[SMTM01]   Satoh Akashi, Morioka Sumio, Takano Kohji, and Munetoh Seiji: A compact
            Rijndael hardware architecture with S-box optimization. In: Advances in Cryp-
            tology, Proceedings of Asiacrypt 2001, LNCS 2248. Editor: Boyd Colin.
            Springer-Verlag, 2001. p. 239-254.

[WoOL02]   Wolkerstorfer Johannes, Oswald Elisabeth, and Lamberger Mario: An ASIC im-
            plementation of the AES S-boxes. In: Topics in Cryptology --- CT-RSA 2002,
            LNCS 2271. Editor: Preneel Bart. Springer-Verlag, 2002. p. 67-78.

Delivering more Secure Software

Ronny Bjones

Microsoft EMEA
ronnybj@microsoft.com

Abstract

This paper is talking about Microsoft's initiatives in delivering more secure software. The first part of the paper defines the Trustworthy Computing initiative and will highlight the security pillar of this initiative. I will explain the security framework called SD3+C and give some examples what we did in each part of this framework.

The second part highlights one specific element of the initiative called STRIDE threat modelling. Under impulse of the Trustworthy Computing initiative, each product development needs to go through STRIDE. We want to encourage designers in general to include threat modelling into the design process. The STRIDE model can be very helpful to achieve this. STRIDE should be seen as a two phase approach. In the first phase, designers will use the model to look to their architectures through the eyes of a hacker. The outcome will be a prioritized list of threats. In a second phase the designers need to mitigate this high priority threats. STRIDE will help them to include threat modelling into their design process and to ask the right questions.

1 Trustworthy Computing

Trustworthy Computing means helping ensure that a safe and reliable computing experience is both expected and taken for granted. It's a vision of computing as intrinsic to productivity and enjoyment of life as water, electricity or the telephone dial tone. Achieving this vision is an industry-wide challenge in which Microsoft must be deeply involved. The company is profoundly refocusing to make Trustworthy Computing its first priority.

Goal of Trustworthy Computing initiative: *'To make Microsoft the trusted vendor of secure, private and reliable computing for everyone'*

Trustworthy Computing has four pillars: security, privacy, reliability and business integrity. In the next section I will go into some more detail on the security pillar.

S. Paulus, N. Pohlmann, H. Reimer (Editors): Securing Electronic Business Processes. Vieweg (2004). 66-72

1.1 Trustworthy Computing Security Pillar

Success for an individual, a business, or a government agency increasingly depends on the ability to securely communicate around the world in real time. The advent of widespread connectivity via the Internet and an array of ubiquitous and powerful mobile devices have changed the face of computing and communications. With the vast benefits of increased connectivity, however, a host of new risks has emerged, risks on a scale that few in the industry anticipated, including Microsoft. To address the need for heightened security in our increasingly connected world, Microsoft has made security its top priority. Based on extensive feedback from customers, Microsoft developed the SD3+C framework to address customer security issues as part of its vision for Trustworthy Computing. The components of the framework are Secure by Design, Secure by Default, Secure by Deployment and Communications.

1.1.1 Secure by Design

To help achieve greater security in design, Microsoft began training developers and other employees to write more-secure code and find vulnerabilities in its products before they ship. Last year the company trained more than 11,000 engineers. We called this the Windows security push and it interrupted product development for two months. This training is now part of the package received by each engineer joining the product teams. Microsoft developers are clearly accountable for the security features of their code — a significant cultural change at the company. Security pushes are now a recurring event, and security audits are part of the product release process. The results of these efforts are available to customers today in the case of products such as SQL Server 2000 SP3, Microsoft Exchange 2000 Server, Microsoft Office 2003 and Windows Server 2003.

Microsoft developed some complete new automated software testing tools, called prefix and prefast. These tools are used to scan the sources of the products we develop. They will find common constructions in the software that can lead to vulnerabilities. It is a flexible framework, so we can add new constructions as they are detected by the industry.

So Secure by Design is about training, improved processes but also about technology. We add a lot of basic architectures to our products to provide more security. Examples are the PKI support, authentication schemes, network security, etc. We are currently working on a complete new foundation for the Windows platform. This is called Next Generation Secure Computing Base (NGSCB). NGSCB is an industry wide initiative that will fundamentally change the way how classic PC motherboards will works with respect to security [Micr03].

1.1.2 Secure by Default

To reduce the attack surface of products, Microsoft now preconfigures them to be "locked down" out of the box, meaning the most security-enhanced options are the default settings. This is another change of cultural mindset: In the past, a feature was enabled by default if there was any possibility a customer might want to use it. Customers have benefited from this change with Windows XP Service Pack 1, where share permissions were changed from "full control" to "read" and the firewall configuration changed so that it is on by default. In addition to work around default settings and modules, free security tools such as the Internet Information Services lockdown tool help customers with existing products reach the equivalent of Secure by Default. Products such as Windows Server 2003 will continue to reduce the attack surface areas.

1.1.3 Secure in Deployment

To help customers deploy and maintain products securely, Microsoft had to offer the proper tools and prescriptive guidance. Over the past year, Microsoft has added to and updated its security tools. Consumers and small businesses can automatically stay up to date on security patches by using the automatic update feature of Windows Update. Last year Microsoft introduced Software Update Services (SUS) and the Systems Management Server 2.0 SUS Feature Pack to improve patch management for larger enterprises. It also released Microsoft Baseline Security Analyzer, which scans for missing security updates and analyses configurations for poor or weak security settings, and advises users how to work on the issues found. Microsoft has introduced prescriptive documents for Windows 2000 and Exchange to help ensure that customers can configure and deploy its products with security enhancements. Customers can visit http://www.microsoft.com/technet/security/ for much more prescriptive and how-to content.

Microsoft launched recently a new initiative related to Trustworthy Computing, called the security mobilization initiative. This initiative will focus to improve heavily the patch management experience people currently have. Some highlights are:
1. Allow customers to better plan the patch management by reducing the frequency of patches to once a month.
2. Reduce the sizes of patches by 30-80% to help people that don't have broadband.
3. Prescriptive guideline on patching.
4. New shielding technology and quarantine concept. This will be a safety net so people don't need to go to an emergency situation even when a critical vulnerability is detected. The goal is not to remove patching but to come to a situation that for seven out of ten vulnerabilities we don't run into critical emergencies.

1.1.4 Communication

To keep customers better informed on security issues, Microsoft made several important changes over the past year. User feedback during 2002 indicated that its security bulletins, though useful for IT professionals, were too detailed for average consumers. Customers also said they wanted more differentiation on security patches so they could quickly decide which ones to apply and how to prioritize them. As a result, Microsoft worked with industry professionals to develop a new security bulletin severity rating system and introduced consumer bulletins in addition to the IT professional bulletins, which provide the level of technical information that customers wanted. A further result of customer feedback is the introduction of an e-mail notification system for consumer security bulletins. Later in 2003, Microsoft will offer the option for customers to subscribe to receive the security bulletins they want. Through direct interaction and participation in customer advisory events like the CSO Forum, Microsoft will be able to improve its overall customer communications.

2 The STRIDE Threat Model

In this section we go into more detail on one specific element of "secure by design" called threat modelling.

Threat modelling was widely introduced into Microsoft's development process during the start of the Trustworthy Computing initiative back in 2002. Threat modelling could be described as a risk assessment technique for designers.

Michael Howard and David LeBlanc [HoLe03] wrote a reference for developers that showed developers how to write code in a secure way "Writing secure code". This book handles the threat model called STRIDE. They define threat modelling as a security-based analysis that helps people determine the highest level security risks posed to the product and how attacks can manifest themselves.

The goal is to determine which threats require mitigation and how to mitigate the threats. The whole point of threat modelling is to push developers to think about the security of their application in a relatively formal way during the design of the system.

The STRIDE model consists of six steps.

1. Identify the assets.
2. Assemble a threat modelling team.
3. Create an architectural overview and decompose the application.
4. Identify and document the threats.
5. Rank the threats by decreasing risk.
6. Choose techniques how to mitigate the threats.

2.1 Identify the Assets

First one needs to define the assets that we try to protect. An asset is defined as a resource of value. This could range from privacy related data such as customer databases to confidential information such as future plans of the organization.

2.2 Assemble Threat Modelling Team

We need to assemble a broad team to do the threat modelling exercise. By having different specialties such as designers, developers, testers, technical writers and project management in one room, you will have different views on the same architecture. This will improve the result of the whole exercise.

2.3 Create an Architectural Overview and Decompose the Application

The next step is the creation (if it does not exist) of an architectural overview. This overview should illustrate the boundaries of the application which will be controlled in the threat modelling exercise. It is important to decompose the application in sub-components and show the dataflow between the components. UML sequence diagrams or dataflow diagrams are a good way of doing this. Data flowing between different components are in a lot of cases assets. This is also the case with data that is stored temporarily or permanently at some location. These assets need to be shown in the architectural overview.

2.4 Identify and Document the Threats

A threat is defined as a potential occurrence, malicious or otherwise, that might damage or compromise your assets.

In order to identify the threats we will use the STRIDE model. STRIDE categorizes threats in six categories. These categories are a great way to steer dedicated questions that one should ask himself about the architecture of the application. One should investigate whether the specific category is a threat to the application under investigation. Let's have a look at the six categories used in STRIDE.

1. Spoofing.
   Spoofing is attempting to gain access to a system by using a false identity. This can be accomplished using stolen user credentials or a false IP address. After the attacker successfully gains access as a legitimate user or host, elevation of privileges or abusing authorization can begin.

2. Tampering.
   Tampering is the unauthorized modification of data, for example as it flows over a network between two computers.

3. Repudiation.
   Repudiation is the ability of users (legitimate or otherwise) to deny that they performed specific actions or transactions. Without adequate auditing, repudiation attacks are difficult to prove.

4. Information disclosure.
   Information disclosure is the unwanted exposure of private data. For example, a user views the contents of a table or file he or she is not authorized to open, or monitors data passed in plaintext over a network. Some examples of information disclosure vulnerabilities include the use of hidden form fields, comments embedded in Web pages that contain database connection strings and connection details, and weak exception handling that can lead to internal system level details being revealed to the client. Any of this information can be very useful to the attacker.

5. Denial of service.
   Denial of service is the process of making a system or application unavailable. For example, a denial of service attack might be accomplished by bombarding a server with requests to consume all available system resources or by passing it malformed input data that can crash an application process.

6. Elevation of privilege.
   Elevation of privilege occurs when a user with limited privileges assumes the identity of a privileged user to gain privileged access to an application. For example, an attacker with limited privileges might elevate his or her privilege level to compromise and take control of a highly privileged and trusted process or account.
   It is clear that this is the worst threat the can result in different other effects categorized by STRIDE.

The next step is to identify the threats and to document them.

Threat Description	Describe the potential threat
Threat Target	Which part of the application is this threat referring to? This should correspond with the used architectural overview.
Threat Category	Record the category type used in the STRIDE model. A threat can fall under multiple categories.
Risk	Make a judgment about the risk. This is done once all threats are identified.
Mitigation technique	Which technique can be used to reduce the risk associated with this threat?
Comment	Any comments can be put here.

Figure 2-1: Template for documenting threats

Figure 2-1 shows a template that can be used to document threats. It is important to use this table in different phases during threat modelling. At this stage we are just identifying the threats. Risk assessment is done once we have identified the different threats (see next step). Don't think about mitigation techniques while identifying threats because this will focus you on solutions instead of identification of possible problems.

2.5 Rank the Threats by Decreasing Risk

We need to rank the identified threats.

We will use the DREAD method for rating the risks associated with the threats. Basically we will ask the following questions for each threat:

1. **D**amage potential: How great is the damage if the vulnerability is exploited?
2. **R**eproducibility: How easy is it to reproduce the attack?
3. **E**xploitability: How easy is it to launch an attack?
4. **A**ffected users: As a rough percentage, how many users are affected?
5. **D**iscoverability: How easy is it to find the vulnerability?

Each of these questions need to be answered by means of a rating High (3), Medium (2), Low (1).

Figure 2-2 shows a template that can be used to rate the risk according to the DREAD method.

	Rating	High (rate=3)	Medium (rate=2)	Low (rate=1)
D	Damage potential	The attacker can subvert the security system; get full trust authorization; run as administrator; upload content.	Leaking sensitive information	Leaking trivial information
R	Reproducibility	The attack can be reproduced every time and does not require a timing window.	The attack can be reproduced, but only with a timing window and a particular race situation.	The attack is very difficult to reproduce, even with knowledge of the security hole.
E	Exploitability	A novice programmer could make the attack in a short time.	A skilled programmer could make the attack, then repeat the steps.	The attack requires an extremely skilled person and in-depth knowledge every time to exploit.
A	Affected users	All users, default configuration, key customers.	Some users, non default configuration.	Very small percentage of users, obscure feature; affects anonymous users.
D	Discoverability	Published information explains the attack. The vulnerability is found in the most commonly used feature and is very noticeable.	The vulnerability is in a seldom-used part of the product, and only a few users should come across it. It would take some thinking to see malicious use.	The bug is obscure and it is unlikely that users will work out damage potential.

Figure 2-2: Source "Improving Web Application Security"; Meier, J.D. et al [NMD+03]

Each threat gets a rating by adding all rating categories together. This gives us a rating between 5 and 15 per threat. Next step is to order the threats by rating. The highest and most risky threats first. Based on this table the team needs to decide which threats to mitigate.

2.6 Choose Techniques how to Mitigate the Threats

Now we come to the final step of the threat modelling exercise and this is the decision whether we accept the risk or if we use a certain technique to mitigate the threat.

3 Conclusions

Delivering Trustworthy Computing is essential not only to keep the computer industry healthy, but to help protect public safety, national security and economic prosperity and improve the quality of life.

Trustworthy Computing is a multidimensional set of issues. All accrue to the four pillars: security, privacy, reliability and business integrity. Each demands attention.

While important short-term work needs to be done, this is a long-term challenge. Hard problems remain, requiring fundamental research and advances in engineering as well as fundamental cultural changes and global thinking.

Hardware and software companies, as well as academic and government research institutions, need to step up to the challenge of tackling these problems.

I highlighed one element of the SD3+C security framework, being threat modelling. Designers need a methodology that helps them to secure their architectures. STRIDE could be an important component in such a methodology.

STRIDE threat assessment is done in two major steps. In the first step, designers need to think about possible threats on the different architectural building blocks of their application. The STRIDE model helps them ask the right questions to identify the threats. The result of this exercise is a prioritized list of threats. In a second step we are going to select the most important threats and choose the appropriate techniques to mitigate the threats.

Threat modelling should become a part of the classical development cycle. Let's start educating our designers how they can use these security methodologies to build safer infrastructures. This is a necessity if we want to benefit of the promises new IT infrastructures will bring us in combination with trustworthy computer infrastructures.

References

[Micr03]   Microsoft: Next Generation Secure Computing Base. Editor: Microsoft Web: http://www.microsoft.com/ngscb, Microsoft, 2003.

[NMD+03]   Meier, J.D. et al. Microsoft: Improving Web Application Security: Threats and countermeasures. Editor: Microsoft patterns & practices Web: http://msdn.microsoft.com/library/default.asp?url=/library/en-us/dnnetsec/html/ ThreatCounter.asp, Microsoft, 2003.

[HoLe03]   Howard, Michael and LeBlanc David Name: Writing Secure Code Second Edition. Editor: Microsoft, Microsoft Press, 2003.

Side Channel Attacks on Smart Cards: Threats & Countermeasures

Uwe Krieger

cv cryptovision gmbh
uwe.krieger@cryptovision.com

Abstract

Countermeasures against side channel attacks – e.g. power attacks, based on an analysis of the power consumption, or electromagnetic attacks, which are based on the measurement of electromagnetic emanation – play an important role in modern implementations of cryptographic algorithms on Smart Cards or other security tokens. This has led to significant higher efforts in the implementation of cryptographic libraries for these platforms. For getting assurance about the security, at least during two stages of the development process, additional measurements on the hardware platform become necessary. After giving a short introduction, this article outlines some of the current threats and possible countermeasures; another topic is to describe, how this problems influences the development process and the resource consumption of components which are appropriately secured against possible attacks.

1 Introduction: Side Channel Attacks

Today, the main reason for using a token like a Smart Card is, that such a device can be seen as a personal security environment; processors used for such cards are so-called Security ICs, they are designed to withstand all kind of potential attacks. In the past, the focus here was on securing the microprocessor and the memory against invasive attacks like micro-probing; additional shielding or the use of sensors (for noticing such an attack and erasing memory with sensitive data) are effective countermeasures in this case.

A new idea – now known for a couple of years – is to attack the device by observing the processors behaviour *while it is in operation*; this is a completely different approach and exposed a lot of potential and surprising weaknesses when it was first introduced. First steps have been to observe the influence of sensitive data on the computation time (so-called *timing attacks*), a major breakthrough has been P. Kocher's work in the years 1997-98. The new idea was to collect information by observing the current consumption of a device like a Smart Card (which doesn't have a battery). This is called *power analysis* today, the method has been extended and improved considerably in the last years.

The most important thing to mention: these are not theoretical attacks. Examples like the PIN or *power break* attack (which can be seen as a successor of side channel attacks) are very easy to mount on cards which contain no adequate countermeasures even if the attacker possesses almost no special knowledge or equipment. Attacks based on power analysis might raise the barrier, because an attacker has to invest in special hardware equipment (like an expensive oscilloscope). But in principle, all of these attacks are working in the real work and for a developer of cryptographic modules, one important question is, against what kind of attacker an implementation should be secured. As it can be seen from the following, integration of all possible countermeasures is not an easy task.

S. Paulus, N. Pohlmann, H. Reimer (Editors): Securing Electronic Business Processes, Vieweg (2004), 73-81

2 Most Important Threats

Side channel attacks normally try to take advantage of the fact, that the behaviour of the computation is at many points directly influenced by the input data; under certain circumstances, this can be exploited if information about sensitive data can be seen from the outside via channels, whose existence are perhaps not realized.

Although it might look a little bit artificial, depending on the nature of the leaking channel one can distinguish between attacks against the hardware or the software which implements the cryptographic routines. In reality, exact distinction lines are not easy to find; practical reason for such an approach is mainly to get a better feeling who (the hardware manufacturer or the developer of the software) is mainly responsible for which kind of problems.

2.1 Attacking the Hardware

Next to pure invasive attacks (e.g. micro-probing for reading out the memory content), current problems are attacks which might interfere with the operations of the processor while it is working on critical operations. For doing this, it is not always necessary to get direct access to the silicon; semi-invasive attacks (where only part of the shielding will be removed) or even attacks which don't really touch the hardware might also work.

But securing a processor against invasive attacks to ensure that an attacker is not able to read out critical data like private keys is not the topic here. Normally, hardware manufacturers are familiar with the possible attacks and try to find adequate countermeasures; they are responsible to make their product tamper-resistant. But of course, perfect security is impossible; a software developer should know about remaining problems. Only then, he is able to consider the respective countermeasures while doing his work.

One classic example of the kind of problems which can come up is an attack against the RSA algorithm based on DFA (*Differential Fault Analysis*). The principle idea of the so-called *Bellcore Attack* is the observation, that somebody can very easily completely break the system if the implementation is using the CRT (*Chinese Remainder Theorem*) as the underlying math and the attacker is then able to manipulate or disturb certain computations.

The idea has first been described by the Bellcore researchers D. Boneh, R. DeMillo and R. Lipton in 1996 ([BDL96]) and was quite a shock at the time. The problem was not, to find possibilities to prevent the attack; once known, it was not too complicated to secure implementations (for example, one simple method are additional checks which prevent the information leakage). The main problem with this experience was, that the weakness was substantial for many implementations and that is has been discovered so late.

2.2 Attacking the Implementation

Next step is to look at non-invasive attacks; this is the area, where software developers have lots of possibilities to improve the security of their work. The most well-known class of attacks in this area might be *Timing Attacks* (TA, see for example [Koc96]): main idea here is, that the attacker tries to use some leaking information about necessary computation times as a side channel.

As an example, one can look at attacks on public key cryptosystems: algorithms used here are normally based on modular arithmetic, it can be seen that it is possible to get some information about operands by observing this special side channel. Reason for this is, that sometimes there is an additional reduction step necessary during a modular multiplication; this additional operation might be detected and helps to gain knowledge about parts of the secret.

But there are also a lot of other side channels which might be attractive (from the attackers point of view), examples are:

- *Power Analysis* (PA): By observing the power consumption of the card, one might be able figure out on which operations the processor is currently working. When talking about *Simple Power Analysis* (SPA), one normally means the attempt to get some knowledge about secret data by directly looking at the power consumption of one single operation (e.g. the creation of a digital signature) on the card.

- *Differential Power Analysis* (DPA) is a more sophisticated approach. By looking at the data of many (eventually thousands) of measurements and using tools like statistical analysis or error correction methods, one can improve the attack considerably.

- *Electromagnetic Analysis* (EMA): Instead of looking at the power consumption, it is also possible to observe the electromagnetic emanation. The source of the information is therefore different, but the methods used are quite similar. Again, there is the distinction between *Simple Electromagnetic Analysis* (SEMA) where one looks in essence at one single run of an operation and *Differential Electromagnetic Analysis* (DEMA) where the attackers tries to use the observed data of many measurements.

A couple of other possibilities of information leakage might exist; so it should be clear, that software developers have to take care of the problems caused by this. All operations dealing with secret data have to be secured; regardless if one talks about symmetric like DES or AES, public key algorithms like RSA or ECC or even "simple" tasks like storing a cryptographic key in a file.

Although in the following it might look like that there is a mayor problem with public key algorithms, this is definitely not the case: the reason for this is simply, that some methods (attacks or respective countermeasures) are somewhat easier to describe for these kind of operations.

3 Possible Countermeasures

Of course, today normally every microprocessor used for Smart Card applications contains some countermeasures implemented in hardware to prevent these kind of attacks. This might be something like bus encryption (which can also be seen as a countermeasure against invasive attacks); other examples are random process interrupts which are automatically induced by the processor (and therefore randomise the steps an operation takes) or inducing noise on the current by additional power consuming devices on the chip.

As already mentioned, focus here are countermeasure which can be integrated in software. In principle, one should distinguish the following two approaches: first, work on the algorithmic level (which should be comparable on different hardware platform), second the use of special coding techniques which should address potential weaknesses of the respective hardware. Of course, some methods doesn't fit in this kind of classification (e.g. additional checks for proving the correctness of an operation to prevent a DFA-like attack), but for getting an idea of what can be done, it makes sense to have a look at these two kind of mechanisms.

But to get an impression of the kind of information available to an attacker and how the results of countermeasures might look like, here an example of a SPA measurement:

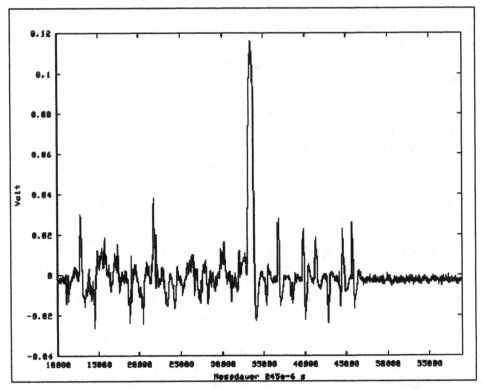

Fig.1: Power consumption of copy operation

In the picture above, one can see a graph describing a typical operation, in this case copying 16 byte data from one memory area to another. The graph shows the difference in the processors power consumption doing the same operation with different input. On the rightmost quarter of the image (showing the almost flat line) the copy operation has been done with identical data as input, so there is almost no difference concerning the power consumption. Next step is to do the same operation, but now with different (random) input. One can see the result in the next quarter of the image: the difference in power consumption, caused by the difference of the input data, is clearly visible. On the other side (i.e. on the left of the peak in the middle), the measurement has been done for the same computations, but in this case with some integrated software countermeasures which should help to disguise operations. Again, the operation has been done twice, one time with identical bytes which are copied, further on the left the same operation with random data. One can see the difference, but a closer look shows that there is still enough potential for an attack; so this result is still not seen as secure.

That this picture is showing a measurement concerning a very basic operation (copying of data between memory areas and not some cryptographic algorithm or protocol) is not by chance: experience teaches, that is often relatively easy to secure complex operation like a modular exponentiation, but there still remain enough possibilities for an attacker on this lower level.

3.1 Randomisation of Algorithms

Actually, randomisation is the most easy and commonly used technique to prevent such kind of attacks. The basic idea is simple: one can try to "scramble" the implemented algorithm. By the use of additional random input it should be ensured, that if a concrete computation is done a couple of times, the performed steps are different from case to case, especially if secret data (like cryptographic keys) are used during the computation.

A typical example is a private key operation using RSA: basically, this is a modular exponentiation where the private key is used as the exponent (and therefore has to be secured against spoofing). Basic idea is to randomise this operation by computing m^{x-R} and m^R for some random number R instead of computing m^x; multiplying these two values gives the correct result, but during the critical operation (the exponentiation) the secret was not directly used.

This method is a classical blinding technique, it can be used in many variations. Especially, if the algorithm used is not consisting of only one basic operation (like it is the case with RSA), but consists of a more complex protocol (e.g. creation of digital signatures with ECDSA), there are normally many opportunities, where the developer can use tricks like this.

3.2 Special Programming Techniques

Most important and basic design principle is of course to avoid the use of conditional jumps where the conditions are depending on secret data; one always has to be afraid that the behaviour of the implementation might be visible from the outside. But this countermeasure alone is not enough for getting a secure implementation, other additional techniques must be considered.

To focus only on modifying the algorithm looks very attractive, especially because this is work which can be used for implementations on many different platforms. But there is one important thing to realize: often the sources of information leakage are very different from platform to platform; so some method which is useful on one processor might lead to a problem on another one.

So one has to know the underlying hardware in detail, if one wants to ensure, that the problems are addressed correctly. This means, that before designing a module an analysing phase becomes important, where the behaviour of basic operations is studied. Problems analysed during this step might be multiplications or copy operations between different memory areas (e.g. EEPROM, RAM, ...) on the chip. In case of the multiplication, there might be a difference concerning information leakage for the two operands; so it is important to know, about which operand an attacker could learn more by doing measurements. In case of the copy operation, either getting information about the addresses used or about the content of the memory can be subject of an attack, and of course it is again crucial to know, which information might leak.

After this preparation phase, there should be enough knowledge about the potential weaknesses of the processor and possible countermeasures for this platform. The following design and implementation phase can then integrate some of the methods which have been mentioned above or additional tricks (like initialisation of registers with random input before using them or parallel operation of host and crypto-coprocessor if something like this is available on the chip).

But the latter is an typical example, which goal can be reached by such kind of work and which problems still might remain: of course, the additional noise created by parallel operation of more than one device on the chip is helpful when looking at the power consumption of the complete processor. But sometimes, this is simply not enough. One problem might be, that the attacker is able to distinguish between various current consumers, e.g. by starting a SEMA / DEMA attack where the location of the probing sensor can be changed in three dimensions and therefore the attacker can get additional geometrical information which helps him to filter out this additional noise. Another problem might be, that (due to the nature of the measurement setup) the data is already filtered according to the frequency; also this could be a big advantage for the attacker.

For the software developers this means, that a really secure implementation normally necessitates the combination of various techniques; this has of course also effects on the size of modules, on running times and on the overall development time.

4 Some Consequences

One important thing to mention is, that the integration of effective countermeasures directly affects the total costs of an implementation. Additional tasks (like measurements on real hardware before starting the design phase) are not for free, the influence on the development can be considerable.

Another problem is the availability of solutions: ideally, a Smart Card using a new version of a microprocessor should be available very soon after the availability of the hardware; of course this is not easy to realize if somebody wants to have a closer look at the hardware before starting the actual development.

In the following, two consequences are described a little bit more detailed: one is, how the product (typically a library for doing cryptographic operations) is affected in terms of code size and other resource consumption; the other topic is, what changes are necessary in the development process.

4.1 Influence on Resource Consumption

Of course, the influence on the resource consumption depends on a couple of circumstances (e.g. the processor used, the clock frequency at which it is working and which countermeasures have been integrated); so all values given in this paragraph can only be seen as a rule of thumb.

There are mainly two important resources: the computing power of a typical microprocessor used on Smart Cards on the one hand, on the other hand the available memory (concerning RAM, EEPROM as well as ROM). In contrast to processors used in modern PCs, Smart Card processors today are quite similar to those who have been around a couple of years ago: normally they are still a based on an 8 bit core, have a few Kbytes of RAM, something like 32 Kbytes EEPROM and up to 128 Kbytes ROM. Typical processors used are the SLE66CX-family of Infineon Technologies or the SmartMX (also named P5) family, manufactured by Philips Semiconductors.

So what about computation times on these platforms? For cryptographic purposes, Security ICs often have some kind of hardware accelerators for the necessary computations; this might be something like a DES engine or a separate crypto-coprocessor for doing modular arithmetic. By using this, a typical operation like generation of a digital signature takes approx. 200 – 400 ms in case of RSA and somewhere in the area of 50 – 100 ms in case of ECC-based protocols (e.g. ECDSA). Compared to the time for the whole process of using a Smart Card, it is not a real problem that these timings can contain an overhead of up to 50% for integrated countermeasures against attacks. The overall performance is sufficient in this case.

But the situation might be a little bit different when looking at other use cases or operations: beneath the use in contactless applications (where speed is really an issue) one especially critical part is key generation in case of RSA. Doing this on the card normally yields to computation times from 5-15 seconds (again for 1024 bit key length). Because this is an operation which is used in the personalisation process of a Smart Card, one might be keen on saving every possible second for this.

Again, the concrete values, how much performance is lost, depend heavily on the countermeasure which has been taken. Sometimes, the only really good method is, to run an algorithm (or part of it) twice. Securing against DFA attacks on symmetric ciphers often works like this: by comparing the two computed results one gets assurance, that the computation has not been disturbed. Of course, such an approach doubles the encryption (or decryption) time.

Concerning memory consumption, the situation is quite similar. Again, integration of qualified countermeasures is not for free and clearly visible in the size of the code. But because of two reasons, this case is a little easier to deal with: first, cryptographic libraries (as a part of the operating system) are normally stored in ROM, and this is the kind of memory, where the constraints are not so problematic. Second, the influence on the code size is not as big as it is in case of computation times, normally one can think about additional 20-30% of code.

But also here, values might be higher in special cases. As an example of what can happen, one can look at a not very elegant but simple and effective coding technique: the developer can implement different code sequences for doing the same task. By randomly chosen one special code sequence (out of 2, 3 or even more possibilities) each time the algorithm is running, the power trace is different every time and DPA-like attacks are much harder to mount. Of course, increase of code size is at the highest for this kind of countermeasure.

4.2 Changing the Development Process

Most important is a complete change in the design phase: knowing the hardware in advance and understanding the whole problem (e.g. the cryptographic aspects) is crucial for getting the highest level of security. So the necessary skill level of the developers is different today: the focus is not only on the engineering skills, mathematical understanding of the whole problem is also important. One has to understand, how attacks work, to find ways to prevent them.

There is one other important point to mention: how can someone be assured, that integrated countermeasures are really effective? In the past, the main approach was to do ones own measurements or have measurements done during an examination of the product by a neutral institution (e.g. in form of a CC or ITSEC evaluation); all of this normally takes place when the implementation is finished or at least almost done. But if somebody is interested in the effectiveness of some special method used, this procedure has a couple of drawbacks: one of the problems is, that at the end there are so many countermeasures integrated that it is hard to decide, what exactly the influence of which method is. At this point of the development it is normally not easy to separate the influence of the mechanism one likes to analyse.

This is the reason, why the development process of such a module should contain another cycle: after finishing one step of the development, one should not only think about quality management in terms of extensive testing, also measurements concerning security issues are necessary. In case of any suspicious behaviour, it is then early enough to correct the problem by redesigning the module.

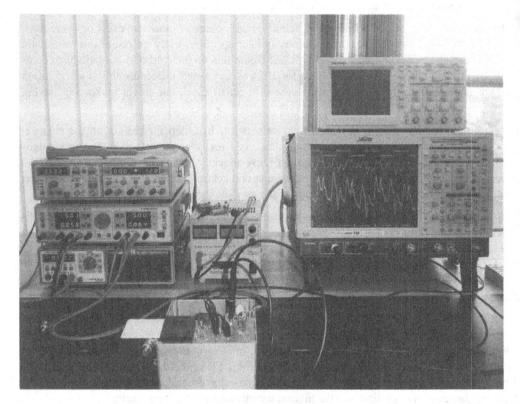

Fig. 2: Simple measurement setup

For doing this kind of measurements, quite a simple measurement setup is normally sufficient: a good oscilloscope with a reasonable sampling rate and enough memory costs somewhere in the range of 50.000 - 100.000 Euro; even equipments available for much lower costs
can be used in practice.

There is one clear advantage for the developer of the software: by working with the mean
over many measurements he is able to simulate a much better (and much more expensive)
measurement setup. An attacker has to work with the Smart Card he wants to break "as it is",
this means he has to deal with all existing countermeasures at once.

5 Conclusion

Some people thought, that with the use of public key cryptography the race between cryptog-
raphers (who are searching and designing secure algorithms and protocols) and cryptanalysts
(who try to break these systems) could come to an end. But problems in the area of side channel attacks are showing, that this is definitely not the case: theoretical security of an algorithm
or a protocol can be something completely different than the security of a real world implementation. This has to be acknowledged.

Of course, something like computational efficiency of operations, code sizes or costs for the
development are all important points; but for a product like a Smart Card, the priority should
lie on the security of the implementation.

References

[BDL97]   D. Boneh, R. DeMillo, R. Lipton: "On the Importance of Checking Computations", Advances in Cryptology – Eurocrypt 97, Springer-Verlag, 1997

[BS97]   E. Biham, A. Shamir: "Differential Fault Analysis of Secret Key Cryptosystems", Advances in Cryptology – Crypto 97, Springer-Verlag, 1997

[KJJ99]   P. Kocher, J. Jaffe, B. Jun: "Differential Power Analysis", Advances in Cryptology – Crypto 99, Springer-Verlag 1999

[Koc96]   P. Kocher: "Timing Attacks on Implementations of DH, RSA, DSS and other Systems, Advances in Cryptology – Crypto 96, Springer-Verlag, 1996

Qualified Electronic Seals
An alternative solution to X.509

Nick Pope · John Ross

Security & Standards Ltd
Chelmsford
CM2 0LG, United Kingdom

pope@securityandstandards.com
ross@securityandstandards.com

Abstract

This paper presents a form of certificate, called a Qualified Seal, which can be used as alternative or addition to public key certificates, as defined in ITU-T X.509, to support the security of electronic signatures such as defined in the Electronic Signature Directive 1999/93/EC. The essential difference is that X.509 certificates support any number of transactions over a given validity period whereas the technology described in this paper certifies a signature key applied to a single transaction. This has a number of significant advantages in efficiency, usability, management and deployment. In particular:

- The validity of the signature key is verified before issuing the Qualified Seal, thereby avoiding the need for further revocation status checks. In addition, the seal includes trusted time, avoiding the need for additional time-stamping services. This simplifies the infrastructure and avoids the relying party to call on additional services.
- A certification service provider can control its liabilities on a transaction-by-transaction basis; unlike X.509 based certificates where liabilities apply to an unlimited number of transactions within the total validity period of the certificate.
- It is possible to assure the validity of qualified seals over long periods by maintaining a trusted archive of each qualified seal.

1 Introduction

Existing electronic signature systems are commonly based around the use of public key certificates such as defined in the standard ITU-T X.509. Such a public key certificate is a statement issued by a trusted authority that a given public key can be used to verify that signatures were created by an identified person or other entity. Whilst European legislation is aimed at being technology neutral, it includes requirements for a form of electronic signature which is supported by a "qualified certificate". The requirements of a qualified certificate includes all the features normally associated with a standard X.509 certificate such as having a validity period and requiring support of revocation information plus a few simple extensions.

X.509 certificates have a number of features that adds significantly to the complexity of their use. Firstly, X.509 public key certificates are issued for a limited period, such as a year and during that period the status of the identified individual, or the security of the private signing key, may change and so the statement made in the certificate would no longer be valid. Hence, when using X.509 certificates the status of that certificate requires checking to insure that it has not been revoked, for example using a "Certificate Revocation List" issued on a

S. Paulus, N. Pohlmann, H. Reimer (Editors): Securing Electronic Business Processes, Vieweg (2004), 82-87

regular basis, or an "On-line Certificate Status Protocol" which provides a real time check on the certificate. This places a significant extra burden on systems using X.509 certificates. When relying on X509 certificates it is necessary for applications to perform some real time check on the validity of the certificate. Public key infrastructures based on X.509 need to support the distribution of revocation information alongside the issuance of public key certificates.

A second complexity in the application of X.509 certificates to electronic signatures, is that there can be a significant difference between the time that a signature is created and when it is verified. For example, there can be a delay of months or even years between the time an electronic contract is signed and the time when the validity of that contract needs to be confirmed in the case of a later dispute. In such situations, the signing time needs to be known and trusted, so that the status of the certified identity and key at the time of signing can be found. If a key is reported to be lost or stolen after the creation of a signature then it is important that any previously signed documents are not invalidated. If a revocation status of a certificate used to support a signature at a given time cannot be later confirmed then signed contracts and other documents are open to "repudiation" by the signatory in the case of a later dispute.

Solutions exist to the problems of obtaining the status of certificates at the signing time for long term signatures. For example, a European standard for "advanced electronic signatures" which have long term validity has been specified in ETSI TS 101 733 & TS 101 903 and also published as an Internet RFC 3126 and a W3C Note. This involves significant complexities in ensuring the appropriate certificate status information is available and the time of signing can be independently assured. Certificates and certificate revocation / status need to be collected and trusted time-stamps applied to the signature to give the necessary independent assurances of the security of the signature.

In addition to the technical complexities of time-stamping and revocation status, the use of .X.509 certificates also has significant impact on the legal liabilities to which the providers of X.509 certificates (i.e. certification authorities) are subject. Under the requirements of the European Directive and the rules of tort in some countries a certification authority can be liable for the accuracy of the information held in a certificate. As X.509 certificates can be used any number of times within its validity period, the liabilities resulting from any errors may be unlimited. An X.509 based certification authority has no ability to control its total liabilities, as it has no means of controlling the number of transactions to which a certificate may be applied.

Thus, use of X509 in support of electronic signatures for long term evidence has the following major disadvantages that significantly effect their costs and usability:

- Additional revocation and validation services are required to confirm the status of a certificate,
- Certificate and revocation information, as applicable at the time of signing, needs to be preserved .
- Trusted time infrastructure services are required to confirm the time of signing,
- Certification authorities liabilities can be unlimited given that an X.509 certificate can be used for any number of transactions.

This paper describes a novel form of certificate which avoids these disadvantages. This certificate, called a Qualified Seal:

- certifies the signatory's public key,
- for a specific transaction,
- at a given time,
- for an identified signatory whose signing key is known to be valid for that transaction.

The Qualified Seal meets the requirements in European electronic signature legislation for Qualified Certificates. Relying parties can use this single object, issued from a trusted authority, without the need for the additional complexities associated with separate revocation or trusted time services. Also, by certifying a single transaction, the issuing authority has direct control over its liabilities.

2 GrowlTech: Seals

The Qualified Electronic Sealing system is based on a system for issuing electronic seals developed by Security & Standards called GrowlTech: Sealing. The seal is an object signed by a trusted authority providing independent proof of the who, what and when (i.e. source, content and sealing time) of any data (e.g. file, graphic, document etc).

The basic operation of the GrowlTech: Sealing system to seal is illustrated in the following figure:

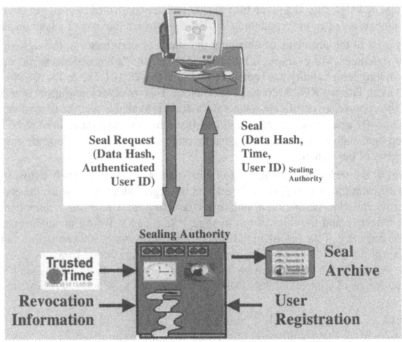

Figure 1: Illustration of GrowlTech Sealing in Operation

The user requiring data to be sealed produces a mathematical digest or hash of the data using a one-way function, such as SHA-1, and sends this in an authenticated request to a sealing authority. The sealing authority checks the user authentication, obtains the current time from a trusted clock and, if the request is valid, send back a digitally signed seal certifying that:

- the data represented by the given hash,
- was held by the identified user,
- at the given time,

and that the 'credentials' (certificate, password ....) used to authenticate the user was correct at that time.

Depending on the strength of authentication required, users can be authenticated to the sealing authority using a range of authentication mechanisms including public / private key pairs or passwords.

The seal and associated data is placed in a secure archive and kept for the period of time required to provide supporting evidence for the sealed data. This seal archive does not compromise the confidentiality of the user data as it only contains a one-way hash, but can be used to validate the authenticity of the data without depending on the long-term security of any keys employed.

This sealing service provides the equivalent of the conventional PKI certificate, time-stamp, revocation-status and evidence archive service in a single component.

The functions of the sealing authority are implemented in a secure server system, with a FIPS 140 compliant cryptographic module and secure links to a trusted time source. The architecture for the GrowlTech: Sealing service allows for full redundancy. In the case of failure of one sealing server, the user requests are directed at alternative trusted sealing servers.

The sealing service is offered by Security & Standards as a public service accessible through the Internet. In addition, customers can operate their own server to act as it own sealing authority, sealing data for members of its own organisation.

3 Qualified Seals

By extending the structure of the GrowlTech: Seal to include the public key that is currently valid for the user a seal can provide a certificate of the user's public key, bound to a single transaction providing a "qualified" seal. The "qualified" seal can be sent as a transaction certificate in support a digital signature, in the same way as an X.509 public key certificate. The relying party wishing to validate the signature can check the signature using the key in the seal, but without having to do any further checks on the validly of the certificate as the seal would not have been issued if the user's key or identity was revoked. Moreover, there is no need for additional time-stamping as the qualified seal includes a trusted time which is bound to the signed data.

The operation of a service providing Qualified Seals is illustrated below:

Figure 2: Illustration of Qualified Seal in Operation

The structure of the GrowlTech: Seal can be easily extended to incorporate the requirements of Qualified Certificates as specified in Annex I of the European Electronic Signatures Directive [Directive 1999/93/EC]. In particular, the public key of the user requesting the seal is added having checked its revocation status. Other additional "Qualified Certificate Statements" required under the directive, such as an indicator that the seal is a form of "Qualified Certificate", can also be added to the structure of the seal without significant changes to the operation of the sealing system.

The Qualified Seal, through a single integrated service, provides the functionality which conventionally requires three separate infrastructure components: certification, time-stamping and revocation status. As the seal binds an identity to a public key, it performs the function of a public key certificate. The seal also binds a trusted time to the signed data, and so provides the equivalent to a time-stamp. Finally, before issuing a seal the users key is checked to be currently valid for the identified user, and thus there is no need for additional revocation checks.

As the Qualified Seal is also copied into a secure archive and periodically countersealed, even if the initial cryptographic key used to protect the seal expires or becomes weak, the validity of sealed data can be checked against the seal retrieved from the seal archive. Unlike public key cryptography whose security depends on computational difficulty, the security strength of the hashing algorithm used to represent the data in the seal does not degrade with time. Thus, the seal can be used to assure the validity of the sealed data years or even decades later. As long as the seal archive is maintained, the authenticity of the sealed data can be verified.

The certification applied by Qualified Seals is particular to an individual transaction carried out at a given time. Hence the assurance given by such as certificate that the information is correct at the time of the transaction is much greater. There is no question as to whether the information used in the certificate is correct at the time of the transaction as the certified data is verified at the time of the transaction. This minimises any uncertainty about the validity of the certificate and negates the need for additional revocation checks.

This feature of a Qualified Seal being applied to each transaction also has significant advantage regarding liability. The authority issuing such seals can control its liabilities on a transaction by transaction basis, and so avoiding the potentially open liabilities that occur with conventional X.509 certificates.

4 Electronic Signatures Directive

The Qualified Seal can be used as a form of Qualified Certificate as defined in the European Electronic Signatures Directive (1999/93). It can include all the contents required in a Qualified Certificate identified in Annex I of the Directive including specific content such as the transaction value. In addition, a Certification Service Provider (CSP) issuing Qualified Seals could meet the requirements of Annex II.

This does not imply, however, the use of qualified seals is limited to any particular legal framework. It supports the protection that is required by any legislative environments requiring authentic electronic signatures.

5 Conclusions

Qualified Seals provide an effective alternative to use of X.509 Certificates in supporting the security of digital and electronic signatures. By certifying individual transactions the security of the signature is improved, and their use is greatly simplified. A single service provides all the user needs where as with existing "qualified certificates " requires a multitude of services including: certification, time-stamping, revocation status and archiving. The liabilities of the authority issuing Qualified Seals can be controlled on a transaction by transaction basis significantly reducing the commercial and legal risks involved. Finally, the sealing system provides the evidence needed to assure the validity of signatures long after a conventional X.509 certificate would have expired.

Where appropriate, X.509 certificates can also be used along side Qualified Seals thereby taking advantages of both systems. For example: where an X.509 public key infrastructure already exists and is used as the authentication mechanism, this can provide the user authentication to the sealing system. The sealing authority can check the validity of the X.509 certificate at the time of the transaction, and then, subsequently, relying parties can use the Qualified Seal is then be used to assure the validity of the key, identity and time associated with a transaction, without the need for additional services. This provides a form of transaction certificate that can be used to confirm validity long after the transaction has occurred, through a single object.

References

[ITU-T X.509]   ISO/IEC 9794-8 I ITU-T X.509 .Information technology - Open Systems Interconnection - The Directory: Public-key and attribute certificate frameworks

[DIRECTIVE 1999/93/EC] Directive 1999/93/EC of the European Parliament and of the Council Of 13 December 1999

[ETSI TS 101 733]   ETSI TS 101 733 – Electronic Signature Formats

[ETSI TS 101 903]   ETSI TS 101 903 – XML Advanced Electronic Signatures (XAdES)

[RFC 3126]   Internet RFC 3126 Electronic Signature Formats for long term electronic signatures Pinkas, Ross & Pope

[W3C XADeS]   W3C Note September 2002, XML Advanced Electronic Signatures (XAdES)

Authorisation Models for Complex Computing Applications

Jim Longstaff[1] · Mike Lockyer[2] · John Nicholas[3]

[1]School of Computing, Teesside University,
Middlesbrough, TS1 3BA, UK
J.J.Longstaff@tees.ac.uk

[2]Teesside University, UK
m.a.lockyer@tees.ac.uk

[3]Tees Health Authority, UK
john.nicholas@tees-shs.nhs.uk

Abstract

This paper presents the **Tees Confidentiality Model**, an authorisation model which is suitable for complex web applications in addition to computer systems administration. It achieves its functionality by combining Identity-Based Access Control (IBAC) and Role-Based Access Control (RBAC) in novel ways. The model is based on a range of permission types, called Confidentiality Permission Types, which are processed in a defined order. Confidentiality Permissions may have negative values (ie they may deny access), and may be overridden by authorised users in carefully specified ways. A single concept of Collection is used for structuring roles, identities, resource and resource type, although the RBAC general and limited role hierarchies can be used if desired. Confidentiality permissions may be defined to inherit within collections, thereby providing a mechanism for confidentiality permission assignment. We use a demanding scenario from Electronic Health Records to illustrate the power of the model.

1 Introduction

An authorisation model, through its implementation within an identity and access management system, provides facilities to enable users, whether they be human end-users or other computer systems, to use resources in specified ways. This can range from using sophisticated application facilities to the simple querying of data.

Identity and access management systems are usually perceived as consisting of three parts: authentication, for establishing the identity of the user; authorisation, for determining the resources that the user is permitted to use; and administration. One application for these systems is to provide access control for distributed web-based applications.

Concerning authorisation, the model that is becoming predominant is Role-Based Access Control, or RBAC. However RBAC has been developed primarily for computer systems administration. In situations where organisations are exposing more sensitive data to growing numbers of users and applications, additional authorisation functionality is often required. Very detailed user-defined constraints, e.g. 'Doctor Smith must not be allowed to see my psychiatric reports', in addition to more conventional RBAC authorisations, e.g. 'an identity

S. Paulus, N. Pohlmann, H. Reimer (Editors): Securing Electronic Business Processes, Vieweg (2004), 88-96

(user) who has activated the role of Doctor is authorised to view and update medical records' need to be handled in a consistent way. In particular a feature needs to be addressed which no authorisation model currently provides (other than the Tees Confidentiality Model, summarized below): that of overriding restrictions to accessing data or using resources in exceptional situations and emergences. Generally we would expect the majority of authorisations to be provided through RBAC, with additional facilities used as required.

We start by outlining a scenario to demonstrate the need for powerful authorisation functionality in healthcare. This is followed by a discussion of RBAC. The Tees Confidentiality Model (TCM) is then outlined and the permission mechanism discussed in detail. Finally we discuss the override issue and draw some conclusions.

2 Healthcare Authorisation Scenario

This scenario illustrates confidentiality issues which have been recently debated in the UK. A model for patient confidentiality is soon to be mandated across the UK [4, 5], which requires the authorisation capabilities illustrated in this scenario.

The scenario was written by a Consultant Transplant Surgeon, and was first discussed in [2]. It concerns a fictitious patient who we will refer to as Alice, and her GP, who we will call Fred. Alice is 50; some of the major events in Alice's medical history are summarized as follows

- She had a pregnancy termination when she was 16
- Was diagnosed diabetic at 25
- End Stage renal failure when she was 45
- Renal transplant at 48
- Acutely psychotic at 49
- Crush fracture of T12 aged 50

Let us now suppose, not unreasonably, that Alice expresses the desire to place the following confidentiality restrictions on the availability of her medical records data about two of these conditions:

1. My GP, Fred, can see all my data. (Here it must be established whether Fred is being authorised as an individual identity, or whether it is the patient's current GP – the normal situation - who is being authorised).

2. Nobody must know about my termination except my GP, any Gynaecological Consultant, and the Consultant Renal Transplant Surgeon who operated on me. (These are all individual identities, with the exception of any identity who has activated the role of Gynaecological Consultant).

3. My GP, Consultant Renal Transplant Surgeon and Consultant Orthopaedic Surgeon can see my psychosis data, but no-one else. (Again individual identities).

Let us also consider the following contrived requirement (but still one which a health records authorisation system must be capable of implementing):

4. I do not wish the members of the hospital team who carried out my termination operation to be *ever* able to see my psychosis data, except if they are viewing in a psychiatric role. This constraint to be in force throughout the careers of those professionals concerned. (The hospital team are a collection of individual identities, as far as this constraint is concerned).

In one of our implementations of the Tees Confidentiality Model, these confidentiality requirements can be specified using electronic consent forms [2].

We must add to these requirements that they must be capable of being overridden in carefully controlled and auditable ways.

Suppose Alice has been scheduled for a transplant. Tests lead the surgeon to suspect a previous pregnancy (if the tissue type of the father is similar to the graft a very serious rejection may ensue). However Alice refuses to confirm a previous pregnancy. The surgeon then elects to use an override facility (Specific Override, as described below), which enables him to discover and view the termination data. A safe treatment can now be planned.

3 Role Based Access Control

The basic principle of the established RBAC model of authorisation is that users acquire permissions by being assigned to roles. Here "permission" means the granting of authority to perform an operation on a resource, e.g. the granting of read access for part of a patient's medical record. This contrasts with Identity-based Access Control (IBAC) in which permissions are assigned directly to users (identities). The IBAC approach suffers from problems resulting from large numbers of permission assignments; the main purpose of RBAC is to reduce the number of permission assignments, and to facilitate their management.

RBAC generally provides the following benefits:

- Increased scalability for numbers of users, and applications, especially for web-based users.

- Improved productivity and efficiency, through speed of response to organisational change, timely availability of resources to authorised users, and delegated authority.

- Separation of duties (a user cannot inappropriately activate two or more roles at the same time).

- Principle of least privilege – users only have the authorisations they actually need.

- 'Extended enterprise' benefits: development of trust relationships between organisations based on role model mappings. Also could be basis of federation: shared methods for authentication and authorisation.

A proposed standard for RBAC has been produced by NIST [1], and this perhaps remains the most comprehensive work in the area. Relevant standards include SAML[6], which allows role authorisations to be communicated over the internet, and also standards for authentication.

4 Tees Confidentiality Model

We now summarise the main concepts and principles of the TCM authorisation model, which combines RBAC and IBAC processing in a simple way, and is capable of supporting the healthcare scenario given above. The TCM has been extensively applied in recent and current UK national programmes (ERDIP [7], and National Implementation Programme for IT – NPfIT[5]), which have the objective of developing a national Electronic Health Record (EHR), among others. We illustrate the use of the TCM principles from its EHR application.

The development of a TCM application involves the following steps:

- Establish the *identities* (users), and *resources* (objects accessed and used).
  For the EHR projects, the identities are Health Care Practitioners (HCPs, e.g. doctors,

nurses), and patients. The resources are patients' EHRs, with authorisations specified at the granularity of DataItem and DataItemType.

- Determine the *identifiers* for both identities and resources.
  Patients in the UK are identified by NHS Number; HCPs by various national and local registration codes. Identifiers for DataItems and DataItemTypes are determined by designers of EHR software.

- Specify *collection types* for identities and resources.
  Authorisations are specified and enforced for members of collections conforming to collection types, by confidentiality permissions. Names for collection types and confidentiality permissions are chosen by the application designer.
  EHR applications enable both HCPs and patients to access health records.
  The collection types associated with identities we will call Identity and Role, and for the EHR resource DataItem and DataItemType.

- Define the practically useful *confidentiality permission types*, generated from the collection types (see below for details)

- Choose the required *overrides* from the full range generated from the confidentiality permission types (see below).

We now give further details of the main concepts and principles involved.

5 Collections

A *collection* has *elements*, which may be *members* or other collections. Collections and elements are uniquely-identified. Collections are inherently hierarchical in that they can contain sub-collections, which in turn can have their own sub-collections. Elements can participate in more than one collection. *Confidentiality permissions* are defined with inheritance properties in collections.

The preferred TCM mechanism for realising Role hierarchies, and hierarchies of Identities, DataItems and DataItemTypes, and for performing confidentiality permission assignment, is based on the concept of collection. However it is possible to assign confidentiality permissions to Roles using general and limited role hierarchies in the established RBAC ways [1].

Some remarks on the TCM EHR application collection types now follow.

Identity Collection

Generally speaking, collections associated with Identities, and containing identifiers for Identities, can be used to model naturally-occurring team/subteam, or committee structures. The assignment of Identities to Identity Collections would mostly be made on the basis of Role – e.g. an anaesthetist is needed at a certain level in a team. Teams may have a temporary existence (being formed for a single task), and may exist in a succession of versions (members being replaced, for whatever reason).

Consider a Surgeon's team, which we will call SurgeonTeam1, formed for the purpose of carrying out emergency operations during a fixed time period; Figure 1 depicts part of this team. SurgeonTeam1 contains all the Identities concerned with carrying out operations, with subteams AnaesthetistTeam1, AnaesthetistAdmin. (Other subteams which are not shown include Theatre Nurses, Ward Nurses). Figure 1 indicates that clinical data can be viewed by SurgeonTeam1 and AnaesthetistTeam1 members only – see later for discussion of the ISC confidentiality permission type. Note that a doctor is only allowed to access a patient's records if he becomes involved in the treatment for that patient. Therefore authorisations must take place at the level of Identity.

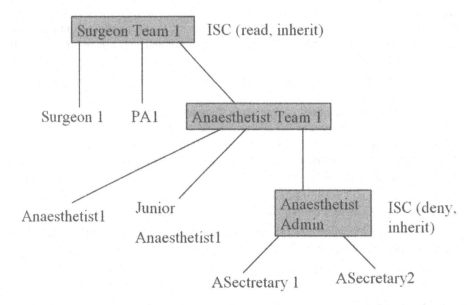

Figure 1 Team/subteam, with permissions

(For a specified DataItemCollection, with downward inheritance to any DataItem subcollections – medical data relevant to operation)

Consider an emergency situation where a junior member of a team, say ASecretary1, needs to have access to the clinical data which has been made available to more senior members. Suppose that ASecretary1 has been granted the privilege of using Team Override (see later for definition) to the level of AnaesthetistTeam1, and she elects to do so. She will now be able to access the data, because AnaesthetistTeam1 and its members inherit the access assigned to this data for SurgeonTeam1.

Role Collection

A Role Collection type structure can potentially contain several Roles as members, which may be regarded as being 'at the same level'. This provides a means of classifying Roles within large applications.

Role Collections facilitate specifying the scope of inheritance for confidentiality permissions, in the way illustrated above for Identity Collections. Therefore if a confidentiality permission is required to apply to part of a Role Collection, this can be accomplished easily.

DataItem Collection and DataItemType Collection

The collection concept, including inheritance of confidentiality permissions, carries over directly to resources. A permission for an identity defined with inheritance within a data-related collection with sub and super collections behaves in the same way.

An example of a DataItem Collection is the EHR for a particular patient. Sub collections can be defined which might correspond to notes, current medication, etc.

DataItemType Collections can be used to model clinical coding systems, e.g. Read Codes.

6 Confidentiality Permissions

We now list the confidentiality permission types of the TCM EHR application in their order of precedence for evaluation (i.e. most restrictive to least restrictive, resource-related within identity-related). The names of confidentiality permission types may be derived from the names of collection types. Note that the definition of a confidentiality permission includes whether it is to be inherited to any subcollections of participating collections [3]. An example of inheritance to subcollections was given in Figure 1.

There are five types of practically useful confidentiality permission, which we briefly describe below, and illustrate in Figure 2.

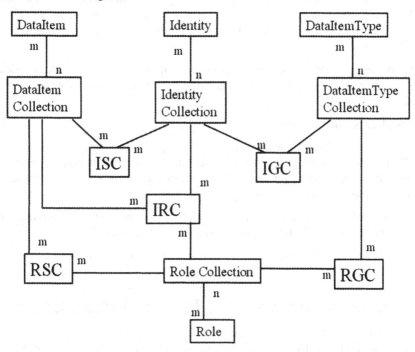

Figure 2 Class diagram for Confidentiality Permission Types

IdentityRoleConfidentiality (IRC)

An IRC specifies an association between an Identity Collection (e.g. a clinical team), a Role Collection (e.g. roles associated with psychiatry), and a DataItem Collection (e.g. psychosis data for an individual patient, including any subcollections such as medication prescribed for psychosis). It grants or denies access to identities acting in specific roles to specific collections of data.

An IRC partially implements confidentiality requirement 4 of the 'Fred and Alice' scenario described above.

IdentitySpecificConfidentiality (ISC)

An ISC associates an Identity Collection (e.g. consisting of a single individual, 'Fred') with a DataItem Collection (pregnancy termination).

Confidentiality requirement 1 in the scenario is represented by an ISC permission, as are parts of requirements 2, 3 and 4.

IdentityGeneralConfidentiality (IGC)

An IGC grants or denies access for Identities (in an Identity Collection) access to DataItems irrespective of Role, and providing the DataItemType is in the DataItemType Collection.

An IGC can grant or deny access for an Identity to particular type of disease data (any patient), e.g. a specialist could be granted access to the use of medication data which has been denied (by RGCs – see below) to several clinician Roles (including his own Role).

There are no IGCs in this scenario.

RoleSpecificConfidentiality (RSC)

An RSC associates a Role Collection (e.g. containing the Gynaecological Consultant Role) with a DataItem Collection (e.g. pregnancy termination). It grants or denies Identities acting in Roles in the Role Collection access to DataItems in the DataItem Collection, irrespective of DataItemType.

Confidentiality requirement 2 from section 3, concerning access for any Gynaecological Consultant, is represented by an RSC permission. Also RSCs deny access to data in requirements 2, 3 and 4.

RoleGeneralConfidentiality (RGC)

An RGC associates a Role Collection (e.g. containing Gynaecological Consultant) with a DataItemType Collection (pregnancy termination data, any patient). It grants or denies access to Identities acting in Roles in the Role Collection to DataItems, providing their DataItemType is in the DatItemType Collection.

This type of permission is used to provide normal access to data, where restrictions have not been specified by other confidentiality permissions processed before RGCs.

It is possible to define other confidentiality permission types from the four collection types specified for the scenario, but these were judged not to be practically useful.

7 Permissions Processing for Healthcare Scenario

Suppose that Fred queries Alice's Electronic Health Record (EHR), with authorisations controlled by the TCM. He will see the data for the termination, because the permissions would be processed as follows.

- IdentityRoleConfidentiality (none for Fred)
  (no match)
- IdentitySpecificConfidentiality (access, for Fred)
  matched, data displayed
- IdentityGeneralConfidentiality (none)
  (overridden)
- RoleSpecificConfidentiality (denial, for GPs)
  (overridden)
- RoleGeneralConfidentiality (access, for GPs)
  (overridden)

Now consider a query by a GP other than Fred. For the termination data:

- IdentityRoleConfidentiality (none for this GP)
  (no match)

- IdentitySpecificConfidentiality (none for this GP)
  (no match)
- IdentityGeneralConfidentiality (none)
  (no match)
- RoleSpecificConfidentiality (denial, for GPs)
  match, data not displayed
- RoleGeneralConfidentiality (access, for GPs)
  (overridden)

Query by a Gynaecological Consultant. For the termination data:
- IdentityRoleConfidentiality (none for this GC)
  (no match)
- IdentitySpecificConfidentiality (none for this GC)
  (no match)
- IdentityGeneralConfidentiality (none)
  (no match)
- RoleSpecificConfidentiality (access, for GCs)
  match, data displayed
- RoleGeneralConfidentiality (access, for GCs)
  (overridden)

8 Override

An identity would generally need to be authorised to use an override, and would have to subsequently justify its use. Electronic notifications would be sent to appropriate authorities when an override is used.

There are four types of override defined for the TCM EHR application.
- *Specific override*, which cancels any negative (denial) effects of IRC, ISC, IGC, and RSC permissions, leaving RGC operating. This will enable the enquirer to see the information he would normally see by virtue of his role.
- *Team override*, which enables an identity to view data read-authorised to a higher-level of Identity Collection (team).
- Role Override, which enables an identity to view data according to the confidentiality permissions granted to a higher-level Role Collection.
- Global Override, which removes all restrictions on data.

Examples of the use of Team Override and Specific Override were given above. In the Specific Override example, the permissions processing for the termination data, for the Transplant Surgeon is as follows:
- IRC (none for this TS)
  (Specific Override)
- IdentitySpecificConfidentiality (none for this TS)
  (Specific Override)
- IdentityGeneralConfidentiality (none)
  (Specific Override)
- RoleSpecificConfidentiality (denial, for TSs)
  (Specific Override)

- RoleGeneralConfidentiality (access, for TSs)
  Match, data displayed

9 TCM implementations

Implementations of the TCM have been constructed at Teesside University using SQL, Active Server Pages/JavaScript/XML, and .NET/C#/XML, in the context of the UK Electronic Records Development and Implementation Programme (ERDIP) [7]. The model was used to control access to data in a Torex GP system, and in an OLM Carefirst Social Services system. We have also demonstrated that it works directly with the XML Referral Messages used in the health service in Scotland.

The TCM has also been implemented by commercial suppliers to the Walsall and South Staffordshire ERDIP projects, by making enhancements to their existing RBAC software.

10 Conclusions

We have used a scenario and examples to demonstrate sophisticated authorisation functionality, which has potentially wide application in modern distributed computing applications. The main concepts presented, which represent additional functionality to that provided by Role-Based Access Control, were:

- the use of a range of permission types which are processed in a defined order
- allowing negative permissions, and
- overriding negative permissions by cancelling denial effects at defined points in the order of processing the permissions.

The Tees Confidentiality Model, which supports the functionality outlined above, has been implemented by several suppliers to the UK health service. It has significantly influenced the specifications for the national Electronic Health Record system to be implemented for England (the ICRS OBS [5]), against which suppliers are currently bidding.

References

D F Ferraiolo, R Sandhu, S Gavrila, D R Kuhn, R Chandramouli (2001) "Proposed NIST Standard for Role-Based Acess Control", *ACM TISSEC*, Vol 4, No 3.

J J Longstaff, MG Thick, G Capper, MA Lockyer (2002) "Eliciting and recording eHR/ePR Patient Consent in the context of the Tees Confidentiality Model", *HC2002 Conference*, Harrogate, England.

J J Longstaff, MA Lockyer, J Nicholas (2003) "The Tees Confidentiality Model: an authorisation model for identities and roles", ACM SACMAT 2003, Como, Italy, June 2003.

UK NHS Confidentiality Workstream (2003)
www.nhsia.nhs.uk/confidentiality/pages/consultation/

NHS National Programme for Information Technology (2003) Integrated Care Records Service, Output Based Specification.

Oasis standards organisation (2003) *Oasis* http://www.oasis-open.org/home/index.php

"ERDIP" (2003) www.nhsia.nhs.uk/erdip.

TruPoSign[*]
A trustworthy and mobile platform for electronic signatures

Michael Hartmann[1] · Levona Eckstein[2]

[1]KOBIL Systems, Worms
hartmann@kobil.de

[2]Fraunhofer SIT, Darmstadt
eckstein@sit.fraunhofer.de

Abstract

Today's PCs and laptops with standard operating systems cannot be considered as secure signature platforms because they are at risk of manipulation when they are connected to public networks. Viruses and Trojan horses can be designed to cause damage in the signature environment. Furthermore, existing concepts do not sufficiently address signature creation in third party environments and working conditions, where documents have to be signed at different workstations. This article presents the Trusted Pocket Signer (TPS), a development funded within the German Federal Ministry of Economics and Labour (BMWA) programme "VERNET – Secure & Reliable Transactions in Open Communication Networks". The TPS device is a mobile and trustworthy signature platform based on common PDA technology. It provides features for a secure wireless communication, trustworthy visualization of documents to be signed and convenient biometric authentication. Common smart cards are used as secure signature creation device.

1 Introduction

Whenever high liability is linked to electronic signatures or highly critical actions are based on them, the security of the signature environment is essential.To address that issue, Germany has introduced the so-called *qualified electronic signatures*. Qualified electronic signatures have the same validity as their handwritten counterpart. It is thus possible to make legally binding statements such as contracts, tax declarations on PCs in service environments, in the office and on home PCs.Therefore, qualified electronic signatures require a Secure Signature Creation Device (SSCD) for protecting the signing key and the signing function and further trustworthy signature application components such as a document presentation component for displaying the signer's document in a secure and unambiguous way. Typically, smart cards are used as SSCD. But typically, signature applications and special signature application components are running on a PC, which is potentially endangered by viruses, trojan horses, worms, etc. Due to this fact, manipulations of the system components cannot be prevented generally.

The creation of an electronic signature in service environments causes an additional problem. The whole hardware and software environment is controlled by the service provider and the signer is not able to verify the system or to take security measures. Therefore the signer can not be sure that he signs exactly the document, which he has seen on the screen. Additionally

[*] BMWA Förderkennzeichen 01MS114

S. Paulus, N. Pohlmann, H. Reimer (Editors): Securing Electronic Business Processes, Vieweg (2004), 97-107

it can not be excluded that signature creations are processed in the background using an already activated smart card.

Besides the above mentioned security problems there still exist some handling problems while using a smart card as SSCD. Users who are changing their workplace frequently probably won't put their smart card in a smart card terminal and then enter the PIN to activate the smart card, each time when they are changing the workplace. For these highly mobile users the described effort takes to much time, is boring and therefore not acceptable.

We will describe a PDA based solution that eases the use of common smart cards and can be easily integrated in existing infrastructures and applications. It provides trustworthy visualization of documents to be signed and supports common cryptographic APIs. Finally, it uses convenient biometric verification as realization of the wilful act to invoke signature creation.

The paper is organized as follows: Chapter 2 describes the objectives of the project. In chapter 3 one example application about how to use the TPS is explained. The technical requirements and the whole system are explained in chapter 4 and 5.

2 Project Goal

The goal of the "Trusted Pocket Signer – TruPoSign" project, which is funded by the German Federal Ministry of Economics and Labour (BMWA), consists of the concept, technical realization and evaluation of a mobile and trustworthy signature platform based on common PDA technology. This device is called "Trusted Pocket Signer" or in short "TPS".

The main features of the TPS are:

- secure, wireless communication with PC based backend system
- all security relevant steps (document and signature attribute presentation, user authentication, wilful act, signature creation) are performed in a secure closed environment
- common smart cars are used as secure signature creation device (SSCD)
- the document to be signed is validated and presented in a secure and unambiguous view
- biometric user authentication via handwritten signature supports data protection and fast, convenient performing of the "wilful act" to enable the signature creation in the smart card (especially suited for professionals who sign frequently)
- the PIN for enabling the signature function in the smart card is never disclosed to the outside world
- software upgrades and the installation of additional features (e.g. organizer functions) are possible using a secure protocol; only certified modules are accepted for download

The TPS can be integrated in all signature applications, which need a trustworthy signature platform. Equipped with a trusted viewer, the TPS can validate and display documents before, for example, an electronic order to repair a car is issued, or a booking for a Caribbean holiday is made in a travel agency, i.e. in an environment not controlled by the signer. At home, too, people no longer need to have any reservation when surfing in the internet and signing e.g. an electronic cheque – currently in development – to electronically transfer the sum paid for an object acquired e.g. in an ebay auction.

The project is running from July 2001 to the end of December 2003. Currently the development is nearly finished and the practical use of the device is to be evaluated by some doctors now. Partners in this project are: Fraunhofer Institute SIT, Darmstadt (biometrics and signature application), Fraunhofer Institute IBMT, St. Ingbert (application and evaluation), SRC

Security Research & Consulting, Bonn (application and evaluation), KOBIL Systems, Worms (hardware and system).

3 Applications

The TPS is especially suited to workplace situations where signatures are needed frequently, possibly even at different PCs, but unauthorized use of the signature function has to be avoided. The health care is in the focus of the TruPoSign project because of its specific usage requirements. Therefore the usage of the TPS in a doctor's practice is described in detail in this section.

Usage of the TPS in a doctor's practice

The healthcare sector is rapidly moving towards the use of information technology for secure electronic documentation and communication. An important element is the Health Professional Card as SSCD. The complex infrastructure of medical institutions and the fact that during a busy working day a doctor has to sign up to 300 forms, letters and other documents require technologies which can be used in a simple and convenient manner and support the mobility of healthcare workers who frequently have to use IT resources in different locations. In the following, we consider as example a doctor's practice which consists of several consulting rooms and other function rooms (e.g. laboratory). Each room is equipped with a networked PC workplace, so that the doctor is able to sign a document at each workplace. Using a stationary smart card terminal on each workplace would mean, that the doctor would be forced to carry his Health Professional Card around and to activate the signature function each time by entering the PIN. This way of using smart cards in practice time-consuming and does not meet existing workflow requirements.. With the TPS the doctor does not need to enter a PIN every time to create a signature. He can simply initiate the signature function by entering a handwritten signature or paraph instead of entering a PIN.

The following brief scenario describes the daily usage of the TPS in a doctor's practice. In the morning the doctor inserts his Health Professional Card into the TPS and activates the signature function by entering the PIN once. The signature function is then enabled. The doctor carries his TPS with him. After a medical exam the doctor uses his practice computing system in the usual way to prescribe the medicine for the patient. After composing the prescription he activates the signature button. The hash value of the data to be signed is visualized as a sequence of easily recognizable symbols (abstract viewing mode) on the PC side and sent to the TPS. The same hash visualization is processed on the TPS side to prove that the same document is received. The abstract viewing mode is especially suited for workplace situations where the signature environment is under the signer's control. Now the electronic signature is required and has to be activated by entering the paraph on the TPS display. The signature function is performed in the Health Professional Card. After successful signature creation the signature is sent back to the PC application.

4 Technical Requirements

The TPS has to be small, lightweight, and handy. It needs a smart card interface, a touch panel for user interaction and an option for entry of the handwritten signature for biometric authentication. For the user's convenience the TPS has to communicate via a wireless interface. To get the users acceptance in mobile use, the TPS needs a battery with high capacity and docking station for fast recharging. This requires an efficient power management to reduce the energy consumption to a minimum. Manipulations of the TPS hardware may destroy the trustworthiness of the TPS. Therefore this device has to be tamper evident, which should be checked easily by an average user.

The user should be able to easily verify the issuer of the installed applications and the currently running application, as well as the status of the application. The content viewer for document visualization may be downloaded separately. Only the applications running on the TPS are allowed to invoke the signature creation function on the inserted smart card. A secure download mechanism assures the trustworthiness of the applications. The operating system has to protect applications and the operating system itself against manipulations of any application.

The TPS must be able to establish a trusted connection between a stationary PC and the mobile TPS device via a wireless communication interface. Authenticity, integrity and privacy must be guaranteed being independent of the selected communication technology, e.g. using well-known SSL technology.

The user has to enrol the biometric reference data once. During the enrolment the biometric features of a handwritten signature are recorded, the reference data are computed and stored in persistent memory. Usually three enrolments each in sitting and in standing position are requested.

The biometric verification needs to be real fast, less than one second. The false rejection rate should be about 5%. To reduce the risk of attacks a retry counter must be implemented. After correct PIN entry the retry counter is reset.

The supported document formats are derived from the applications, for which the TPS is used. The general requirement for the content viewer is to ensure that the signer sees what he signs. The content viewer has to ensure:

- correctness: the viewer shall warn the signer, if the document cannot be presented accurately according to the content format
- completeness: the viewer shall warn the signer, if the document can not be presented completely
- uniqueness: the viewer shall warn the signer, if the presentation is ambiguous

Within the project an ASCII Viewer is implemented as standard viewer. The concept also allows to download further application specific content viewers, such as PDF, XML, etc.

Additionally an abstract viewing Mode is required. In the abstract viewing mode the hash value is visualized as a sequence of easily recognizable symbols or digits on the PC side and on the TPS. This special viewing mode is designed to avoid scrolling within large documents, which do not fit in the display in a whole and for which no special content viewer is installed. This viewing mode is useful especially in signature environments under signer's control (e.g. doctor's practice), where the signer sees the document on his own screen but the signature creation should be done in the secured TPS environment.

A mandatory requirement on the TPS system is to provide an API which is suitable to integrate the TPS in existing and newly developed signature applications. On the one hand an API for easily communication with the TPS signature application is necessary. On the other hand this API has to support common cryptographic interfaces (e.g. PKCS#11, CryptoAPI) for integration in commercial security products.

5 Architecture

An overview of the TPS system architecture is given in this chapter.

The TPS system environment consists of the following base components:

- the PC, where the signature application is running
- the Trusted Pocket Signer (TPS) based on PDA technology taking care of visualization and wilful act,
- the signature smart card, where the electronic signature is created

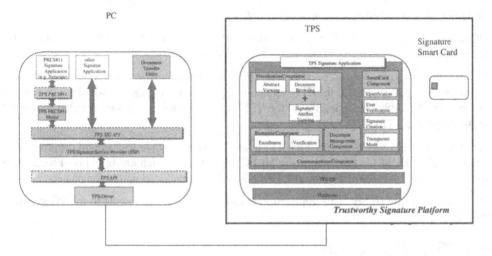

5.1 Security Levels

Depending on the necessary security different security models for the TPS are available:

- **Sealed TPS:** No additional applications can be downloaded on a sealed TPS. TPS is not freely programmable, this means the user can not download any application on the TPS. In the rollout other applications besides the TPS signature application may be installed. It is not possible to download any new functionality, but already installed application may be updated (e.g. current document viewers for the new document content types, new smart card profiles,...).

- **System controlled TPS:** The TPS allows to download applications, which are verified and signed by authorized instances. These authorized instances are defined by the TPS issuer. The user can not influence this.

- **User controlled TPS:** The TPS allows download and installation of applications only after verification of the applications signature. But in difference to the system controlled TPS the user has to decide if he trusts the issuer of the application or not.

For different application environments, the TPS supports the following user modes:

- **Single User Mode:** The TPS is used by a single person only. Normally the TPS belongs to this person and is personalized to her.

- **Multi User Mode:** The TPS is used by several persons. Normally such a TPS belongs to an institution, which provides a unique TPS to some employees. The TPS is personalized to all of these users.

- **Unknown User Mode:** The person using the TPS is not known. Normally the TPS belongs to a service provider, who offers the TPS to its customers in the office for signature creation, if the customer does not possess an own TPS. In this user mode no personalization is done.

5.2 PC Components

On the PC side the following components exist:

TPS-Driver / TPS-API: The TPS driver connects the TPS with the PC and handles the communication. The functionality of the driver is provided by the TPS-API.

TPS Signature Service Provider / TPS-SIG-API: This module realizes the communication between the PC application and the TPS signature application using the TPS-API for communication with the TPS. The functions of the TPS signature application are provided to the PC application by the TPS-SIG-API.

TPS PKCS#11 Module: The TPS-SIG-API is not a real alternative to standard cryptographic interface like PKCS#11. For supporting all PC application, which are based on PKCS#11 a special PKCS#11 wrapper based on the TPS-SIG-API is developed within the project.

Document Transfer Utility: This application is used to transfer documents to the PC stored in the TPS.

5.3 The TPS Device

The TPS signature application is the main application of the TPS. The TPS signature application provides a secure signature creation environment in conjunction with the TPS hardware, system software and the signature card. Other TPS applications can reside together with the TPS signature application on the TPS. But these applications are not in the focus of this project. The TPS signature application consists of the following parts:

Visualization Component: this component has to present the data to be signed on the reduced visualization capabilities of the TPS in an unambiguous view. It is differentiated between document browsing and abstract viewing. In the document browsing mode the data to be signed are visualized depended on the document content type. Additionally the signature attributes are shown on demand. In the abstract viewing mode the hash value is visualized in an abstract way (e.g. graphic, sequence of symbols, sequence of digits,...), to avoid document scrolling. This visualization mode is useful in secure environments (e.g. doctor's practice), where the signer verifies the document on his PC, but signs it without any time delay on the more secure TPS environment.

Biometric Component: if signature dynamics is used for the wilful act, the biometric component performs the enrolment and verification of the users reference data. Only after a successful biometric user verification the signature creation can be processed on the smart card.

Smart Card Component: this component has to control the interaction with the smart card. In a first step the smart card has to be identified and the corresponding smart card profile has to be selected. Since currently only PIN protected signature cards are available, knowledge based user authentication is one of the main tasks of this component. For signature creation the data to be signed has to be hashed and the requested signature input format has to be prepared. Based on the selected smart card profile this component has to build up the sequence of command APDUs and send them to the smart card for signature creation. Besides the already mentioned functionality this component also controls the access to other smart card functions and objects, e.g. reading a certificate..

Document Management Component: signed documents are stored in the TPS for further investigation by the user, using this component. This is used to sign documents in an environment not controlled by the user. The user can carry the signed document inside the TPS and transfer it to a trusted environment for archiving.

Communication Component: this component establishes a secure communication channel between the TPS and a PC via a wireless interface for exchanging data.

The TPS device is realized, using a dedicated hardware.

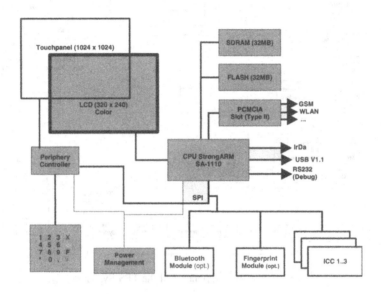

Fig. 2: TPS Hardware

The TPS is based on an Intel StrongARM SA-1110 CPU, with each 32MB SDRAM and flash memory. All communication channels which do not lead directly out of the CPU are connected via an SPI bus. These are the periphery controller for input via function keys and touch panel, the optional bluetooth module[BT], an optional fingerprint sensor and the ICC interfaces. Currently the TPS supports IrDA [IRDA], USB V1.1 and two PCMCIA / Compact Flash slots to connect additional communication modules (GSM, WLAN, ...) or memory extensions. A 320x240 pixel colour display is used for visualization.

The TPS software system is roughly divided in three parts:

- The Linux based operating system with memory management, process management, device drivers and file system.

- Native applications, which are the Java CVM, the biometric components and the system update application.

- Java applications, all TPS specific applications are implemented in Java.

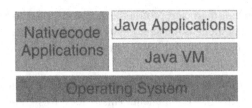

Fig. 3: General concept of software components

5.4 Detailed Description

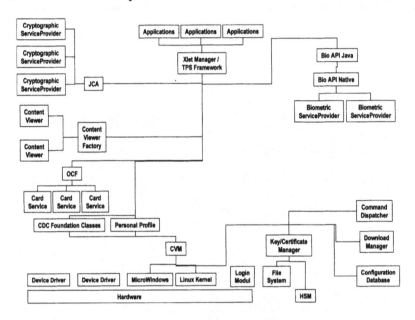

Fig. 4: Components of the TPS Systems

All components of the TPS system and their relationships between each other are shown in figure 4. The functionality of each component is described in detail in the following section.

Linux Kernel

The TPS operating system is build upon a Linux port on StrongARM processor based on the Familiar Distribution [FD]. The advantage of Linux is it's continuous development, the open source and the non existent licence fee. The open source allows to fit the operating systems to the special needs of the TPS.

CVM

Sun Microsystems provides the Java technology in several editions, which are designed for the specific needs of different device classes. TPS uses Java 2 Micro Edition (J2ME), which is optimized for resource-limited environments. J2ME is available in two configurations, CLDC – Connected Limited Device Configuration and CDC – Connected Device Configuration [CDC]. Both configurations provide their own virtual machine, which has to be ported to the target platform. For CLDC the virtual machine is called KVM and for CDC its called CVM. TPS uses CDC and the CVM.

Device Driver

The device drivers address the peripherals. Special device drivers are necessary for the function keys, the touch panel, the ICC interfaces, IrDA, etc. The device drivers are linked statically to the kernel or loaded dynamically during runtime.

Content Viewer Factory

The content viewer factory instances the content viewer objects. Each content viewer implements a visualization for a specific document content type. All content viewers provide an identical look and feel. During the project content viewer for ASCII documents, an abstract viewer and a signature attribute viewer are implemented.

OCF

For integration of smart cards in java applications the Opencard Framework (OCF) [OCF] exists. In OCF the functionality of a smart card is encapsulated in some Java classes called card service. To map the signature function of the smart card in OCF each card needs it's own card service implementation. During the TruPoSign project a generic card service is implemented. This generic card service detects the smart card and selects the appropriate smart card profile. It is not allowed that a PC communicates directly with the card through a transparent channel.

Bio-API

The TPS offers the feasability of biometric user verification. As a standard framework for biometric functionality BioAPI [BioAPI] is used. Within the TruPoSign project the Fraunhofer Institute SIT developed a signature dynamics algorithm which is optimized for the TPS platform. This algorithm is implemented as a Biometric Service Provider (BSP) compliant to BioAPI. Due to performance reasons this is implemented in native code. For easily integration in Java applications a Java wrapper for the BioAPI is developed. The use of BioAPI allows the extend the biometric functions by providing a new BSP, e.g. for biometric user verification by fingerprint recognition.

Configuration Database

The Configuration Database (CDB) manages all information about the installed applications like version, paths, author and packet dependencies. The CDB is implemented in native code.

Download Manager

The Download Manager (DM) has to install downloaded packages. The DM receives an update package from the command dispatcher. This update package is TLV coded and contains three parts, header, payload and Data Authentication Pattern (DAP). The header describes the payload (TPS application (e.g. TPS signature application, calendar, address book, etc.), Java library (e.g. JCA provider), operating system component (e.g.BSP, device driver, etc.), paths, versions, package dependencies). The payload contains the data to be installed. The DAP contains a certificate of the author and an electronic signature of the hash value from header and payload. The DM verifies the DAP. After successful verification of the DAP the DM decides (expansions stages "sealed TPS" and "systemcontrolled TPS") or requests the user ("user controlled TPS") if the package should be installed or not. If the packages will be installed the DM generates the necessary files, configures the CDB and restarts applications, CVM or the complete TPS if necessary.

Command Dispatcher

The Command Dispatcher (CDP) controls the external interfaces of the TPS. The complete communication of the TPS with the outer world is done via the CDP. The CDP receives XML coded commands, analyses them and dispatches them to the according operating system component or application. Internal components and application of the TPS also use the CDP to transfer data to the external world.

Login Modul

The login module is present or absent depending on the user mode (single user mode, multi user mode, unknown user mode). The login module allows the user to log in with username and password or by signature dynamics (after enrolment of the reference data). Later on the login module will support fingerprint and smart card login.

Personal Profile

The J2ME Personal Profile specifies a platform for development of applications for mobile devices like PDAs. Personal Profile supports the whole AWT for building graphical user interfaces. Personal Profile also provides API for applets and xlets. Personal Profile is used in conjunction with CDC and the according Foundation Profile.

CDC Foundation Profile

The CDC Foundation Profile of the CDC contains the necessary classes for CDC application development.

JCA

The Java Cryptography Architecture [JCA] was specified to provide cryptographic functions to Java applications. The JCA specifies a framework where cryptographic service provider can be simply included. These providers can be implemented in pure Java or in native code, addressed through the Java Native Interface JNI to increase performance.

Key/Certificate Manager

The Key/Certificate Manager manages the keys and certificates which are necessary to verify signatures of update packages and other cryptographically secured information. The private and public keys and certificates can be stored in the file system as well as in a hardware security module (HSM).

Xlet Manager / TPS Framework

The Xlet Manager / TPS Framework (XM) takes the management of the real TPS applications, which are implemented as xlets. The XM loads, starts, stops and terminates the xlets. Thereby the XM controls the status bar of the TPS where the user can find information on the currently active application, and the corresponding data stored in the configuration database (CDB). The user can also choose any application from this status bar and give this specific application the control of the TPS. Only one application can be active at the same time. Only the active application can access the peripherals of the TPS (display, keyboard, inserted smart card).

Micro Windows

To treat the limited TPS resources with care Micro Windows [MW] is used to cover the graphical user interface and the AWT functionality.

6 Summary

The TPS device is a mobile and trustworthy signature platform based on common PDA technology. It provides reliable visualization for documents to be signed by using common smart cards. Biometric user authentication is used for the wilful act to invoke signature creation on the smart card. It can be used in open and closed user groups. It eases the use of electronic signatures and increases their convenience and acceptance. It can be easily integrated in existing infrastructures and applications by supporting common cryptographic APIs.

Currently the development of the system is nearly finished. The TPS device is available as a prototype and a PKCS#11 module is implemented. The whole system will be evaluated now at some doctor's practices.

We will organize a workshop in early 2004 to present some more application scenarios to interested people.

References

[BioAPI]   BioAPI Specification 1.1. The BioAPI Consortium. March 2001
             http://www.bioapi.org/

[JNI]   JAVA Native Interface Specification. Technical documentation. SUN Microsystems, Inc. March 1997. http://java.sun.com/products/jdk/1.2/docs/ guide/jni

[OCF]   Opencard Framework OCF V1.2 http://www.opencard.org

[FD]   Familiar Linux Distribution http://familiar.handhelds.org

[JCA]   Java Cryptography Architecture
             http://java.sun.com/j2se/1.4.1/docs/guide/ security/CryptoSpec.html

[CDC]   Connected Device Configuration – CDC http://java.sun.com/products/cdc/

[IRDA]   Infrared Data Association. Serial Infrared Link Access Protocol (IrLAP), 1996
             http://www.irda.org

[BT]   Bluetooth SIG. Specification of the Bluetooth System (Core), Feb. 2002.
             http://www.bluetooth.com

[MW]   The Microwindows Project http://www.microwindows.org

Biometric System Security

Brigitte Wirtz

Guardeonic Solutions
brigitte.wirtz@guardeonic.com

Abstract

The terrorist events of 11th September have resulted in an increased focus an security technologies, not only for Internet technology, but also for secure travel, ID documents and government applications. It seems that the usage of biometrics over the last few years has clearly shifted to a solution and application-oriented approach. The adoption of integrated solutions using smart cards, PKI and biometrics will make today's and tomorrow's world much more secure.

Although still a relatively new technology, biometrics has been promoted as the ultimate security panacea that an its own fulfils all security needs, making a system simultaneously convenient and secure. But recently the hype seems to have shifted to the opposite point of view, the publications of Matsumoto [14] or similar papers [9,16,17,20,21,23] have proven how easy it has been to spoof fingerprint systems with faked fingers. Even if such findings have already been reported some time ago, these recent publications seem to aggressively towards a general condemnation of the technology, doubting its usability at all.

This paper gives an overview of the major aspects of biometric system security, trying to draw a broader picture an security issues of systems using biometrics. Security will be defined and analyzed in a general IT security setup. A special focus an the categorization of attacks and appropriate preventative measures leads to a system solution understanding of biometric system security and thus enables a more distinct view an the applicability and limits of the only technology available today that can really identify humans: biometrics.

1 The Role of Biometrics for the IT Security

In today's networked and digital world, system security is of vital importance. A big part of our professional life is based an some form of electronic transactions, so securing a company's digital assets and identities is a prerequisite for financial success. Ignoring IT security increases the risk of major losses to any company or private person moving through this electronic world.

So what is security and how can it be achieved? Generally speaking, security can be described as the absence of risk. In the context of today's IT systems security it has four major aspects:

- Secure authentication, which guarantees that only legitimate users can access certain data or perform specific actions,

- Confidentiality of data using data protection, such that personal or sensitive data is protected from non-legitimate users,

- Data integrity, which ensures that available data is not purposefully changed by non-legitimate users, and

- Data availability, i.e. measures ensuring that data, supposed to be accessible an a specific server to a defined public remains so.

These four aspects of IT security are typically implemented by different system security measures - authentication can for example be done by using password or PIN mechanisms; Confidentiality can be achieved by encryption: IT security is a Set of security measures to ensure the overall system's security targets. Privacy and security are System design tasks - dependent an the system and also the application's security objectives. Applying security measures within an application environment requires a holistic approach, that takes into account the application specifics, the available security measures that could be used to provide security, as well as an analysis of the given security needs. The security measures represent a wall against the potential attacker - and thus must be appropriately balanced with respect to cost and strength.

Secure system design means the consideration of a broad spectrum of attack scenarios from different directions. Generally speaking, a single security mechanism will not provide appropriate security. Combinations of various security mechanisms will normally lead to synergistic effects, and determine the security of the overall system. Thus all single mechanisms must be well balanced and at the Same level, since usually the weakest and cheapest path will be subject to attacks. The picture of the security wall, which is equally high at all points, or of the security chain, where all links of the chain are of equal strength, are well-known analogies in this context.

Secure system components are manifold, and consist of one or several of the following security components such as: a security policy, a security architecture, the operating system security, the physical tamper resistance of devices, the tamper resistance of the involved Software, the communication security, cryptography and security protocols, and last but not least user identification. User authentication can be single or multi-factor (using different methods) for example, something you possess like a smart card and/or something you know like a PIN and/or something you are, like a biometric feature. And so it becomes apparent that biometrics is not a secure system by itself (even if this impression seems to have been generated in the industry all too often) but just one component in an overall secure system design. Biometrics is just one possible way of user identification in an overall security application. It is not the only possible way of user identification - although it is the only method that allows for person identification, given that the overall security policy of the application has proven the claimed person's identity in the first place[1]. Secure system design implies that absolute system security does not exist. Analyzing and breaking a security system is a matter of experience, equipment and effort (e.g. cost). Secure system design means that the costs of a successful attack must be considerably higher than the potential profit from breaking the System. Furthermore, security is always a process of continuous improvement in order to remain ahead of the hacker. New attack scenarios may decrease the cost of a specific attack from one day to the other dramatically. Moreover, the application's security requirements may also change to cover attacks not anticipated or previously considered unimportant.

Ultimately, secure system design for biometrics means that we are talking about general IT secure system design, plus the security issues introduced by biometrics. Later in this article, the security analysis of possible attacks and countermeasures in systems with biometrics will Show that secure biometric system design is heavily characterized by traditional secure sys-

---

[1] Actually it would be more correct to call biometrics the only method to prove "person continuity": biometrics is the only method that can check a person's identity based an the identification of a real person by comparing biometric features against so-called reference features. If, however, the person's real identity has not been established by appropriate means in an overall security framework, biometrics still cannot guarantee real person identification, but only the continuity of matching the person that got enrolled into the System in the First place. See security policy and general functioning model of biometric systems later in this article.

tem design. A thorough analysis of the attacks involved leads to a clear understanding of which attacks are introduced through the biometric technology, and must consequently be dealt with by the biometric system itself.

- **Security should not be assumed – Biometric Common Criteria Certification**

The end-user of any security system probably has just three questions: is the system secure, how secure is it and what is the cost? The answer should not just be stated by the application provider, but rather be proven.

An acknowledged industry standard for Security certifications is the Common Criteria Protection Profile Process [6]. Standardized Protection Profiles ensure quality and provide a neutral security assessment for the end-user. Following the Common Criteria (CC) guidelines any Hardware, Software, or System can be defined as a so-called "Target of Evaluation" (TOE). A Protection Profile then establishes an internationally approved Set of protection requirements to apply for this TOE. Furthermore, a Security Target defines the Security enforcing functions to cover the Security requirements originating from the Protection Profile. Thus CC offers a standardized evaluation methodology to Set industry-wide security and quality standards for similar products. The standardized Protection Profiles can be used for collecting and merging information about security threats, requirements and Standards.

The development of biometric protection profiles is currently under way - draft versions of an American, Canadian as well as British biometric protection profile are available and currently being voted and reworked [2,3,5]. Although the existence of three versions in today's global world is to some extent troublesome, mechanisms for the security assessment of Systems with biometrics following Common Criteria do exist, and will be further developed and fine-tuned in the fixture. In contrast to the Security evaluation of "regular" IT Systems, biometrics does however introduce some specialties. As all biometric systems are statistical pattern recognition systems in an abstract sense, the implication is that their evaluation also has to obey statistical requirements, which are not relevant in traditional secure system design. The Common Criteria evaluation of Systems with biometrics is inherently linked to the statistical performance evaluation of biometric systems. Although it is not yet an internationally accepted standard, it is accredited practice in the biometric world to follow the so-called "Best-Practice of Biometric Testing" [1] for testing and proving a system's biometric performance. While these methods might have been well known in the biometric field for some time, they are still not easily transparent to either end-customers or independent evaluators of IT systems, such as Common Criteria, or local organizations such as TÜV or BSI in Germany for example. As such, best practices still require translation into measurement functions easily integrated in a security evaluation. (See [2,3,1].)

- **Biometric System Security – Analysing the Security in Systems with Biometrics**

2 The General Biometric System Model

Biometric systems verify the identity of an individual by checking personal characteristics. This is done by applying pattern recognition methods to compare given biometric features against corresponding previously stored reference patterns, associated with the Same individual.

The match score describing the similarity between a current template and the respective reference template, is the input for the identification decision. Whereas all computations starting with data collection at the biometric sensor to the final recognition decision belong to the so-called biometric subsystem, the recognition decision is normally transported to the application and its security policies.

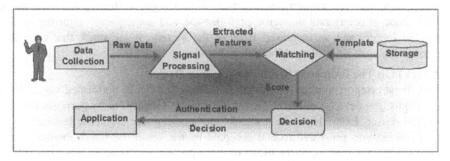

Figure 1: The General Biometric System Model

The biometric system model allows for any particular configuration with respect to its System components. For example, the biometric reference data can be stored either centrally in the application server database or locally an a smart token that is in the user's possession. The configuration of the biometric system has a direct impact an the security of the resulting application. Storing the reference data an the smart token for example increases both user acceptance, as well as security and privacy.

For the security analysis of the general biometric model, we currently assume a general distributed system, i.e. all components are locally distinct and mutually connected via insecure communication channels (which is a reasonable scenario e.g. for PCs, were all buses can be accessed quite easily). Thus all parts could be subject to attacks and must be secured. The user of the application inputs his/her biometric data via an insecure data acquisition device, which subsequently provides the raw biometric data to the biometric subsystem.

3 Threat Categorization in the General Biometric System Model

In this section we will go through a rough categorization of the possible attacks to a security system using biometrics. In this article we will focus an a generic view for the benefit of a general security analysis. For an exhaustive list of possible distinct attacks to biometric systems, refer to the current draft version of the British Biometric Protection Profile for Common Criteria evaluation of biometric systems [2,3].

The biometric subsystem performing the biometric recognition is based an the above general biometric system model. The biometric subsystem is integrated into an application with its own security policy. For the general threat analysis, all communication channels are assumed to be open and insecure.

- **Organizational, Insider, And Physical/Software/Electrical Attacks On All System Components**

  As with any IT security system, the security policy has to deal with organizational and insider attacks, since social engineering opens the door to most powerful system intrusions. The Same is true for physical, Software or hardware attacks an all application system components. Since this article focuses an biometrics and the Integration interface to the host application, we will not go further into these attacks. The interested reader is referred to such well-known literature as [15,19].

  One exception though does exist, which is insider and organizational attacks an the biometric performance. Since the biometric subsystem basically consists of statistical pattern recognition algorithms, such systems usually have parameters to control and optimize biometric recognition performance. Any changes to these parameters purposefully made to deteriorate biometric performance, and consequently allowing easier access to forgers and an increased FAR of the system, is an attack that is generated through the specialties of the biometric subsystem.

- **Attacks On The Biometric Sensor/Acquisition Device**
  This threat category applies for any kind of attack that can be performed via the biometric acquisition device - either at the human-sensor interface, or by purposefully changing the sensor. Examples of such attacks are spoofing live biometric features by using artificial features presented to and accepted by the sensor device (a method currently discussed by the media), or the usage of disembodied dead features like a cut-off finger in the fingerprint case. Changing the sensor device itself to a device that accepts canned or artificially created features, rather than accepting live biometric features, is a further example (an attack that has in the past been applied to ATM machines!).
  Attacks At The Biometric Software Level This category also consists of two scenarios. The first is the scenario of viruses or Trojan Horses introduced to parts of or the complete biometric Software. The biometric Software or parts thereof could be substituted by bogus Software, which Shows a desired performance and produces pre-defined recognition results. It is important to note, that this holds true for any modules and functions of the complete Software package, as long as it is not guaranteed that all functions are run in the Same process of the computational platform.

- **Attacks On The Biometric Reference Data**
  Attacking the biometric reference data can be a passive or an active attack, and consequently "only" leads to a loss of privacy for the respective person, or to further attacks, if the intercepted data is subsequently actively re-introduced into the System.

- **Communication Channel Attacks**
  As in any IT security system, there is a possibility of attacking the insecure communication channels between any two components of the system involved. To remain general, we will not distinguish here between the different communication channels, because the general attack (and the solution, which is well known from the IT security world as well) is always the Same: attacking the communication channel by well-known so-called Man-in-the-Middle attacks. Generally two kinds of interception attacks an the communication channels can be distinguished. The first would be just eavesdropping, leading primarily to a loss of privacy. With respect to biometrics, this attack is of special interest if the channel in-between the sensor and the feature extraction unit or the one between the reference database and the matching unit would be attacked, as this leads to the attacker gaining knowledge of the biometric data - either as raw or template data. Even if this knowledge could not be used (since appropriate security measures would prevent a re-introduction of such data into the System), eavesdropping leads to a loss of privacy for the respective user. The second possibility is the active attack, that not only eavesdrops, but purposefully uses or changes the intercepted data for subsequent introduction back into the System.
  It should be noted here, that these attacks - with the exception that possibly intercepted biometric data an the user side is often perceived as very important personal data - are not any different from similar attacks in any distributed security system. For example, the often cited USB-Sniffer attacks an biometrics in recent publications [23] is not actually a biometric attack, but "only" a traditional attack an communication channels, such

as IP sniffing, which should and can be solved by regular cryptographic security measures.

- **Combination Of The Above Attacks**
  Following the categorization above, it can be Seen that attacks to the biometric subsystem often require successful attacks an several system components. Introducing the canned biometric data of an enrolled person, instead of live data into the communication channel in-between the capturing and the signal processing device for example, requires that either the biometric reference data has been successfully attacked, or the algorithm has been re-engineered to be able to re-create arbitrary data templates to be subsequently re-introduced into the System via an active Man-in-the-Middle attack. The same holds true for the so-called biometric Hillclimbing attack, which will be described later in the section an Biometric Attacks.

Reviewing the above broad categories leads to several conclusions well-worth keeping in mind when designing systems using biometrics. Firstly, system security requires a system solution where component security an all levels and for all components must match - and where biometrics is only one part of the overall security architecture. Thus secure biometric system design deals primarily with "regular" secure system design, plus the additional measures that have to be taken to cope with the vulnerabilities that are specific to biometric systems. A regular security architecture comprises the overall security policy and organizational directives, the security of the operating system integration, as well as the security of System components with respect to physical, Software or electrical attacks and the security of the communication channels. Concepts for securing the integrity of mutual communicating devices, as well as the confidentiality of the communication through Challenge-And-Response based integrity protocols and cryptography, are well-known in the field of IT-security and smart cards. They can and must be used in conjunction with biometrics - the biometric subsystem must actually be integrated into an overall security scheme, otherwise biometrics can at most add convenience, but not security to an existing application.

Only a few of the above-described attacks are purely associated with biometrics, and thus the biometric subsystem or its system integration must handle these biometric attacks!

- Thus in the remainder of the chapter, we will have a closer look at the inherently biometric attacks: Attacks an biometric system performance in order to achieve higher intrusion rates using increased biometric error rates. These attacks stem from the general functioning principle of biometrics as statistical algorithms, which are typically influenced by the special environmental conditions at the human-Sensor interface, and could be generated through:
  - deliberate physical environmental changes,
  - deliberate generation of bad enrolment templates,
  - exploiting knowledge an biometric algorithms and functioning.
- Fakes and Non-Live Biometric attacks at the biometric measuring device.
- Attack on biometric data through Hillclimbing.

Furthermore, it can be observed (also common in IT security) that successful attacks often require intrusion into more than one part of the system. For example, to introduce an impostor template into an ongoing verification process, requires access to the respective communication channel, and knowledge about the feature extraction process, as well as the template data format. Due to the proprietary pattern recognition algorithms in current biometric technology, biometrics adds a certain level of knowledge required for non brute-force attacks. This security-by-obscurity of biometric algorithms should however not be seen as a security measure, but rather as a hint to the easier threat locations in a biometric security system - again it is well-known in the cryptography field that the secrecy of an algorithm at best increases the time taken for the completion of a successful attack. Special attention must therefore be given to the zero-knowledge biometric attacks, such as spoofing at the sensor or a brute-force attack at the raw biometric data level.

Thus we can summarize, that we need "classical" cryptography and System security such as digital signatures against "normal" system attacks (spoofing and non-legitimate change of data along communication channels). Cryptography can and should be used for privacy of the biometric data, acknowledging the special nature of biometric personal data - but not necessarily for security. In contrast to secret keys usually used for identification by knowledge, biometric data must be considered as public data, since most biometric data can be observed to some extent in the public (such as latent fingerprints, faces, etc.). The integrated security protocol of the application system must ensure, that biometric data can only be introduced via a living human at an integer sensor.

An excellent guideline to secure biometric system design can be found in the ANSI X9.84 [4]. The scope of X9.84 is the use of biometric technology for identification and authentication of banking customers and employees. But far from just providing a security protocol for banking applications, the ANSI standard serves as a security integration profile for biometric application integration. As such, it deals with the security and management of biometric data and physical hardware, the application of biometric technology for logical and physical access, the encapsulation of biometric data, as well as techniques for secure transmission and storage of biometric data. The X9.84 could probably be called the first available biometric security and application integration profile.

Another solution for secure biometrics is integration into security controllers, offering a platform for secure data storage and processing. The European IST project FingerCard [7] developed a security framework for such an integration, using standard security controllers, as well as security class3 smart card readers.

4 A Closer Look at Biometric Attacks

- **Artificial and "Dead" Biometrics**

A considerable amount of publicity has recently been generated an the subject of the susceptibility of biometrics to fakes - and since fingerprinting seems to be the prevalent biometric, a lot of the publications have been elaborating an how to generate artificial fingerprints from different "rubber" fingers. Even if such findings have been covered before [9,10,11,14,16,17,21], these publications probably not only reflect the trend of certain publishers to go from general hype to the fear of absolute insecurity and inapplicability, but also reflect more security focused expectations of biometrics, as they might have evolved over the last few years. Given the continuous events in the world today, (also for biometrics) a shift from convenience oriented applications to secure applications has happened or is at least desired. Biometrics is seen as a secure form for travel, national ID and governmental applications. This puts higher security demands than previously anticipated an some of today's biometric applications, especially in unsupervised scenarios.

Table 1: Threats Through Fakes In The Different Biometric Systems

Biometrics	Threat	Live/Fake Measures
Fingerprint	Artificial or dead fingerprints, video, latent prints	Fake/live detection by additional hardware or signal interpretation
Face	Pictures, artificial heads, video	3D- and texture imaging
Iris	Pictures, artificial iris, video	3D- and texture imaging
Retina	Pictures, artificial retina, video	3D- and texture imaging
Hand Geometry	Artificial hand, video	3D- and texture imaging
Static Signature	Re-drawn image	Forensic science, limited
Dynamic Signature	Signature robot	Motion science, off-line limited
Voice	Recording	Text-prompted verification, limited when speech dependent
Typing Rhythm	Typing robot	Motion science, off-line limited

Let us here try to focus an some general implications.

Firstly, it is a fact that any biometric system can be subject to fakes - and thus any biometric system must also cover respective measures for the detection of faked biometric features. Table 1 gives a general overview an the possibilities of and measures used against faked biometrics.

In general, the fake scenarios can be categorized in two ways; the one of artificial features, such as artificial fingers, heads, etc.; and the one of "dead" or disembodied features, such as cut-off fingers etc. Live detection is often treated as a subset of fake detection, as in most cases both scenarios can be treated with similar mechanisms.

With respect to the fake scenario, it should be noted that the potential success of the majority of forging scenarios is application-scenario dependent, since the respective attack would only be feasible in an unsupervised scenario. Certainly in the supervised scenario, behaviour-based biometrics can often be regarded as a weak inherent form of live and fake detection.

Furthermore, there must be a differentiation between attacks: those that demand the co-operation of the legitimate user, and those that do not. In the context of an overall security concept "easy forgeries", that can be generated without the co-operation of the user (such as the re-vocation of a latent Fingerprint or pressed-through signature or the use of an unnoticeably taken print) must be considered more likely than those that demand a high degree of co-operation and cost. The latent problem however, can be easily solved, due to the statistical nature of biometric algorithms: no consecutive acquired feature set will normally be the same as a recent one. Anti-latent detection can easily be implemented by a piece of software, that checks for subsequent identical biometric features.

Whereas quite elaborate descriptions of how to generate artificial fingers with and without the cooperation of the user exist, it has also been shown through experiments by criminological experts trying to introduce latent prints into a biometric system, [10] that the theoretical procedure of reusing prints in the non-cooperative user scenario is very limited in practical use, due to the bad resulting image quality.

In general we can conclude that fake detection is also a system issue and thus requires a system solution. It can be implemented by measures in the acquisition hardware, additional hardware, measures in Software, or even measures in the integrating application or its API. Biometric systems can and have been made secure in the past - for example 3M once produced a fingerprinting device, that asked the user to use both hands, so that simultaneously the ECG could be measured as a fake detection measure. Security is always a question of cost, usability and the security requirements of the application scenario. In the past, the focus of convenience applications such as PC login has been an low cost and biometric performance, and fake detection has often been considered too expensive and too difficult to overcome in terms of verification time and ease-of-use for the end-user in such cases.

- **Attacks On Biometric System**

Table 2: Threats When Attacking Biometric System Performance

Factor	Threat	Measures
Bad enrollment templates	Generate bad biometric performance, higher FARs	Quality verification on enrollment templates
Lowering or disabling security settings , changing system parameters	Generate inconsistent system performance, higher FARs	Security policy, administrator control
Exploit reference adaptation	Change an enrolled template to become the impostor's template	No/restricted (supervised) adaptation of template
Deliberate change of environmental factors to limits of biometric system	Generate bad biometric performance, higher FARs	Self-test functions, additional equipment, security policy/supervision

- **Hillclimbing**

A well-known biometric attack is Hillclimbing, and it is described in detail in [22]. It demands successful Man-in-the-Middle attacks an two communication channels, for example an active one an the channel in-between the capturing and the signal processing device, as well as a reading one an the channel in-between the matching and the decision module. One could also call this attack a focused brute-force attack an the biometric data level. (Having access to the respective communication channels, the Same attack could be applied an the biometric feature level - in minutiae-based fingerprinting for example based an minutiae, which would make the search space much smaller compared to image points.) See Figure 2.

Any biometric system that offers the score at the application user interface is susceptible to this attack. The solution however, is fairly easy and has already been given as a recommendation in the unified biometric application interface standard BioAPI - to only provide the decision scores in a quantized form. The quantization process itself is dependent an the specific biometric technique.

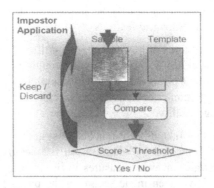

Figure 2: Biometric Hillclimbing Attack

5 Biometric Security - a System Solution

Are biometrics offering ultimate security? The clear answer is No - biometrics only offers a person-centered way of identification to bind the link between devices and Services to real people instead of tokens or knowledge. No more and no less. Biometrics must therefore be integrated into the Security architecture of the surrounding application. Biometric system security is a system solution consisting of a portfolio of Security components and measures - in hardware, Software or the Security policy of the application - of which only a small part is inherently biometric:

- The application specific risk analysis determines the choice of a multi-factor biometric security scheme, which could be

  - multi-factor authentication, combining different technologies (PIN plus/or PKI plus/or biometrics plus/or smart cards ...) for Security and data protection,

  - multiple biometrics,

  - fake detection in the biometric subsystem or application.

- In Client-Server systems a mutual time-stamped integrity protocol for any two components (hardware, Software modules) and their communication links is required. Digital signatures must be used for the security and integrity of the components, whereas encryption should be used for sensitive data (including biometric templates) for privacy.

- The application must be integrated into the Security concept of the platform's operating system.

- SystemOnChip (Card, Token) can enhance security and privacy through sensitive storage and processing in a secure environment.

- Fake and live detection belong to most biometric systems used in unsupervised modes.

- Optimum biometric system performance must be continuously optimized and assured.

The biometric attacks reported in recent publications have not appeared out of the blue for this still young industry, or for Infineon. In contrast to the smart card arena, where certification schemes have already been available for some time, in the case of biometrics they are currently evolving.

Biometric systems of the first generation were clearly focused an convenience and ease-of-use an the application side and an biometric performance as well as low cost an the biometric subsystem side. A current potential shift towards high-end security will certainly be reflected in the respective design of biometric components - however, the focus shift to security may possibly impact an ease of use and cost an the other side.

Security (also biometric security), is a continuously developing target, and integral security concepts being formulized and standardized by acknowledged certification criteria will accelerate the adoption of secure biometrics for the application scenarios where this is required. Thus -just as in the security controller arena - at Infineon, the development of future security products does not only reflect current certification criteria, but is also based an platforms against possible future attack scenarios.

Biometrics can be made secure today at the price of cost and usability - the challenge for Infineon, as for the whole biometric industry, will be to enable this level of security in an integrated and miniaturized way.

References - Useful Website Sites

American National Standards Institute, ANSI, www.ansi.org

BioAPI Website: http://www.bioapi.com

Biometric Consortium: http://www.biometrics.org

Biometrics Working Group (BWG) of the CESG:
  http://www.cesg.gov.uk/technology/biometrics/index.htm

NIST Biometric Consortium Biometric Interoperability, Performance and Assurance Working
  Group (BCWG): http://www.nist.gov/bcwg

TeleTrusT Deutschland e.V., http://www.teletrust.de

US National Biometric test center: http://www.engr.sjsv.edu/biometrics

References - Selected Readings

[1]   Best Practices in Testing and Reporting Performance of Biometric Devices, T. Mans-
       field and J. Wayman for the UK Biometrics Working Group, NPL, Report CMSC 1402,
       Version 2, August 2002.,
       http://www.cesg.gov.uk/technology/biometrics/media/Best Practice.pdf

[2]   Biometric Device Protection Profile (BDPP), UK Government Biometrics Working
       Group, Draft Issue 0.82 - 5 September 2001

[3]   Biometric Evaluation Methodology Supplement, Produced by the Common Criteria
       Biometric Evaluation Methodology Working Group, Version 1.0, August 2002

[4]   Biometric Information Management and Security, American National Standards Insti-
       tute, ANSI X9.84-2001, www.x9.org

[5]   Biometric Technology Security Evaluation under the Common Criteria, Version 1.2,
       September 2001 (CSE, Canada).,
       http://www.cse-cst.gc.ca/en/documents/services/ ccs/ccs_biometrics121.pdf

[6]   Common Criteria Common Methodology for Information Technology Security Evalua-
       tion, Common Criteria

[7]   Deliverables of the European IST-2000-25168 project FingerCard, Infineon Technolo-
       gies AG, Omnikey, Stralfors AB, University of London, NOVACARD GmbH, Univer-
       sity of Kent at Canterbury, HSB Cards & Card Systems B.V., Deutsche Bank AG, Na-
       tional Physics Laboratory

[8]   Smart Cards and Biometrics in Privacy-Sensitive Secure Personal Identification Sys-
       tems, Smart Card Alliance White Paper, 2002

[9]   Spoofing survey, Biometric Technology Today, Elsevier Science Ltd., Vol. 2001 (10),
       pp. 9¬11

[10]   M. Bromba, Biometrie und Sicherheit, Siemens Biometric Security Web Pages,
       http://www.bromba.com/knowhow/biosich.htm, August 2002

[11]   R. Brüderlin, Einbruch per Fingerabdruck? Eine Stellungnahme, ETH Zürich,
       http://www.bioservice.ch/Einbruch per Fingerprint.htm

[12]   G. Hachez, F. Koeune,1-J. Quisquater, Biometrics, Access Control, Smart Cards: A not
       so Simple Combination, Results from the IST-project BANCA

[13]   G. Laßmann, (Ed.), Bewertungskriterien zur Vergleichbarkeit biometrischer Verfahren ("Kriterienkatalog "), Version 2.0, TeleTrusT Deutschland e. V., http://www.teletrust.de/publikat.asp?id=40600

[14]   T. Matsumoto, Importance of Open Discussion an Adversarial Analyses for Mobile Security Technologies, ITU-T workshop an security, Seoul, May 2002, http://www.itu.int/itudoc/itut/workshop/security/present/s5p4.html

[15]   R.K. Nichols, D.J. Ryan, J.J.C.H. Ryan, Defending Your Digital Assets, RSA Press

[16]   T.v.d. Putte, J. Keuning, Biometrical Fingerprint Recognition: Don't Get Your Fingers Burned, Proc. IFIP TC8/WG8.8 Fourth Working Conference an Smart Card Research and Advanced Applications, Kluwer Academic Publishers, 2000, pp. 289-303, http://www.keuning.com/biometry/

[17]   T.v.d. Putte, Spoofing Fingerprints - As Easy as 1,2,3?, Talk given at the Biometrics 2001, London UK, November 2001

[18]   N. K. Ratha, J. H. Connell and R. M. Bolle, A Biometrics-Based Seeure Authentication System, IBM Thomas J. Watson Research Center, {ratha, jhc,bolle}@ watson.ibm.com [19] B. Schneier, Secrets & Lies, Digital Security in a Networked World, Wiley Computer Publishing

[20]   B. Schneier, Biometrics: Truths and Fictions, Crypto-Gram, August 15, 1998, http://www.counterpane.com

[21]   B. Schneier, Fun with Fingerprint Readers, Crypto-Gram, May 15, 2002, http://www.counterpane.com

[22]   C. Soutar, Biometric System Security, BioScrypt Inc., Secure 1/2002

[23]   L. Thalheim, J. Krissler, P.-M. Ziegler, Körperkontrolle, c't 11/2002, pp. 114-123

Reprinted from BIOMETRIC TECHNOLOGY TODAY, Brigitte Wirtz, Vol 11, No 2, pp 6-8, 2003, "Biometric System Security, part 1"; Vol 11, No 3, 2003, pp 8-9, "Biometric System Security, part 2", with permission from Elsevier.

BIOVISION – Recent Results of an Exciting European Roadmap Project

Christiane Schmidt

SOFTPRO GmbH,
csc@softpro.de

Abstract

In preparation for the 6th Framework of support for R&D in key technologies, the European Commission has asked for the compilation of roadmaps to identify the critical challenges in key technologies. Biometrics has been identified as one such critical technology. Biometric methods offer a very wide range of opportunities, some of which have been trialed in limited applications. The BIOVISION project (full name: BIOVISION - Roadmap to successful deployments from the user and system integrator perspective) commenced on 1 June 2002 and finished on 31 July 2003. In order to join many facets of applications and services using biometric technologies to a whole the project group considered aspects of system integration and standardisation, legal and regulatory issues, security and testing, medical and safety dimensions as well as end user perspectives of the biometrics sector in Europe.

During their work the project group has examined three specific application areas: a long (2006-10) and nearer (2003-5) term perspective. The focus of interest has been the use of biometrics for physical access control, their application in travel and identity documents, and the potential for their use by financial institutions. Other sectors like health care and home security have been considered. The resulting prioritised research agenda offers the biometrics community in Europe pointers to a successful deployment at both national and cross-national levels.

The final element of the BIOVISION project was the launch of the European Biometric Forum, a body that would act to address the issues that had been identified in the work of the partnership and act as a focus for future activities to reduce the fragmentation of the community involved in biometrics in Europe.

The BIOVISION consortium is listed in Annex 1. Kindly note that this paper could present only a subset of the whole work. The most recent public version of the roadmap [BVN] will be available at http://www.eubiometricforum.com together with further public documents.

1 Introduction

Biometrics as a technology has taken a long time to become established in practical applications and still has some way to go before gaining mass acceptance levels. The fascination with the biometric technology of the last decade has now moved to a more objective thinking about the use of biometrics in typical everyday applications. Vendors are more aware of biometrics and how they might be used to their advantage. It is understood that desired response time, available performance or required accuracy rates are playing an important role in the decision process. But until now, a more in depth understanding of human factors has obviously been neglected. This difficulty is compounded by the fact that vendors, consultants, systems integrators and users seem to speak a different language, leading to misunderstanding and confusion. To encourage a wider public acceptance and thus usage of biometrics, it is extremely important to develop systems that are easy to understand and easy to use. All too often, information is not easy to find, not comprehensive and not in an understandable form.

S. Paulus, N. Pohlmann, H. Reimer (Editors): Securing Electronic Business Processes, Vieweg (2004), 120-128

In contrast with many other technology-focussed roadmaps, the aim of BIOVISION was to balance the understanding of developments in the technology with the potential applications that will make use of them. In particular, BIOVISION was interested in those factors that will determine the success of future deployments, especially those in the European Union. The BIOVISION members have reviewed the main biometric technologies from such perspectives.

2 Studies Relating Critical Areas

To provide validated inputs into this primary activity, a number of supporting studies were undertaken, in those areas that were seen to be critical to the understanding of the future direction of the European biometrics scene. These were:

- End user perceptions
- Security
- Medical Perspectives
- Technology and Applications
- Legal and Regulatory environment
- Standards

2.1 End User Perceptions

The study work [BVN-WP3] introduced guidance for operators and system integrators on improving on the usability and user user-friendliness of systems using biometric methods. The User Psychology Index was introduced as a tool for those specifying and designing such systems. This would partly address the goal of increasing the acceptance by users of biometric applications. The activity also considered the impact of user behaviour on the security of such systems and indicated possible avenues for future research. Further key elements of work were:

- Analysis of field trials with regard to end user perceptions
- Identification and analysis of relevant existing and developing work for taxonomy of impact factors
- Taxonomy – human factors issues in real-world implementation of biometrics proposed
- Future Workshop of End-User-Perception in Health Care
- Work out of research necessities on usability and performance aspects

Most of the users interviewed as part of the empirical research would welcome personal applications that enhance safety or convenience, e.g. for mobile phones, cars, access control on shared computers in the home (e.g. to control children's access to certain sites, or access to financial/work files), or provide enhanced security with higher convenience in commercial sectors such as online banking. For the latter applications, users' confidence would be enhanced through a clear contract specifying how the data will be used and kept safe by the commercial organisation, and legal and financial recourse if the contract is broken intentionally or unintentionally.

Whilst some (generally older) users in our studies also welcomed the idea of biometrics to enhance public safety and security applications (passport/border control/immigration, surveillance) – the general perception being is that "it would help to catch illegal immigrants and criminals, the ordinary citizen has nothing to worry about."

This study shows furthermore that interaction takes place in a particular context - a physical, organisational and social environment. The context affects the interaction between user and system and can vice versa be affected by it. For example: Systems working for a single user in a quiet office may not work in a busy environment in a shared office. On the one hand side a user interface works quite well when users can focus on the task without interferences, on the other hand the interface shows a bad performance when users are disturbed in their attention. An increasing number of systems have groups of users who interact with each other.

2.2 Security

The main driver for using biometrics is improving security, or improving usability while maintaining security. There are several security issues that have yet to be fully addressed if biometrics is to be deployed more widely:

- Few high security applications: To date most biometric deployments have relatively low security requirements, either by design, or by the nature of the application. Security would also need to be strengthened when the same biometric is used for a variety of applications.

- Long-term integrity of biometric data: As people cannot generally change their biometric signal in the same way that they can change their password every few months, it follows that the biometric data must remain secure over a far longer period than PINs, passwords or tokens. Indeed this information may need to be secure over a person's lifetime.

- 'Live and well' features: There is a pressing need to improve biometric products to make it much harder to spoof the devices by artificial means, or by mimicry.

- Template protection & consent: Work has commenced on template protection techniques that can bind a biometric template to a particular application, disabling its use by any other application (without the application provider's consent).

- People and security: People are often the weakest link in a security system.

- Security evaluations: For biometrics to become accepted as a security technology it would seem appropriate that biometric systems are formally evaluated for security.

The study offers taxonomy of the vulnerabilities of biometric devices and systems. It detailed how such issues are currently being addressed by the biometrics industry, and identified serious concerns that remain and require further work.

2.3 Medical Perspectives

This activity provided an introduction to the medical dimension in the application of biometrics. Two principal aspects were addressed: Direct Medical Implication (DMI) and Indirect Medical Implication (IMI).

- Direct medical implications: There are, of course, international standards for the safety of many of the components used in biometric systems, and these should be used wherever possible. Nevertheless, care will be required in the interpretation of these in the context of novel technologies. These considerations are termed the DMI (direct medical implications) of the application of biometrics and their impact should be examined for those systems that are likely to be most widely used.

- Indirect medical implication: There is another class of medical concern, termed IMI (indirect medical implication), where physical or mental characteristics or conditions might be deducible from biometric measurements.

2.4 Technology and Applications

This work considered a number of general aspects of the selection and use of biometric systems from an analytic perspective. In the 'economic' dimension it viewed the determinants of the diffusion of biometric technologies from the points of view of financial outcomes, marketing, the emergence of new organisational units and the optimisation of processes. Testing requirements were assessed in the light of current experience and a discussion paper produced. The failure in take-up of these technologies is partially ascribed to the difficulty of matching the requirements of the application to the capabilities of the biometric technologies and an adaptation guide is proposed that will support both designers and suppliers in the matching process. This study offers a framework for considering the matching of functional requirements with what a commercially available system can offer [BVN-WP6].

2.5 Legal and Regulatory Environment

The legal and data protection issues surrounding biometrics have given rise to much comment and concern. These concerns have arisen from the user community due to worries that their biometric data will not be properly protected, may be accessed or stolen and used for criminal or fraudulent purposes or indeed that that they may be tracked and traced while going about their daily activities.

A report was written as a first assessment of EU and Member State regulatory environments from a biometric viewpoint in the light of legal and e-signature requirements. It provides an outline of guidelines covering the data protection requirements of biometrics for users, suppliers, manufacturers etc. It also offers a draft code of Best Practice for the development, manufacture and use of biometrics from a legal and regulatory standpoint [BVN-WP7].

2.6 Standards

The wide range of different methods, and the ways in which such methods implemented by the 200+ suppliers fails to allow for complete standardisation. During the period of the project, a new standards body was launched, ISO/IEC JTC1 SC 37, with the aim of advancing current standards (BioAPI and CBEFF) to an internationally agreed level, and proposing new standards as required: data exchange standards, profiles, vocabulary, testing and reporting the results of tests and the cross-jurisdictional and societal issues surrounding the introduction of biometric systems.

3 Research Activities

There have been many research projects in this field that have enabled the participants to gain a better understanding of the algorithms and sensor aspects. The research community has recognised the limitations of single conventional biometric methods and substantial work is underway to use multi-modal and multi-classifier systems; other proposals look at the modelling of features such as the face in three dimensions and others discuss the place of intelligent agents. However, relatively little effort has been devoted to fundamental work on cross cutting issues such as design methodologies that take account of the particular aspects of biometric deployments. Future research projects should therefore address this imbalance, so as to ensure that these issues are considered and that the results of the research are communicated to the rest of the biometric community in a clear way. The following listed samples of research are identified by the project (The whole list is published in the Roadmap.).

3.1 Systems and Design

- Successful implementation of systems using biometric methods requires an inter-disciplinary design approach. There are few specialist designers able to put together an integrated design that addresses the already documented issues and concerns.

- Methods are required to evaluate and compare the security of biometric systems. Schemes other than the Common Criteria framework should be investigated for their suitability. The level of security should appropriate to the application and the risks involved. In particular the binding of the application to the result of the biometric authentication has to be secure. In view of the value of databases of biometric identifiers to other people and organisations, these may need to be secured against both internal and external threats using state-of-the-art techniques. Appropriate security is also required for the templates during their transmission between database and application. All security measures subject should be periodically subject to a review.

- Development of design methodologies that support the secure integration of biometric data in applications such as the Criminal Justice Sector, while limiting the opportunity for misuse and 'function creep'. These could make use of binding of the user's identity, the application, template and user's expression of consent as well as validation by external Trusted Third Parties.

- The impact of a high profile failure in the application of a biometric method could impact on the willingness of other customers to specify such methods, and adverse media comment could increase the resistance to their use by individuals and groups.

3.2 End User Perceptions

- There is no clear ethical framework for the development and use of biometrics. To some extent this will be determined by individual societies and cultures. However, currently, the agenda is set by cost-benefit analysis for improved security, without reference to a more fundamental assessment of the advisability of cross-application unique identification of individual citizens and consumers.

- Social and socio-psychological research should be encouraged to understand how identities and personas are used at present, and the implication of the use of biometrics on legitimate expression of such multiple identities.

- Integration of user-centred, business and security analysis into requirements analysis and specification for a daily use

- Detailed social science studies of evolution of perception and acceptance in individuals and groups including a study of long-term risks of extended use

3.3 Technology Aspects and Testing

- A programme of database construction and testing should be initiated especially for those biometric methods for which such a large scale databases are still not collected or publicly available. Certain biometric methods (e.g. multi-modal biometrics) will require specific algorithm testing schemes and research may be required to devise the most appropriate methods.

- The status of those unable to use the preferred biometric solutions should be recognised, whether these are in the private or in the public sector. Solutions are required that will limit the long terms exclusion of such individuals from the opportunities offered by uniform secure authentication.

- Transparent - yet not covert - systems with excellent adaptive user interface, delivering apparently 'instantaneous' authentication for end users.

- R&D effort is required to improve the operational performance of existing biometric systems. In some cases, the error rates are substantially below what is required for the applications for which they are sold, and 'quantum' improvements in their performance may be required.

- Research into the limits of performance with various methods of implementing specific biometric techniques

3.4 Legal Aspects

- Further development of the Best Practices, based upon experience of similar codes in other fields. One specific application could be in the integration with Privacy Impact Assessments, together with advice to auditors confirming the adherence to such a Code.

- Further studies should continue to monitor the progress towards a uniform interpretation of the privacy issues surrounding the use of biometrics in the countries of the EU (including the Newly Accessioning States), and support the activity of the Article 29 Working Party with impartial information about developments in biometrics. Users' experience in the application of biometrics should be collated and interpreted with the aim of either lobbying for a revision in the legal regime or for retention of the status quo.

3.5 Standards

- Interface standards are needed for all aspects of the operation of systems using a biometric. These should be in a form that is easily used by the design community and readily applicable to the variety of applications that are described in this roadmap.

- The prime driver of standardisation appears to be early application to border security and towards improvements in the physical security of transportation systems (especially in airports). Will this impact upon the usefulness of such standards in other application areas?

- Work to support the standards activities in testing, validating, accrediting and accepting deployed systems at the hardware, algorithm and user acceptance levels.

4 Conclusions

On the basis of the studies undertaken in the BIOVISION project, a large number of issues have been tablet. The project group has generally not looked at the challenges posed by individual technologies, nor considered the economic arguments for take-up.

The project group has noted that biometric technologies should be viewed as mechanisms that address one aspect of an application. Whether the use of biometrics enhances or reduces personal privacy, improves or worsens security, makes authentication more or less convenient, will depend on other features of the application. This is no different from many other technologies. It follows, therefore, that discussion of biometric performance, legality or usability should be in the context of a specific application. Moreover, the value of biometric methods - in improving security, convenience, etc - should be judged from the perspective of operators of services using these methods, and from the experience of the end users of such services.

For many governments, the most significant element in their relationship with citizens is the establishing of a unique and usable identity. Most governments, even in the European Union, still have distributed identity systems, resulting in the absence of a coherent single view across all their services. With their commitment to electronic delivery of services, it is likely that governments will want to unify these systems. Inevitably, this will impact on commercially delivered services, through the blurring of the boundaries between the public and private sectors, and the use of more reliable identities and services developed by the state. Undoubtedly the main driver for the more widespread use of biometrics in travel documents in the near future has been the decision of the US Congress to mandate their inclusion on the one hand in visas for travellers to the US and on the other hand in passports for any country currently exempted under the Visa Waiver programme.

The leading EU countries involved in the development of biometric methods in identity and travel documents have been the UK, the Netherlands, Germany and Italy. In the summer of 2002, the Home Office in the UK issued a consultation document on 'Entitlement Cards', strongly linking the proposal for a new type of card to the increasing incidence of identity fraud. The consultation, which closed at the end of January 2003, focussed strongly on the use of biometrics in reducing the opportunity for multiple applications for identification documents.

The tourist industry is one of the largest in the world, contributing approximately 10% of the world's GDP. Biometric authentication can play a role in increasing the security in travel in a number of ways:

- Restriction of physical access to parts of airports, railway stations, etc to those who have been vetted and then authorised to enter such
- Authentication of pilots, drivers of trains, buses and trucks, stewards and those involved in supporting operations such as air traffic control.
- Issue of tamper-resistant visas to immigrants and visitors in their home countries, an authentication at border entry and exit.
- Authentication of holders of passports at ports of entry and exit (as well as ticket purchase if required)
- Operation of watch lists for specific individuals who may be travelling with false documentation or under aliases.
- Reconciliation of baggage with passengers at boarding, in transit and on arrival
- Tracking of individuals and groups of people at airports and railway stations, and observance of unusual activities.

These samples illustrate the complexities in deployment of biometric solutions. In complex applications of biometrics, it is important that the numerous stakeholders appreciate the different perspectives before decisions are taken. In addition to sharing the understanding the significance of the factors that have been highlighted, and the information gained from the numerous trials, the European Biometric Forum should provide a resource for those who are newcomers to the field. This can be in the form of vendor-independent summaries of the results, presentations and displays on current best practice, ands access to consultants who are recognised as having the requisite experience.

Further key issues identified in the roadmap include privacy, confidentiality, reliability and effectiveness. The fragmentation of responsibilities and budgets within the health services of individual countries is likely to limit large-scale deployment of such systems, unless legislation mandates improvements across the sector. In the USA, the recognition of the need to improve security of patient records moving between the various stakeholders in the sector resulted in the Health Insurance Portability and Accounting Act (HIPAA), which requires greater attention to authentication (but not requiring the stronger security potentially offered by biometric solutions). The list of applications is extensive and only a selection is listed below to illustrate the range of services:

- Remote management of home systems: alarms, heating, appliances, etc.
- Payments: at petrol stations, etc.
- Remote bank transactions over the phone or Internet
- Medical surveillance for disabled and elderly people, especially in closed environments: home, hospitals, etc.

The European Biometric Forum could act as a catalyst to highlight the opportunities in this sector, offering an independent vision and source of reliable information. Lessons can be learnt from one application that is likely to be heavily promoted in the US: the security of hospital patient records. Although the HIPPA legislation does not mandate the use of biometric authentication, it is probable that many solutions will make use of these technologies.

5 Outlook

The BIOVISION members are interested in receiving suggestions from the biometric community, whether in the EU or elsewhere, for additions or alterations to the Roadmap. An interim update of the Roadmap will be published in November 2003, taking into account any comments and corrections received by 15 October. A workshop is planned for 23 February 2004 in the UK, after which it is envisaged that a second issue will be distributed.

6 Acknowledgments

This work has been supported by the 5th Framework program of support for R&D in key technologies of the European Union. I thank Marek Rejman-Greene and Martin Walsh for leading the BIOVISION project to a successful conclusion. I would like to express my appreciation to everyone of the BIOVISION project group for their constructive critique and useful contribution during that project.

References

[BVN]   Rejman-Greene, Marek: BIOVISION - Roadmap for Biometrics in Europe to 2010. www.eubiometricforum.com

[BVN-WP3]   Schmidt, Christiane: BIOVISION – Final Report on End User Perceptions

[BVN-WP6]   Behrens, Michael: BIOVISION – Technologies and Applications

[BVN-WP7]   Albrecht, Astrid: BIOVISION – Best Practices in Biometrics

Annex 1 - The BIOVISION Consortium

The Consortium consists of the following principal partners:

- Joint co-ordination, system integration, standardisation and socio-technical design BTexact, the research, development and consulting arm of BT, Marek Rejman-Greene, marek.rejman-greene@bt.com (United Kingdom)
- Joint co-ordination, legal and regulatory issues Daon, an Irish identity management solution provider, Martin Walsh, martin.walsh@daon.com (Ireland)

- Security CESG, Communications-Electronic Security Group,
  Philip Statham, philip.statham@cesg.gsi.gov.uk (United Kingdom)
- Security and testing NPL, National Physical Laboratory,
  Tony Mansfield, tony.mansfield@npl.co.uk (United Kingdom)
- Medical and safety dimensions CNR, the National Research Council of Italy,
  Mario Savastano, mario.savastano@unina.it (Italy)
- Technology and applications CWI, Centre for Mathematics and Computer Science,
  Ben Schouten, bens@cwi.nl (Netherlands)
- Technology and applications, university research, University of Applied Sciences Giessen-Friedberg, Michael Behrens, michaelbehrens@compuserve.com (Germany)
- User perspectives Nationwide Building Society, a major financial institution in the UK,
  Will McMeechan, will.mcmeechan@nationwide.co.uk (United Kingdom)
- User perspectives and legal and regulatory issues TeleTrusT, a German association set up to promote information security in an open systems environment,
  Christiane Schmidt, csc@softpro.de (Germany)
- Other members of the consortium include:
  - Avanti: Julian Ashbourn (United Kingdom)
  - Angela Sasse (United Kingdom)
  - B&L Management Consulting (Germany)
  - Fraunhofer IGD (Germany)
  - A number of specialist groups are also involved: the Association for Biometrics (www.afb.org.uk) and the Dutch Biometric Forum.

Application

E-Invoicing and New VAT Directive – Challenges for Cross Border Transactions

Stefan Engel-Flechsig

Chairman CEN/ISSS focus group on electronic invoices and VAT
CEO Radicchio
Stefan.engel-flechsig@radicchio.org

Abstract

CEN/ISSS has been asked by the European Commission in 2002 to examine the issues surrounding standards relating to e-Invoicing and VAT in relation to the new Council Directive 2001/115/EC, which has to be implemented by Member States by 1st January 2004. CEN/ISSS has created a focus group on electronic invoices and VAT (e-IFG) which will publish its final report in October 2003.[1]

Council Directive 2001/115/EC, details the requirements on taxable persons and their service providers to the guarantee of integrity of content and authenticity of origin of electronic invoices for VAT purposes. This relates mainly to the invoices exchanged electronically and to the storage of invoices.

Based on a questionnaire the e-IFG report describes the main issues around the implementation of electronic invoices for VAT purposes in the European Member States; the report identifies standards available and makes recommendations for usage of electronic invoices across Europe.

The report is based on the contributions from the members of the e-Invoices Focus Group and on the contributions received during the Open Conference held in Brussels, where some 150 participants reviewed the first draft of this report. Some 53 comments were received following the Open Conference.

1 Introduction: The Regulatory Environment

The Council Directive (2001/115/EC) regarding invoicing requirements for the Member States is intended to simplify and harmonize VAT regulations across the Member States. Businesses operating in EU Member States should have simplified invoicing regulations and procedures harmonized at EU Community level as of January 2004. This will naturally flow through onto new acceding Member States in time.

Invoices have a pivotal role in the VAT system for Member States. They indicate the possibility of VAT refund by the receiver of an invoice and the VAT regime applied. Through a more systematic introduction of e-invoicing, tax administrators may be able to implement new tools and procedures to carry out alternative controls that are less intrusive on the trading partners.

The regulatory environment which on the European level directly related to these issues, is mainly built upon:

- the European Directive 2001/115/EC,
- the European Directive 1999/93/EC, and
- the European Commission Recommendation 1994/820/EC.

---

[1] The final version of the report will be available at: www.cenorm.be

S. Paulus, N. Pohlmann, H. Reimer (Editors): Securing Electronic Business Processes, Vieweg (2004), 131-137

1.1 The European Directive 2001/115/EC

The European Directive 2001/115/EC clarifies the implementation of e-Invoicing through the Member States and aims to introduce harmonised procedures for e-invoicing (and paper invoicing) across Member State borders in a homogenous home market.

The Directive 2001/115/EC, details the requirements on taxable persons and their service providers to the guarantee of integrity of content and authenticity of origin of electronic invoices for VAT purposes. This relates mainly to the invoices exchanged electronically and to the storage of invoices.

With regards to the **exchange of invoices** for goods or services by electronic means, the exchange shall be accepted by Member States provided that the **authenticity of the origin and integrity of the contents** are guaranteed:

- By means of an advanced electronic signature (AES). Member States may however ask for the advanced electronic signature to be based on a qualified certificate,

- or by means of electronic data interchange (EDI) as defined in Commission Recommendation 1994/820/EC of 19 October 1994 relating to the legal aspects (See annex 7.3 for the recommendation);

- Invoices may, however, be sent by other electronic means subject to acceptance by the Member State(s) concerned.

Although the Electronic Data Interchange (EDI) invoice message has been defined and adopted by several industry and trade sectors in Europe, it has not been implemented to its full potential. Paper invoices were usually maintained to overcome difficulties surrounding the VAT regulation. Several Member States introduced special procedures to allow EDI paperless invoicing but still requiring companies to apply for permission from tax administration and in some cases to exchange summary VAT control messages, electronically or on paper. For cross border electronic invoicing, companies are exchanging electronic invoices for company administration application, but are forced to parallel the exchanges with paper invoices for Member State VAT requirements.

1.2 The European Directive 1999/93/EC

The European Union has introduced a legal framework to guarantee EU-wide recognition of electronic signatures – a prerequisite for ensuring the security of data that is transmitted electronically (Directive 1999/93/EC of the European Parliament and of the Council of 13 December 1999 on a Community Framework for Electronic Signatures). The purpose of the Electronic Signature Directive is to facilitate the use of electronic signatures and to contribute to their legal recognition. It establishes a general framework for **electronic signatures** and certain **certification services** in order to ensure the proper functioning of the internal market.

The commercial invoice is the most important document exchanged between trading partners. In addition to its commercial value, the invoice is an accounting document, it has legal implications to both transacting parties, it is the basis for VAT declaration and reclamation, statistics declaration for intra community trade, export and import declaration for extra community trade.

While the EDIFACT Invoice was the first message to be accorded UN Recommendation status, companies have chosen to implement other trade messages instead (Orders, Despatch advice) and limiting the implementation of electronic invoice just for inter company accounting application. Implementation of electronic invoice is being held back because of the diverse, often restrictive and conflicting legislation in some Member States. This is one of the weakest link in the electronic trade chain which limits competitiveness of European firms and impedes the development of electronic commerce.

1.3 Commission Recommendation 1994/820/EC October 1994

The Commission Recommendation from October 1994 was developed on the request of European trade and industry EDI user groups to provide the required legality, acceptability and security in the use of EDI in European Member States. The Recommendation includes the **'Model European Interchange Agreement'**, which was developed in line with the work carried out by the International Chamber of Commerce and several major industry sectors, e.g. automotive, electronics, retail and distribution. Trading partners prior to commencing the exchange of EDI messages are advised to agree and sign interchange agreements based on the European model.

2 The CEN/ISSS e-Invoicing Focus Group

The scope of the CEN/ISSS e-Invoicing Focus Group (e-IFG) has been:

- To provide an overview of the standardization aspects of electronics invoicing
- To assess existing standards and their implementation
- To provide proposals for additional activities should these be considered necessary.

The group should also ascertain that the standardization framework ensures 'Authentication and Integrity' requirements as stated in Directive 2001/115/EC are met in a cost effective manner, whilst maintaining an adequate level of interoperability and functionality.

Particular attention should be paid to the electronic signature and EDI standardization issues, as well to those posed by technology advances, e.g. web services. The group should also examine archiving.

2.1 The Report and Recommendations of the e-Invoicing Focus Group

Following the review and approval of the e-Invoicing Focus Group Terms of Reference, the group indicated that four – five meetings would be sufficient to prepare the report and requested CEN to contract a Technical Editor to take responsibility for compiling the report. The participants in the e-IFG have represented a broad range of expertise:

- Electronic signature
- Law practice specialising in legal aspects
- Tax administrator
- e-Business and EDI experts
- Business process experts
- Third party service providers
- International accounting practice with expertise in e-Invoicing
- Financial institution

Approval was given by the group to develop a 'Questionnaire template' proposed by France for collecting information from Member States. The European Commission, DG Taxation, provided the names and details of the contact persons to whom the template was addressed. The Editor was requested to gather the responses from the Member States.

Furthermore, the group invited experts to give presentations on specific topics, e.g. the national examples in Finland and Belgium, the study carried out by PWC on behalf of the European Commission which identifies the status of e-Invoicing in Member States in 1999, acceptance or non acceptance of e-Invoicing, conditions and facilities.

Submissions from experts were compiled into the report and the first draft was distributed for review on 7 May.

The 'Conference Draft' was made available on the CEN/ISSS website on 27 May and notification was sent out with the invitation to the Open Meeting for June 3rd 2003. It is planned to accept comments up to June 20th, following which the final version will be prepared. The comments will be reviewed by the e-IFG and approval given for inclusion in the report.

The final version of the report is expected to be ready for distribution by the end of June 2003. The report has to be accepted by the CEN Forum beginning October 2003 and the final version wil then be published on the website: www.cenorm.be.

2.2 Scope of the Report

The e-IFG identified four layers for developing the report:

1. **Content**
    The content layer relates predominantly to the data in an e-invoice message independent of the technology, EDI, XML, attachment to an e-mail.

2. **Infrastructure**
    The infrastructure layer relates predominantly to Legislative issues, electronic signatures Documents, end to end exchange format, and security.

3. **Means**
    The Means layer refers to such issues that are software specific e.g. translators, archiving technique, networks, total solutions as developed in some countries, e.g. Finland, Belgium.

4. **Business**
    The Business layer will present the place of the invoice in the enterprise as discussed in the section on End to End Control.

Based on these four main criteria, group members were invited to propose key topics that would be developed by 'champions' and submitted for input into the report. Some 31 subjects were identified and most were allocated to champions. Also, several papers were submitted by champions to debate issues where the group felt there are possibilities of conflict within the Directive, and between the Directive and positions being taken by some Member States.

The report is compiled from the contributions received from members of the e-IFG, based on their knowledge and expertise.

The report also includes information based on the responses from Member States on how and when they intend to implement the Directive. The e-IFG have received responses from ten Finance Ministries and a few more are expected when the work to transpose the Directive is completed. Several Member States have indicated that some amendments may be required as the administrations are holding discussions with trade and industry. The following topics emerged as major issues:

- Cross-border issues
- Storage of invoices
- End to end control between application systems
- National examples of e-Invoicing in Finland and Belgium, Austria, Norway and Greece,
- Details of several 'Use cases' from simple cases to complex cases involving market places
- National legislation overview template per country and a summary of responses with comments and recommendations from e-IFG
- Self billing
- Conversion process

3 Summary of Recommendations

The following recommendations are being brought forward by the e-IFG, some of them are directly pointing to necessary standardisation efforts, some of them are pointing towards activities to be addressed to the European Council.

3.1 EDI and e-Business Standards

a) To bring Commission Recommendation 1994/820/EC October 1994 up to date with the requirements of Directive 2001/115/EC and present day e-Commerce practices.

b) The invoice content details identified in the Directive should be submitted for the creation of the relevant UN/CEFACT ebXML Core Components.

c) To permit the use of internationally recognised organization identifiers and product identifiers in electronic invoices as alternatives to the name and address of an organization or the description of a product or service.

d) To develop codes, standardised at community level, to replace standard clauses (text) being inserted in messages, that usually require human intervention for processing.

e) The term 'EDI' in the Directive 2001/115/EC should have the widest possible meaning of formatted exchanges, not dependent on a specific 'technology' (EDIFACT, X-12, XML, etc..), nor limited to specific international, national or sector standards.

3.2 Electronic Signature

a) Care should be taken not to inadvertently restrict the use of advanced electronic signatures ("AES") to natural persons to achieve authenticity and integrity of the electronic invoices as it may render current practice with automatic generation of invoices impracticable/.

b) In cases where communications are channelled through an intermediary service provider (e.g. in the context of a marketplace or a hub), and AES are used, there may be a need for re-signing (or re-"stamping") the invoice between parties. This should be taken into account so that, if AES are to be considered, the law allows the use of re-signed AES.

c) It must be indicated, that additional work needs to be carried out to further detail the standardisation objectives of authentication for the purpose of using them in electronic invoicing. This recommendation assumes that the current review of the electronic signature Directive will not result in any major changes. The detailed proposals for standardization should therefore take full account of the findings of the review.

3.3 Specific and Fiscal Procedures

a) In view of multinational companies having central computer operation, possibly outside the EU, e-IFG recommends that provisions be introduced to allow electronic storage of invoices in non Member State provided the required conditions for inspection and data protection are.

b) Explore the possibility for remote access to 'audit of traders' computerised tax records and/or downloading transaction files from traders onto tax administration systems will disturb traders far less and allow administrators to work freely.

c) In furtherance of the objective of the EC Directive on Invoicing "to establish a number of common arrangements governing the use of electronic invoicing", it is recommended that the competent authorities in all EU Member States should consider further opportunities for implementing the Directive in a compatible way, in particular, for cross-border electronic invoicing.

3.4 National Examples of e-Invoicing Application

The Belgian and Finnish examples of an integrated solution are presented in some details as the e-IFG group feels the models could be used in other Member States rather than similar local development being developed. Other examples have been added to the report from contributions received from Austria, Norway and Greece.

4 Conclusions

The overall conclusions of the CEN/ISSS report of can be summarized as follows:

- With e-Business being established in large and small enterprises, there is an urgent requirement from business and tax administration to have a standardized approach to e-Invoices, which meets the needs of all business and tax administrations and is of central importance for the success of e-commerce.

- Although standards on EDI and on electronic signatures are available to a certain extent, too many issues on interoperability surround especially cross border electronic invoicing and VAT, and too diverse legislation on electronic signatures and VAT in Member States prevent business and administration to make adequate use of European harmonisation in electronic commerce.

- The e-Invoices Focus group would therefore like to ask the European Commission and the appropriate European Standards Organisations to carefully take notice of the detailed recommendations of the e-IFG and to establish a proper follow-up of the recommendations.

- The e-IFG suggests that this follow-up should happen within an "Electronic Invoices Forum Europe", which should:
  - link and network the various national electronic invoices fora,
  - look specifically into developing the appropriate required standards
  - continue to improve existing standards and bring them up-to-date.

Useful Links:

1. CEN/ISSS Final Report of the eInvoices Focus Group, adopted by the CEN/ISSS Forum on October 7th, 2003, http://www.cenorm.be

2. Council Directive 2001/115/EC of 20 December 2001 amending Directive 77/388/EEC with a view to simplifying, modernising and harmonising the conditions laid down for invoicing in respect of value added tax *Official Journal L 015, 17/01/2002 P. 0024 - 0028*

3. Directive 1999/93/EC of the European Parliament and of the Council of 13 December 1999 on a Community Framework for Electronic Signatures, *Official Journal L 013, 19/01/2000 P. 0012 - 0020*

4. Commission Recommendation 1994/820/EC of 19 December 1994 relating to the legal aspects of electronic data interchange, *Official Journal L 338, 28.12.1994, p. 98*

A Pan-European eID Card ?
Recent Standardisation Projects

Ulrich Stutenbäumer · Gisela Meister

Giesecke & Devrient GmbH, Technology Center
Security/Evaluation
Ulrich.Stutenbaeumer@de.gi-de.com
Gisela.Meister@de.gi-de.com

Abstract

World wide standardisation projects in the field of electronic ID cards have to specify interoperable solutions in the framework of national and international legal guidelines.

An interoperable European ID smart card based on the EU directive on electronic signature is aim of the eEpoch project. The specific technical objectives of eEpoch include the realisation of a demonstrator for demonstrating workable solutions to apply electronic signatures with a secure signature creation device (SSCD) at different European pilot sites. The specification of an IAS (Authentication, Identification, Signature) services module within the Smart Card is the central component of the demonstrator project.

The requirements of relevant EESSI standards / documents (e.g., ESIGN Area K) and the results of the global Interoperability Framework Group (GIF) of the Smart Card charter (eEurope) are considered as well.

The CEN/ISSS technical committee TC 224 will specify a European Citizen card to harmonise the different identity support of European countries with the most stringent level of security against fraud.

The CEN/ISSS eAuthentication workshop output is intended to be a multi-volume multi-part CEN workshop agreement and aims for an international harmonization on eAuthentication in cooperation with Japanese and US American smart card interests.

The ICAO technical advisory group on machine readable passports has specified electronic travel documents which are used with the US enhanced border security and visa entry reform act and specify the physical characteristics of biometrics.

1 Introduction

Presently within the EU several activities are initiated to promote

- multi-application smart cards based on public key services and biometrics, eventually,
- particularly in connection with ID cards, citizen cards or sector specific cards (health, banking, mobile environment).

These services are intended for the direct use of the card holder as for the creation of electronic signatures, key decipherment and/or client-server authentication. On the other side they are intended for protecting the communication with or the access to the smart card, for instance in retrieving or storing personal tokens, e.g. a biometric template, a personal file, or a public key certificate.

Thereby it is necessary to agree on a common specification describing these services on a "bit & byte level" based on international smart card standards

S. Paulus, N. Pohlmann, H. Reimer (Editors): Securing Electronic Business Processes, Vieweg (2004), 138-146

- to rely on a common and sharable public key functionality on a card
- to be used in different application fields.

A side effect for the card issuer is than the possibility of getting a second source for his application.

A proposal for such a specification, to be presented in this paper, will be a deliverable of the eEpoch project [Epoch], a citizen card based on the EU directive on electronic signatures. This card will be designed to support electronic signatures created by a secure signature creation device (SSCD).

The specific technical objectives of eEpoch include the realisation of a demonstrator to present workable solutions at different European pilot sites. The specification of an IAS (Authentication, Identification, Signature) module within the Smart Card is intended to support the above described services and presents the central component of the demonstrator project.

This project is based on results of the EESSI specifications (e.g., ESIGN Area K and the deliverables of the Global Interoperability Framework Group (GIF) of the Smart Card charter (eEurope)) to avoid duplication of work and respect already existing projects (see figure 1). Therefore the full paper will give an overview over these projects.

The integration of rather new activities as the new scopes of CEN TC 224 and the CEN eAuthentication Workshop into the eEpoch project will be subject for future discussion and work, but nevertheless a short preview will be presented in the full paper as well.

2 CEN/ISSS ESIGN Area K

The CEN/ISSS ESIGN Area K specification [ESIGN] is part of a series of standards for secure signature creation devices (SSCDs), designed to support the EU-directive on electronic signatures. The key issue of this document is to enable interoperability, so that smart cards from different manufacturers can interact with different kind of signature creation devices but with the same application interface.

The security policy of the ESIGN K specification follows quality requirements of the EU directive. Please refer for instance to ESIGN F [ESIGN] for qualified electronic signatures [EU] and interoperability requirements concerning

- the selection principle of the application (application-identifier according ISO/IEC 7816-5) [ISO/IEC]
- input- and output- formats of a respective subset of ISO/IEC 7816-4/8 [ISO/IEC]
- reference of the data objects on the card (key, certificates, root-certificates) by use of a description application according to FDIS ISO/IEC 7816-15 (based on PKCS #15) [ISO/IEC]
- PKI algorithm suits inclusive padding and hash mechanisms - inclusive task sharing e.g., the last rounds are hashed by the card or hashing is performed completely by the PC or terminal - according to national and European catalogues
- provision of a trusted channel for the key and signature generation under inclusion of cryptographic protocols, e.g., according ISO/IEC 9798 (device-authentication/Secure Messaging according ISO/IEC 7816-4)

- user-authentication (according ISO/IEC 7816-4/11), password authentication and/or Biometric Match On Card (MOC)

- services for the card holder like electronic signature and key generation, key-decipherment, client-server authentication, (according ISO/IEC 7816-8 /11).

The personalisation of the application is out of scope of the ESIGN application, but a profile is present in an informative annex with distributed roles between card manufacturer, issuer and certificate authority (CA).

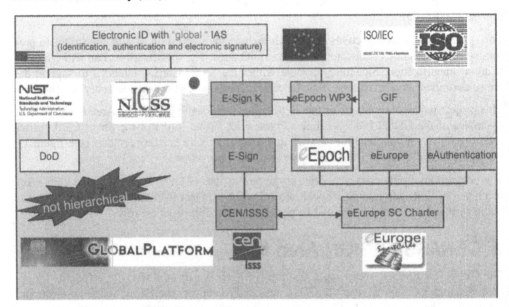

Fig. 1 European and International Standardisation Bodies and Participants for Electronic Signatures for Smart Cards

So far in various CEN working groups like ESIGN Area AA, D2, F and G1 deliverables, so called CEN Workshop Agreements (CWA), were submitted for release by the Article 9 Committee, a political study group designated by the EU to the conversion of the EU directive on electronic signature.

The results of the working group G1 (requirements for signature application environments) and ESIGN F (protection profiles for signature application) have been worked directly into the ESIGN K deliverable.

Additionally already existing national specification like the DIN pre-standard [DIN] are taken into account so that no compatibility problems arise with national standards and specifications. Signature applications are also of interest for the deployment in platform-oriented multi-application-cards. Therefore the CWA of ESIGN K is designed also for the use of Global Platform cards, e.g., for JAVA cards.

In the ESIGN K specification, the signature application is designed following the requirements according to ESIGN G1. Thereby it is oriented on the well known international standard series for contact oriented cards, the ISO/IEC 7816 series for smart cards. Especially the cryptographic command set is based on ISO/IEC 7816-8 , res. CD 7816-4.

The G1 specification ESIGN G1 distinguishes two different types of environments – a trusted and an untrusted one, the decision is to be taken by the signer, for instance in a mobile environment the signer will trust his own mobile phone.

The communication to and from the SSCD user interface shall be performed by a trusted path[1] required by the Protection Profile for the SSCDs, see the CWA of ESIGN F [ESIGN].

In case of an untrusted environment the protection of the interaction sequences shall be performed by means of a trusted channel [2] between the smart card and an authentication module inside the Secure Signature Creation Application (SSCA) e.g. a smart card chip inside a smart card reader, which is under control of the SSCA.

Thereby to support a trusted channel the card and the SSCA establish a protected communication e.g. by cryptographic means, the strength of function valid for a successful evaluation.

In the ESIGN K specification special techniques are mentioned to achieve such a trusted channel by defining suitable authentication protocols with the establishing of session keys to protect the further communication on asymmetric or symmetric bases. The latter case can be used if the authentication module and the smart card can rely already on a common key.

3 eEpoch

The aim of eEpoch (eEurope [eEurope] Smart Card Charter proof of concept and holistic solution) [Epoch] is to demonstrate interoperable and secure smart card based digital identification systems, which provide the levels of trust and confidence necessary for citizens to interact digitally with their national and municipal administrations and other European institutions. Interoperability will enable cross-border electronic signature for legal purposes, offer reliable identification based on data in government databases, and ensure secure authentication of cardholder and device on the basis of PIN, biometrics, and PKI mutual authentication.

eEpoch's primary technical objectives are to enable interoperability between e-service communities within and between the EU member states while maximising the freedom of technology and business choices for the sites.

The core objective of the eEpoch project is to create a pan-European interoperability demonstrator for the use of smart cards for IAS (Identification, Authentication and electronic Signature), based on pilot sites in different countries and to accumulate the interoperability experiences and expertise of the pilot sites, in order to prepare mass deployment of smart cards for IAS in e-government and e-business applications.

---

[1] Trusted path — A means by which a user and a TSF can communicate with necessary confidence to support the TSP (TSF- Security Functions of Target of Evaluation, TSP- Security Policy of TOE)

[2] Trusted channel — A means by which a TSF and a remote trusted IT product can communicate with necessary confidence to support the TSP.

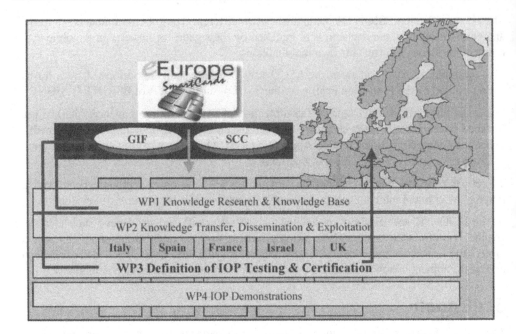

Fig. 2 eEpoch organisation structure [Epoch]

In figure 2 the general organisation structure of the eEpoch project is displayed. The Global Interoperability Framework (GIF) of the smart card charter (SCC) of eEurope and the ESIGN Area K specification are the bases of the design of the IOP (interoperability) demonstrator which will be tested in the six pilot sites in different European countries and Israel.

Necessary in- and outputs to/from work packages (WP) of the eEpoch project are:

- WP 1 generated GIF documents (part 1-4) are to be considered as the architectural model for IAS interoperability.

- WP 3 disseminated a first draft of the "Functional Mapping of GIF on ESIGN Area K" to the pilots to get their feed back throughout a questionnaire on this topic. The comments from the sites will then be included into the IOP specification of the IAS module after verification.

- WP 4 will use the Guidelines for the Pilot sites of WP 3 to create a smart card system with successfully working IOP AIS services.

The expected outcome of WP3 will be an IAS and IOP interface specification for the Pilot sites to achieve interoperability for their IAS services with testable profiles for the sites.

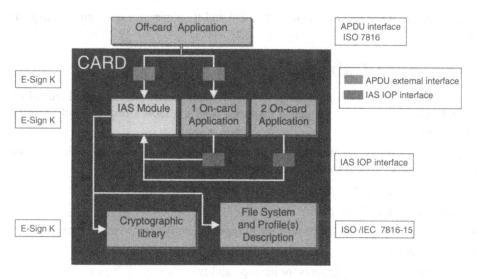

Fig. 3 Implementation of the IAS Module for Java Cards [Epoch]

Figure 3 displays an alternative implementation of the IAS functionality for Java-Cards as discussed in the WP 3 documents of eEpoch. The IAS module is part of an application (or applet) and the off-card application communicate through the APDU (application protocol data unit) external interface with the IAS module or through on-card applications.

The IAS module accesses the cryptographic functions to secure the retrieving and/or storing of personal tokens as identity files or biometric templates by means of

- Internal/External Authentication
- Secure Messaging including calculation/verification of MAC after encipherment/decipherment of the message
- User authentication
- Hash computation and
- Signature computation

The communication of the off-card application with the IAS module (and personal tokens) will be specified according to E-Sign K and FDIS ISO/IEC 7816-15.

The IAS IOP interface has been specified in WP 3 of eEpoch, i.e. the communication of the services/application with the IAS module to secure the access to personal data on the card following security levels as

- Level 0: no protection
- Level 1: User authentication only
- Level 2: Dynamic authentication with/without secure messaging
- Level 3: Level 1 with additional computation/verification of Signature over the personal token (see above)
- Level 4: Level 3 with qualified signature according to the EU directive on electronic signature.

Different profiles (following ISO/IEC 7816-15) for the five different levels of security are designed and can be specified for each site and application on the card.

The card checks if the security status is fulfilled and if so executes the corresponding functions

4 European Citizen Card

The CEN/ISSS technical committee TC 224 [CEN] will specify a standard to harmonise the different identity support of European countries with the most stringent level of security against fraud.

The group will identify the minimum set of data necessary (civil status) to achieve functions of electronic citizen services and may offer an interoperable format.

The specification will define the following functions of smart cards:

- physical security features
- visual artwork in compliance with the European directive on driving licence
- biometric formats
- minimum set of data elements for interoperability
- set of command, mechanism and data access

The European Citizen card will consider all appropriate card technologies (Contact IC, Contactless IC, Optical Memory) also with the possibility of multiple technologies being used on the same card.

The description for the use with one technology or multiple technologies could be included on annexes allowing each government to choose the appropriate technology.

The European citizen card will rely on existing standards for instance PKI, smart card, biometrics and will especially respect the work performed in ESIGN, eEpoch and in the new founded workshop on Electronic Authentication.

5 CEN/ISSS Workshop on Electronic Authentication

The CEN/ISSS eAuthentication workshop [EAUTH] output is intended to be a multi-volume multi-part CEN workshop agreement (CWA):

- CWA eAuthentication Part 1: European Public Electronic Identity functional architecture and required IAS (Identification, authentication and electronic signature) characteristics
- CWA eAuthentication Part 2: Business models, legal framework and technical prerequisites for interoperable multi-application cards and systems
- CWA eAuthentication Part 3: User interface best practices manual for multi-application Smart Card IAS applications

This European workshop aims on an international harmonization on eAuthentication in cooperation with Japanese and US American smart card interests. The Workshop will cooperate with CEN/TC224, ESIGN and other relevant organisations and will rely on existing specifications.

6 ICAO Technical Advisory Group on Machine Readable Passports (TAG/MRTD)

The ICAO technical advisory group on machine readable passports has specified electronic travel documents [ICAO] which are used with the US enhanced border security and visa entry reform act. This acts declares that every passport of any Visa Waiver Program traveler issued after October 26, 2004, must contain a biometric identifier that meets standards set by ICAO. The TAG/MRTD specifies the physical characteristics of biometrics and uses the Common Biometric Exchange Format specified by ISO SC 37.

7 Outlook

It seems an enormous task to harmonise different PKI projects on smart cards. However, the European activities will exactly follow this direction and hopefully will obtain results to be steps towards an international harmonisation as indicated already in the eAuthentication CEN workshop. This will be essential for the world-wide usage of PKI smart cards.

References

[CEN]   CEN/TC 224, Machine-readable cards, related device interfaces and operations
            http://www.cenorm.be/isss/TC/Default.htm

[DIN]   DIN V66291-1: 1999, Chipkarten mit Digitaler Signatur-Anwendung/Funktion
            nach SigG und SigV, Teil 1: Anwendungsschnittstelle, Ausgabe: 2000-04
            DIN V66291-2: 2000, Chipkarten mit Digitaler Signatur-Anwendung/Funktion
            nach SigG und SigV, Teil 2: Personalisierungs-Prozesse, Ausgabe: 2003-01
            DIN V66291-3: 2002, Chipcards with digital signature application/function accor-
            ding to SigG and SigV, Part 3: Commands for Personalisation, Final Draft, Sep-
            tember 2002
            DIN V66291-4: 2000 Chipkarten mit Digitaler Signatur-Anwendung/Funktion nach
            SigG und SigV, Teil 4: Grundlegende Sicherheitsdienste, Ausgabe: 2002-04
            http://www.din.de/set/ds

[EAUTH]   CEN/ISSS WS e-Authentication, E-AUTH N0006, Report of the e-Authentication
            kick off meeting held in Brussels on 2003-04-23
            http://www.cenorm.be/isss/Workshop/eAuthentication/report-mtg2003-05-23.pdf

[eEurope]   GLOBAL INTEROPERABILITY FRAMEWORK FOR IDENTIFICATION,
            AUTHENTICATION AND ELECTRONIC SIGNATURE (IAS) WITH SMART
            CARDS
            Part 1: Contextual and conceptual modelling, August 2002 V. 2.01
            Part 2: Requirements for IAS functional interoperability, November 2002 V. 2.01,

            Part 3: Recommendation for IOP specifications, August 2002, V. 0.96,
            Part 4: Deployment strategies for generic IAS, November 2002, V. 1.0
            http://www.eeurope-standards.org/

[Epoch]   http://www.eepoch.net/

[ESIGN]   ESIGN-F, CEN/ISSS WS/E-Sign Workshop Agreement Group F: Secure Signa-
            ture-Creation Devices, CWA 14169, March 2002

ESIGN-G1, CWA 14170: Security Requirements for Signature Creation Applications, CEN Working Agreement, July 2001

ESIGN-K, CWA: Application Interface for Smart Cards used as Secure Signature Creation Devices, CEN Working Agreement, 26th March 2003, Draft Version 0.17
http://www.cenorm.be/isss/Workshop/e-sign/commenting14167.htm

[EU]   EU Directive 1999/93/EC of the European Parliament and the council of 13 December 1999 on a Community framework for electronic signatures
http://europa.eu.int/eur-lex/pri/en/oj/dat/2000/l_013/
l_01320000119en00120020.pdf

[ICAO]   International Civil Aviation Organisation, Technical Advisory Group on Machine Readable Passports (TAG/MRTD), Doc 9303, Part 2,1994
http://www.icao.int/icao/en/atb/fal/mrtd/guide.htm

[ISO/IEC] ISO/IEC 7816 Identification cards - Integrated circuit(s) cards with contacts
ISO/IEC 7816-4: 1995, Information technology - Identification cards - Integrated circuit(s) cards with contacts , Part 4: Interindustry commands for interchange, IS 1995, FCD December 2002
ISO/IEC 7816-8: IS 1998, Information technology - Identification cards - Integrated circuit(s) cards with contacts - Part 8: Security related interindustry commands , IS 1999, FCD August 2002
ISO/IEC 7816-9: 1998, Information technology - Identification cards - Integrated circuit(s) cards with contacts, Part 9: Additional interindustry commands and security attributes, FDIS 2000.
ISO/IEC 7816-15: 2002, Information technology - Identification cards - Integrated circuit(s) cards with contacts, Part 15: Cryptographic information application, FDIS 2002, December 2002
http://www.iso.ch/iso/en/ISOOnline.openerpage

Secure Financial Reporting through XBRL and Electronic Signatures

Marc Sel

PricewaterhouseCoopers
Generaal Lemanstraat 67
B2018 Antwerp, Belgium
marc.sel@pwc.be

Abstract

This paper will discuss where financial reporting is heading, how such financial reporting according to EU standards should be done in XML and XBRL technology, and why electronic signatures such as XMLDSIG and XAdES should secure this.

1 The Business Problem

Companies aim at effectively and efficiently playing a part in the overall value chain. In this context, they need capital to operate. The EU aims at an efficient and cost-effective functioning of the capital market. EC regulations want to enable Community companies to compete on an equal footing for financial resources available in the Community and in the world capital markets. Financial reporting is a cornerstone in the functioning of the capital market. A common example is the case of an IPO (Initial Purchase Offering), when a company decides to become registered on a stock exchange. Another typical example is the quarterly and annual reporting towards shareholders.

- Tier One: A set of global generally accepted accounting principles;

- Tier Two: Industry-specific standards for measuring and reporting performance, consistently applied and developed by the industries themselves;

- Tier Three: Company-specific information including strategy, plans, risk-management practices, compensation policies, corporate governance and performance measurements unique to the company;

S. Paulus, N. Pohlmann, H. Reimer (Editors): Securing Electronic Business Processes, Vieweg (2004), 147-154

The Three-Tier Model of Corporate Transparency

Fig. 1: The Three-Tier Model of Corporate Transparency

In this context, there is an objective of achieving a single set of global accounting standards, which is supported by the EU. A more transparent and unified accounting and financial reporting framework will facilitate good business practices and corporate governance, both in the public and private sector. On 13 June 2000, the Commission published its Communication on EU ‚Financial Reporting Strategy', which proposed that all publicly traded Community companies prepare their consolidated financial statements in accordance with a single set of accounting standards, namely International Accounting Standards (IAS), at the latest by 2005. This is important since it indicates there is no tendency to create a particular European version of such standards, which would lead to a significant administrative overhead for many companies. Rather, the Commission aims at a single set of globally accepted accounting standards.

The International Accounting Standards Board (IASB) sets these standards. The IASB issues the IFRS (International Financial Reporting Standards) - which were previously called IAS (International Accounting Standards). These standards define a common vocabulary, which will allow a unified interpretation and a comparison of financial reports such as balance sheets, cash-flow statements or similar across national borders. Today such comparisons are rather difficult to elaborate. Comparing Italian figures with Danish ones is not a trivial task.

Within the EU, the main body to endorse accounting standards is the Accounting Regulatory Committee (ARC). This summer (i.e. 2003), they voted unanimously in favour of adopting IAS, including the SIC (standard interpretations). Two IAS standards (IAS 32 and 39) were not endorsed since they are in the process of being revised. Their endorsement is expected later.

So starting January 2005 at the latest, publicly listed organisations will legally have to report according to the new IFRS. And since in many cases, historical data (e.g. on past valuations) has to be included, the actual conversion needs to start one or two years earlier – which means today. It can be assumed that once the legal reporting has been converted, other reporting such as for the creation of the prospectus to become registered on the stock exchange will follow soon.

Another new wave of new financial reporting can be expected from the Basle II agreement. The BIS (Bank for International Settlements, based in Basel - Switzerland) issued a number of guidelines on how financial institutions should manage their risk, with a focus on capital requirements. Financial institutions should take into account market risk, credit risk, operational risk, ... etc. The three pillars of Basle II are minimum capital requirements, supervisory reviews, and market discipline. Pillar 2 establishes a control environment for risk management addressing a. o. operational risk, for which the following definition is applied: *"Operational risk is the risk of loss resulting from inadequate or failed internal processes, people, and systems or from external events."* The better an institution manages all applicable risks (including operational risk), the lower their capital requirements will – which means the lower their basic costs will be.

The European Union thinks along comparable lines as the BIS, and issued directives such as the CAD ('Capital Adequacy Directive'). As such directives are translated into national legislation, they become legally binding. It is clear that Basle II and the EU CAD will exercise a widespread influence, covering banks, financial institutions, as well as their service providers such as SWIFT, Euroclear, Europay, etc. This will equally apply to the national service providers (e.g. payment services).

It is equally clear that operational risk will have a many different components, including organisational and technological aspects. We will now focus on one particular technological aspect, the use of XML to arrive at a unified 'language' for representing financial information - XBRL. This technology is taking up role in virtually all kinds of financial reporting, and is gradually being embraced by important vendors and a recent survey of XBRL US finds two-thirds of accounting software vendors have released or are in process of releasing XBRL-enabled products, XBRL being seen as 'de facto' Technology Standard for Reporting Financial Information (http://www.xbrl.org/newsandevents) . Subsequently we will discuss how to secure it. Here XBRL will significantly benefit from the concepts of electronic signatures, as introduced in the corresponding EC Directive and national legislation. The conceptual work that was done at the level of the Directive was (and still is being) complemented by technical work at the level of the three European standardisation bodies (CEN, CENELEC and ETSI). In this way, a true convergence is emerging where financial reporting needs to be done according to IAS standards, with XBRL as a technical instrument, and electronic signatures as a highly effective security solution.

2 XBRL – Business Aspects

The IFRS standards describe financial concepts in plain terms, using English words. Computer programs cannot interpret such a description. One way to overcome this problem is to use a language such as XML, as developed through the W3C (World-Wide Web consortium). By mapping IFRS definitions onto a number of XML tags, the producers and consumers of this information can agree upon common meanings for data elements. This mapping takes place through an XLink reference linkbase. A group of corporate reporting supply chain participants gave rise to XBRL International, a consortium responsible for XBRL - eXtensible Business Reporting Language.

Consider the case when a company wants to act as a creditor towards a client. In most countries, national law prohibits making loan decisions without the paper documentation of the client's financial position. Obviously, a well-designed and adequately secured paper-less system would offer significant business benefits. XBRL is a strong facilitator for such systems.

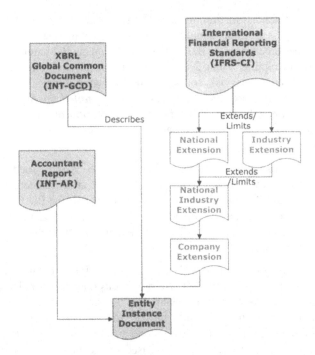

Fig. 2: The XBRL Taxonomy Model

As outlined in figure 2 above, the XBRL taxonomies define common data elements required for financial reporting under a specific set of accounting standards such as IFRS. These taxonomies can be further extended to meet specific needs of an industry group or a particular company. . A client's report is referred to as an instance document (Entity Instance), and can include all or a selection of elements from all the above. In this way, the three tiers of a corporate reporting framework can be implemented in practice (remember those three tiers were: 'globally accepted', 'industry based', and 'company specific').

Obviously, the definition of XBRL was a global activity. This was driven through the XBRL consortium (www.XBRL.org), via collaboration among all participants in the supply chain (preparers, software vendors, accountants and auditors, distributors and aggregators, bankers, and analysts) – over 220 organisations in total. The 2nd version of the XBRL specification was published in December 2001, and today many taxonomies including G/L (General Ledger – a general purpose format), IAS/IFRS and US GAAP are available.

Many large financial organisations are now going the XBRL-route, including the FDIC (the US Federal Deposit Insurance Corporation - www.fdic.gov). This is the US government agency that insures $3.1 trillion in bank deposits. They engaged a joint Unisys / Microsoft / PwC team to implement XBRL for purposes of collecting, managing and distributing reporting by its member banks. XBRL will be the information format for the monthly 'call' reports submitted from each of the 8500 member banks. There is also a significant interest from various tax authorities with the UK Inland Revenue and the Tokyo National Tax Agency already adopting XBRL for e-filing purposes.

3 XBRL – Technical Aspects

For reporting purposes, financial information is often structured into main categories such as balance sheet, income statement, cash flow statement and statement of changes in equity (ref IAS 1, paragraph 7 and IAS 34, paragraph 8).

If we take a balance sheet, which reflects the financial situation of a company at a certain point in time, we notice it is structured into two major categories, called 'assets' and 'liabilities and equities'. When a company is established, the shareholders bring in their part, which gets registered as equity. The company may obtain a loan, and hence becomes liable against the creditor. The "equity and liability" funds are put to use in the company. A building may be bought, raw material purchased and salaries paid. Some cash may remain in the bank. So while at the moment of establishing the opening balance the 'assets' and the 'liabilities and equities' will match, the balance will be upset when money gets made or lost. Historically, a new balance sheet was only calculated after twelve months because it involved so much work. However, today the tendency is towards closing the accounts and establishing a balance sheet much more often (quarterly, monthly, weekly or ultimately even daily).

XBRL is a great facilitator and allows to speed up the creation of a balance sheet to significant extent. It also facilitates data re-use. Of course the balance sheet is not the only mechanism to understand the financial position of a company. Even more important is the cash flow position. If you know that you will make a big profit 6 months from here but you cannot pay your salaries next month due to lack of cash and the impossibility to obtain a loan, you will go bankrupt nevertheless. Hence the cash flow statement is also an important document.

Let us now briefly describe how it works from a technical perspective. The most fundamental component of XBRL is XML as defined by W3C. This includes XML 1.0, XML Namespaces, XML Schema 1.0 and Xlink 1.0. XBRL is defined in the XBRL specification, which is written as 5 XML schemas plus some accompanying description. The specification defines a number of XBRL taxonomies and the schema for an instance document. XBRL taxonomies have names such as PFS (Primary Financial Statements), GL (General Ledger), etc. The PFS taxonomy is structured into balance sheet, income statement, statement of cash flows and statement of changes in equity. The PFS taxonomy does not contain definitions with regard to the meaning of its elements. Rather, it relies on IAS through a reference linkbase for these definitions.

Instance documents will contain actual company data such as the balance sheet of Novartis for 2003. Instance documents contain data expressed as XBRL elements: group, item, tuple, and context. Finally, an XBRL instance document can be represented under a style sheet, to make it accessible under a viewing or editing program. Here's a small XBRL code snippet of an instance document:

```
<?xml version="1.0"?>
<group xmlns="http://www.xbrl.org/2001/instance"
       xmlns:xsi="http://www.w3.org/2001/XMLSchema-instance"
       xmlns:link="http://www.xbrl.org/2001/XLink/xbrllinkbase"
       xmlns:xlink="http://www.w3.org/1999/xlink"
       xmlns:sample="http://www.sample.org/xbrl/2001-12-31"
       xsi:schemaLocation="http://www.sample.org/xbrl/2001-12-31 ..\sample_taxonomy.xsd">
```

```
<sample:assets.cash numericContext="numC1">52000</sample:assets.cash>

<sample:assets.netReceivables numericContext="numC1">1800</sample:assets.netReceivables>

<numericContext id="numC1" precision="18" cwa="true">

<entity><identifier scheme="http://www.stockMarket.com/">SMPL</identifier><segment /> </entity>

<period><instant>2001-11-30</instant></period>

<unit><measure>ISO4217:USD</measure></unit>

<scenario name="Actual values">

<sample:scenarioType>actual</sample:scenarioType>

</scenario>

</numericContext>

</group>
```

The <group> statement is the XML root of the document. It establishes the namespaces and the schema location. The first namespace points to the XBRL instance namespace. The last namespace will resolve the <sample: assets.cash ...> statement. This statement carries the information value of „52000". We then must use the numericContext „numC1" to see it refers to a value in US dollars, and for the period „2001-11-30".

Of course most of today's financial systems internally use other formats than XBRL. The production of XBRL documents could be addressed by the introduction of "converter" tools. However, the most recent versions of e.g. ERP systems (for example SAP) and of common tools such as MS-Office (Excel) are becoming XML and XBRL enabled.

4 XBRL Security

As XBRL is based on XML, it is inherently vulnerable to many attacks. However, a significant effort has already been invested in making XML more secure. The same techniques that can secure XML, can be used to secure XBRL. The first and most relevant technology is electronic signatures. Of course it is equally possible to use encryption technology.

Within Europe, we have already witnessed the arrival of a single currency. We are now witnessing the arrival of electronic ID-cards, which greatly facilitate individual electronic signatures. The combination of XBRL and electronic signatures (e.g. based on electronic ID cards) can lead to fast and secure financial reporting. It will allow the publication of financial reports, statutory audit reports, analysis, etc with the joint benefits of the XML/XBRL format and the electronic signature security.

For the electronic signature technology, the use of XMLDSIG or XAdES is envisioned. This can be applied to XBRL. Creating a fully electronic and electronically signed report document can be done quite easily in technologies such as Java or .NET. The major steps involved are:

- The XML processing (e.g. element selection, link-base expansion, ...);
- Optional style-sheet processing (e.g. if an html representation is also desired);
- Electronic signature creation – with the required canonicalisation etc;
- Electronic signature verification.

The W3C 'xmldsig-core' specification provides an XML schema for digital signatures. It defines three types of signatures:

- Enveloping signature (where the signature is the parent node of the XML document);

- Enveloped signature (where the signature is a child within the XML document);
- Detached signature (where the signature makes a reference to a separate document).

The XMLDSIG approach can be summarised as: signatures are applied to arbitrary digital contents (objects) via indirection, whereby the data objects are digested, the result is placed in an element (with other information) and that element is digested and signed.

In a European context, the basic format for the electronic signature in defined in ETSI's TS 101 733 specification document (ASN.1). For XML, there is the ETSI TS 101 903 XML Advanced Electronic Signatures (XAdES) specification. The XAdES specification essentially builds on XMLDSIG, but allows the inclusion of much more qualifying data such as time-stamps or validation information.

The XMLDSIG or XadES implementations will handle the signing and verification in standard ways. For example in Belgium, as the Belgian Government started an Electronic Identity card pilot in March 2003, the signing can be performed with the private key on the national id card. PricewaterhouseCoopers Belgium already demonstrated in March 2003 how to create and sign a statutory audit report in XBRL, using a national Electronic ID card (for more information, feel free to contact marc.sel@pwc.be).

One prototype make use of an XML parser (Xerces), a processor (Xalan), an XMLDSIG toolkit (IAIK's IXSIL) and a PKCS11 provider (also from IAIK). The XBRL report is processed at XML level, taking into account the XBRL-specific namespaces, linkbases, references and the like. Visual mark-up can be applied through XML-stylesheets. The XMLDSIG toolkit builds the XMLSignature object, while the PKCS11 provider allows the actual signing to take place on the smart card. As the XBRL instance document is an XML file, it can easily be mapped onto a DOM-document. The signature is then applied to the DOM document, which is again serialised into a file. Another prototype is currently being constructed on the basis of .NET, with Microsoft's XAdES library.

Of course, many issues remain to be further addressed. When one considers the possible scenarios for reporting to the public at large, to the shareholders, to the central bank, to the stock exchange etc, many different expectations will have to be met. For example, who will store the instance documents, the taxonomy schemas, the linkbases etc – what goes where, and how will it be stored? And for how long? Also, what about style-sheets, canonicalization and "what-you-see-is-what-you-sign"? Finally, how about selective access to parts of the XBRL information?

5 Conclusion

The acceptance of XML technology on which XBRL is based, is still increasing. Deployments such as in the Estonian e-government portal illustrate how powerful XML architectures can be when combined with adequate security mechanisms. The fact that more applications become XML-enabled will facilitate the processing of XBRL. As governments and stakeholders require faster and better financial reporting, XBRL will most likely become more and more embedded in our software infrastructure.

The current initiatives and applications already demonstrate that combining the power and versatility of XML and electronic signatures with the work done in the XBRL field, lead to a new more effective platform for providing business information to management and stakeholders. This information will be provided in a more reusable and more secure manner than they experience today. It can be considered mandatory that sound cryptography-based security measures be applied to XBRL in order to make such information sufficiently trustworthy.

The adoption of secure XBRL can further help us make Europe a competitive player on the global field.

References

Information with regard to XML can be found at www.w3c.org

For all information with regard to XBRL, please visit www.xbrl.org

For accounting standards and how they come to fruition, visit www.iasb.org.uk

Visit PricewaterhouseCoopers' XBRL web site at www.pwcglobal.com/xbrl

To witness how XBRL can change the organization of a stock exchange, visit the NASDAQ demo at www.nasdaq.com/xbrl;

Also, many other demos can be found at www.xbrl.org/demos/demos.htm

Additional information with regard to financial reporting can be found at www.buildingpublictrust.com as well as at www.pwcglobal.com/xbrl .

Mobile Payment Transactions

Paul Vanneste

Global e-Business & Emerging Technologies
MasterCard International
paul_vanneste@mastercard.com

Abstract

Mobile payment transactions are not fundamentally different from classical e-commerce payment transactions. Although the inherent limitations of mobile devices may render difficult the support of both the purchasing experience and the whole payment phase, their personal nature and their built-in authentication capabilities make them an attractive channel to support cardholder authentication by the payment card issuer. Such an authentication is a prerequisite for the non-repudiation of payment transactions, and therefore for a liability shift from the merchants to the issuers. Mobile devices may be used as authentication tokens within the framework of modern e-payment architectures, such as SPA/UCAF or 3-D Secure. The techniques used range from robust but rather complex and costly systems, e.g. based on symmetric or asymmetric cryptography and SIM or WIM cards, to less sophisticated, but easy to deploy, means, e.g., the use of passwords with SMS messages.

1 Introduction

The mobile channel opens new possibilities both for electronic commerce and for electronic payment. The increasingly popular use of mobile phones and Personal Digital Assistants (PDAs) has changed consumer expectations. Consumers now want to be able to conveniently purchase, and subsequently pay, at any place and at any time. Mobile payment transactions may help in meeting part of these new expectations.

Mobile payment transactions may be defined as payment transactions conducted by means of a radio-based wireless device. Two main classes of mobile payment systems may be distinguished:

- The proximity payments, and
- The remote payments.

The main characteristic of proximity payments is that the consumer is physically present at the point-of-sale. As such, proximity payments are very similar to classical credit or debit card payments. The main difference is that the transaction is conducted using a wireless device, such as a contactless card. Because of the presence of the consumer in the merchant premises, the infrastructure for this kind of payment is often based on an existing Point-of-Sale infrastructure, where contactless card readers, e.g. based on the ISO14443 standard, are added to existing payment terminals.

Remote mobile payments on the other hand are mobile payment transactions where the consumer is physically remote from the point-of-sale. Therefore, they are closer to Internet payment than to classical card payment. Because they usually require a somewhat heavy infrastructure to allow for a wide acceptance, they are likely to be based on existing communication networks that are already deployed for another purpose, such as the GSM network.

S. Paulus, N. Pohlmann, H. Reimer (Editors): Securing Electronic Business Processes, Vieweg (2004), 155-163

Both kinds of mobile payment share common characteristics with Internet payment:

- They are all a form of electronic payment.
- They are conducted over networks that are either public (the Internet) or easy to eavesdrop (radio waves).
- They may use all or part of a set of common protocols, like SSL, 3-D Secure, etc.

However, they are some specificities of mobile payment that deserve a particular attention.

2 Mobile Payment

Although mobile payment systems are not intrinsically different from other Internet payment systems, three main aspects differentiate them from other systems:

- They are based on *wireless communications*. This kind of communications is likely to suffer from more security vulnerabilities than wired communications whose security has been more extensively scrutinized. Furthermore, most of the wireless networks used for mobile payment have been designed for other purposes than transmission of sensitive digital information.
- They usually involve *new players*, such as the telecommunication operators, in an area where banks were traditionally the only actors.
- They feature a unique characteristic in that they make an extensive use of *personal mobile devices*. This makes them very attractive to both the banks and the consumers.

Obviously, several of the particularities of these personal mobile devices must be taken into account, that impact the design of mobile payment systems:

- *Scarce resources*. Mobile devices usually possess somewhat limited resources from a bandwidth or computing power perspective. With the current state of technology, these limitations may preclude the implementation of some solutions, e.g. those relying on the use of fat wallets.
- *Limited user interface*. Limited or impractical user interfaces may make data entry tasks difficult, such as the entry of credit card details (in particular, the non-numerical fields). In such a context, server wallet-based solutions have a definitive advantage.
- *User interface security threats*. From a security point of view, impractical user interfaces may also create new security threats. For example, some security-related information, like the URL of the visited site, may be only partially displayed, or even not displayed at all, making man-in-the-middle attacks possible.

However, they also offer a unique opportunity to secure the payment transactions. The security of traditional Internet payment relies on a number of implicit but rather questionable assumptions. The main one is that the consumer platform behaves as expected. Unfortunately, the security of this consumer platform, usually a PC, is difficult to ensure, as typically only minimal security mechanisms are available. Not only the security of the transaction relies on the consumer awareness of the underlying security features at the time of the transaction[1], it also relies on the integrity of his PC. Trojan horses may for example compromise passwords. Even the use of simple IC card readers is not sufficient, as a compromised application running

---

[1] For example, the consumer should be able to check the status of an SSL connection or to assess the validity of a particular SSL server certificate.

on the PC could send fraudulent data to the IC card. Therefore, there is a definite need for so-called Personal Trusted Devices. Most modern mobile devices are suitable for this role, as:

- These communication devices are *programmable* and feature a built-in *display and keyboard*.

- Their *personal nature* reduces the need for tamper-evidence or tamper–resistance. It makes them particularly suitable for performing security functions, e.g. PIN entry, as they are unlikely to be vulnerable to techniques like tampering or keyboard sniffing.

- Their *widespread ownership and use* is of great help for solving the cost and distribution issues associated with massive rollout of tokens or specific hardware, e.g., smart card readers.

- Their relatively *modest cost* and their *pervasive nature* make them very attractive to consumers.

Such devices may be used as the cornerstones when building the security services required for secure payment transactions:

- *Authentication*, allowing the merchant, the acquirer bank or the issuer bank to verify the consumer credentials.

- *Confidentiality*, to protect the security-sensitive data, such as the payment card account number, and to protect the consumer's privacy.

- *Data integrity*, to ensure that the payment data are not altered after the consumer agrees to the terms of the transaction

- *Non-repudiation*, so as to bind the parties to the transaction.

However, the particularities of the channel used, i.e., the over-the-air link, and of the protocols used, have to be considered carefully. Implementation issues may create security flaws that have no counterparts in the wired world. In addition, the rapidly changing wireless standards may be a significant concern for wide adoption.

The lack of standardization in these areas, as well as the rapidly evolving technologies, is also a significant concern for interoperability. Mobile payment applications are usually implemented by an ad hoc combination of techniques such as GSM encryption, SMS, SIM Toolkit applications, Wireless Application Protocol (WAP) and WML scripts.

3 Basic Mobile Security

When comparing mobile payments with classical electronic payments over the Internet, the following security aspects have to be considered:

- The lack of *security on the over-the-air link*, both for voice or message data transmission, and

- The lack of *security on the operator network*.

These shortcomings usually require the ad hoc implementation of end-to-end security through specific means, e.g., SIM Toolkit (STK) based applications or WAP/WIM-based solutions.

Due to the rapidly evolving mobile technology and standards, designing such systems is far from being obvious, and their intrinsic security has to be carefully assessed. In addition, in most cases, payment card issuers and acquirers have to collaborate with telecom providers. This delegation of some security elements to external parties introduces new risks. Therefore, specific mechanisms have to be put in place in order to avoid the loss of control of the system security.

Several constraints have impacted the design of the security services available on GSM mobile devices:

- *Timing constraints*: the delay of the initial call set-up must be kept as short as possible, for convenience reasons.

- *Bandwidth limitations*: the additional bandwidth requirements must be as small as possible.

- *Computing resource limitations*: the system must be kept simple, as it has to operate on platforms with limited computing power, e.g. a SIM card.

- *Costs constraints*: the cost impact on the mobile device must be limited.

These constraints, combined with the weak requirements for full end-to-end security of voice transmission led to the design of specific, proprietary algorithms. Sufficient details about these secret algorithms, i.e., COMP-128, A5/1 and A5/2, have been released to allow extensive research on their security security – see, for example, [WaWr02]. Several attacks, either by direct access to the SIM card or by over-the-air queries to the phone, have shown intrinsic weaknesses of these algorithms. However, these attacks are not necessarily so simple to launch (and some networks have never used COMP-128), and it could be argued that in many ways GSM suffers from less problems than, say, using SSL/TLS.

Also, the communications between the base station and the mobile switching centre (MSC) and the Gateway MSC (GMSC) are not cryptographically protected – of course, this is not an 'open' network, although gaining the physical access necessary to intercept communications may not be very difficult. Furthermore, unencrypted transmission of data and keying material may take place over-the-air between the base stations and the base station controllers. For example, the various security zones in a WAP transaction conducted over a GSM network are illustrated in Figure 1.

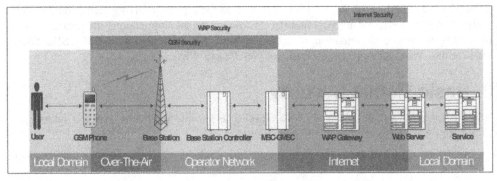

Figure 1: GSM Security Zones.

The SMS messages are protected in exactly the same way as the voice channel. As such, they suffer from the same weaknesses as the voice communications. In addition, the store-and-forward nature of the SMS network allows even easier access by the network providers. Other security weaknesses exist, e.g. linked to the protection of the SMS public gateways. Furthermore, the absence of delivery guarantee may be of concern when implementing reliable payment protocols.

As shown above, the basic GSM security protocols suffer from several weaknesses that prevent their exclusive use in a lot of security applications. The two main weaknesses are:

- The lack of *communication privacy* against the network operator, and

- The lack of *end-to-end security* for Internet connectivity.

GPRS does not feature any significant improvement with respect to security. UMTS will very probably provide a better level of security, e.g., by the use of publicly reviewed and approved algorithms and by a more sophisticated authentication procedure (see, for example, [Blan02]), but it will take several years before the use of UMTS becomes general.

In order to overcome the weaknesses of basic GSM security with respect to authentication or support of payment applications, several providers have developed proprietary security systems. Most of these implementations rely on the use of the STK. STK allows programming of the SIM with an application that may interact with the phone. STK is standardized and the major handset manufacturers offer STK-compatible handsets. The services that may be implemented using STK range from games to on-demand information and mobile banking. When WAP is not available, STK is a necessary tool to install value added services on top of bearer services.

From a bank perspective, using STK-based systems has a major drawback: the SIM card belongs to the telecom operator. That is, telecom operators keep total control of the applications, including over when they are downloaded, and when they should be removed. Therefore, agreements have to be sought between issuers and operators.

In closed environments, such as e-banking systems, STK applications may contain embedded secret keys for use with symmetric cryptographic techniques. These keys may then be used to ensure end-to-end confidentiality and integrity of data exchange, e.g. through SMS messages. However, in open environments or in order to provide additional services such as non-repudiation, it is of interest to implement public key cryptographic functionalities within a SIM Toolkit application. Such applications typically contain a private key that is unique to the user. Certificates for the corresponding public key of the user may be publicly distributed. The private key is used to sign messages received as SMS messages. Obviously, this signature operation is subject to the entry of a dedicated PIN. The application responds by sending back the signature in another SMS message. Such systems are generally implemented in combination with server wallets, which send payment approval requests for a transaction to the mobile for signature. By verifying the signature received, the server wallet performs in one single step both the cardholder authentication and the validation of the cardholder approval for that particular transaction.

Although the use of proprietary, application-specific systems allows the limitations of the basic GSM security to be bypassed, it is usually preferable to rely on standards. For example, WAP could have been a suitable platform to avoid dependence on proprietary solutions. In addition to the confidentiality service available at the bearer level, WAP offers additional security services:

- The *WTLS protocol*, which is the mobile counterpart of TLS, supports confidentiality, data integrity and authentication between two communicating entities. Just like TLS, WTLS is implemented at the transport layer.

- An *application-level cryptographic library*, allowing digital signature and encryption. These functions may be accessed through WML Script function calls.

Both security services rely on the use of a WAP/Wireless Identity Module (WIM) – see, for example, [Ertl03]. The WIM is a tamper-resistant device, typically an IC card, that:

- Carries PIN-protected *asymmetric keys* and the related certificates,
- Perform *on-board encryption and digital signature* operations, and
- Implements support for *WTLS authentication and encryption.*

At minimum, the WIM stores two private keys, a key used for WTLS authentication, and a key used for signature of data by use of the WMLScript SignText function. This key, the so-called non-repudiation key, can only be used after the input of a dedicated PIN, called the non-repudiation PIN. The non-repudiation key provides an elegant way to verify transaction approval by a specific cardholder. However, the limited diffusion of WAP-based applications has restricted the use of this technique in the financial sector.

4 Other Mobile Environments

In the future, GSM and UMTS will by no means be the only available carriers for wireless payment information. Other possible technologies which could be used for transporting trans-action information include Bluetooth and Wireless LAN (WLAN), and there are also a variety of alternative network architectures, some much less well-defined that the current telco-oriented architectures for GSM and UMTS. Possible future scenarios for connecting a mobile payment device to a remote payment server include:

- The use of a *Bluetooth* link to a 'conventional' telecommunications network infrastructure, e.g. UMTS or a fixed network;
- The use of a *WLAN hot spot* to connect to a 'conventional' telecommunications network infrastructure, e.g. UMTS or a fixed network;
- The use of an *ad hoc network* of devices communicating via wireless means, with one node in the network providing access to an IP-based network infrastructure.

In the first two cases similar security vulnerabilities arise to data transferred between the mobile payment device and a remote payment server. These arise firstly because the wireless link between the mobile device and the point of access to the infrastructure may be insecure, and secondly because the payment data will be vulnerable at the point of access itself. Examples of the first type of issue arise with WLAN or Bluetooth, given the known security issues with the techniques currently in use to protect these types of network (documented extensively – see, for example, [GeNy03]). Issues of the second type are similar to those discussed above, and also arise with the use of schemes such as WTLS, where a separate protected session is required for the wireless part of a communications link.

The existence of these vulnerabilities supports the desirability of the provision of application-layer security mechanisms, much as is the case when a GSM network is used. Even if the 'main' network could itself provide a secure communications environment, these vulnerabilities mean that security must also be considered as part of the design of the payment system.

In the third case, issues similar to those immediately above again apply. However, in this environment there are yet further vulnerabilities. One of the characteristics of mobile ad hoc networks, as discussed extensively in the literature (see, for example, [YaSd03]), is the lack of any centralized network infrastructure to manage functions such as routing. This means that routing of data within such a network relies on co-operation by network nodes, which may only trust each other to a very limited degree. This raises serious issues relating to denial of service, and/or deliberate truncation of transaction traffic. This means that payment protocols running over such networks need to be made robust against malicious behavior of this type. In particular, repeated selective deletion, re-ordering, and/or insertion of traffic, should not put at risk the availability of the payment system.

5 Mobile Payment Architectures

The very concept of a mobile payment system actually covers two significantly different notions:

- The full mobile implementation of e-payment systems, i.e., the use of mobile phones or of other mobile devices, e.g., PDAs, as access devices to the Internet supporting the whole payment phase.

- The use of mobile devices as support tools, i.e., the use of mobile devices for the support of other, classical e-payment systems. For example, the supported systems may include server wallet-based implementations of SPA/UCAF or 3-D Secure, which perform most of the payment-related tasks. In such a case, the mobile is not necessarily the access device to the Internet and plays a limited role in the payment transaction.

In the first case, the mobile devices may support various techniques and protocols, including SSL-protected transmission of credit card details or client implementations for SPA/UCAF or CAP/UCAF protocols. As already stated, scarce resources, limited user interfaces and user interface security threats may limit the suitability of mobile devices for the implementation of such demanding protocols.

In the latter case, the mobile device is used in most implementations for authentication purposes. In that context, it may assist modern payment protocols like SPA/UCAF of 3-D Secure in achieving authentication in several ways:

- By acting as an *authentication factor*. The mobile device is usually accessed through a call-back mechanism. In such a case, the mobile, or rather the embedded SIM card, becomes itself an authentication factor. Such a call-back mechanism may be based on voice server call-back, but also on receiving one-time passwords through SMS messages, to be used subsequently on the access device.

- By acting as *support for authentication mechanisms*. The mobile device may support authentication mechanisms based on several factors. For example, it can act as a PIN entry device, and communicate this PIN to a DTMF server or send it through SMS messages. It can interact with a classical payment card, and be used for offline PIN verification.

The wide variety and the ad hoc nature of most mobile payment schemes make an exhaustive description of such schemes difficult. However, several trends may be identified.

The mobile payment models can be categorized as follows:

- In the *acquirer-centric model*, the merchant is in charge of handling the interactions with the mobile device by means of a mobile-specific protocol. An example of this is the dual slot model. When a second IC card slot is available on the handset, it can be accessed by an STK application. When the second slot is an external one, it is possible to implement POS-like functions within the mobile, e.g. to perform EMV (Europay-MasterCard-Visa – see www.emvco.com) transactions with an EMV-compliant card inserted in the second slot. This virtual POS terminal receives the transaction details and communicates the results of the EMV processing through SMS messages. In such a dual slot model, the main payment-related tasks are performed by the mobile itself. The merchant server must be aware that a mobile phone is used for payment and proceed accordingly. Usually, for ease of implementation reasons, the merchant routes the transaction to a dedicated payment server, which handles the exchanges with the mobile phone and the communication with the payment scheme network on-behalf of the merchant. This system supports multiple cards and offers the cardholder a payment experience similar to the one he/she is used to in the classical POS or ATM environment. However, cost and form factor issues may preclude a large deployment of dual slot handsets. In addition, as for any STK-based solution, such systems require close collaboration between issuers and telecom operators. An example of this model is illustrated in Figure 2.

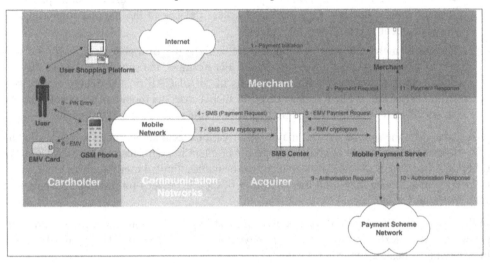

Figure 2: Architecture Example in an Acquirer-centric Model.

- In the *issuer-centric model*, the merchant is unaware of the mobile nature of the payment, and the issuer handles the interactions with the mobile device. In this kind of solution, the mobile acts mainly as a support for the authentication mechanisms that allow the server wallet to verify the presence of the legitimate cardholder and his approval of a particular transaction. The key issue in such an architecture is the implementation of an efficient routing service component responsible for directing the payment messages to the relevant server wallet. The implementation of such a routing service depends on the capabilities of the mobile device and on the nature of the interfaces between the mobile, the server wallet and the merchant. When the mobile is able to perform the routing task, implementation of payment protocols like SPA/UCAF or 3-D Secure becomes possible. With SPA/UCAF, the details on the location of the cardholder server-side wallet are provided at the mobile level. The details of the location of the cardholder server wallet can either be pre-configured at the mobile device level or rather be entered by the cardholder when a transaction takes place. The clientless nature of 3-D Secure makes it more suitable for mobile architectures. The main requirement is that the device supports a HTTP-like redirection, allowing the merchant to contact the issuer Access Control Server (ACS). An example of this model is shown in Figure 3.

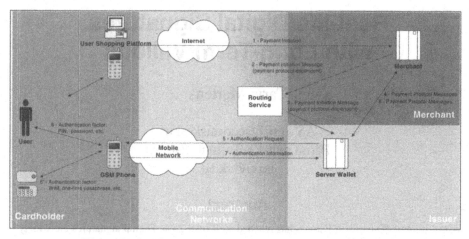

Figure 3: Architecture Example in an Issuer-centric Model.

6 Conclusion

For each of the models presented above, several schemes may be implemented, depending on the capabilities of the mobile devices. Until suitable standards emerge, ad hoc proprietary architectures will remain the basis for mobile payment systems implementation. The challenge of the future in this area will be to define and implement a unified architecture based on robust, standardized end-to-end security services.

References

[Blan02]   W. Blanchard, 'Wireless security'. In: R. Temple and J. Regnault (eds.), *Internet and Wireless Security*, Chapter 8, pages 147-162, IEE Press, 2002.

[Ertl03]   H. Ertl, 'Secure mobile tokens – the future'. In: C. J. Mitchell (ed.), *Security for mobility*, Chapter 5, IEE Press, to appear.

[GeNy03]   C. Gehrmann and K. Nyberg, 'Security in personal area networks'. In: C. J. Mitchell (ed.), *Security for mobility*, Chapter 9, IEE Press, to appear.

[WaWr02]   M. Walker and T. Wright, 'Security'. In: F. Hillebrand (ed.), *GSM and UMTS: The creation of global mobile communication*, Chapter 14, pages 385-406, John Wiley & Sons, 2002.

[YaSd03]   P.-W. Yau and V. Sdralia, 'Towards the security of routing in ad hoc networks'. In: C. J. Mitchell (ed.), *Security for mobility*, Chapter 10, IEE Press, to appear.

Real-life Digital Signatures with Long-Term Validity

Tarvi Martens

AS Sertifitseerimiskeskus
Pärnu mnt.12, Tallinn, Estonia
tarvi@sk.ee

Abstract

The penetration of ID-cards in Estonia has reached well over 25%. Digital signatures are widely used in a variety of situations and treated equally to handwritten signatures by law. In this presentation we look into reality-proven infrastructure and end-user tools required to create digital signatures with long-term validity. The infrastructure is lightweight as compared to competing solutions, and is based on already existing industry standards and protocols. Use of OCSP responder as an electronic notary and secure logging system providing auditable security are explained. Some end-user tools that are based on the XAdES standard will be described.

1 Introduction

National PKI with compulsory ID-card is a blessing for a PKI designer. One can forget about "reaching critical masses" or "inter-PKI-interoperability" – we can assume that all Estonians have the same common card, issuance and PKI validity services are controlled centrally. This allows us to concentrate on ID-card applications area and leave behind other issues.

There is not much to invent in applications making use of PKI for authentication. Configuring Web server to accept ID-cards and providing LDAP, CRL and OCSP services for validity information is not exactly a rocket science. Of course, service providers need to be encouraged and educated to allow every public or private service to accept ID-card for client authentication, but this is it.

The picture is different in digital signature field. Digitally signed document can be treated as a "smallest self-contained trusted data entity" usable universally. Of course, if it is provided by PKI design and services, legislation and common understanding of "what is a digitally signed document and how to make sure it is authentic". This is true in Estonian case.

2 Infrastructure First

Our company – AS Sertifitseerimiskeskus (Certification Centre Ltd., hereinafter: SK) issues, suspends, and revokes certificates of Estonian ID cards as usual CA practice. We also provide validity information through different methods – LDAP and CRL to be mentioned first.

Estonian national PKI is a real-life example of CRL concept shortcomings. About 10% of cardholders suspend their certificates when receiving the ID-card and therefore CRL has grown well over 1 MB. Starting from April this year we abandoned CRL immediate update policy and CRL is renewed every 12 hours. Using CRL is therefore not suitable for serious applications.

The most convenient method of verifying certificate validity is SK's OCSP [RFC 2560] service. It can be used for simple certificate validity confirmations, but also for validity confirmations ("notary confirmations") to digital signatures. SK provides a standard OCSP service compliant with RFC 2560. An important detail is that according to the RFC, OCSP responses are supposed to be based on CRL-s and therefore may not necessarily reflect the actual certificate status. In contrast, SK has implemented its OCSP service in such a way that it operates directly off its master CA certificate database and does not use CRL-s. Thus, SK's OCSP responses reflect actual (real-time) certificate status.

3 OCSP and Time-Stamping

For legally binding digital signatures, time is an extremely important factor. According to the Estonian DSA as well as common sense, only signatures given using a valid certificate are to be considered valid. On the other hand, to provide remedy to the risk that the signing device (ID card) may be stolen together with PIN-s and digital signatures could be given on behalf of the user by someone else, users have the chance of suspending their certificate validity using a 24-hour telephone hotline operated by SK. With these two concepts combined, users must be able to clearly differentiate the signatures given using a valid certificate from those given using a suspended or revoked certificate. Thus, there is a need for a time-stamping and validity confirmation service that binds the signature, time and certificate validity.

Another important concept concerning signature validity is that the signature must be valid also when the certificate has already expired or been revoked. If a certificate is suspended by the card holder or anyone else, the card holder can reactivate it at a bank office.

SK chose to base its time-stamping implementation on standard OCSP. This enables the service provider to conveniently deliver certificate validity and time information in one convenient query response. The OCSP protocol query format contains a Nonce field, which protects against replay attacks. Instead of cryptographically random data, the Nonce field is set to contain the hash of the data to be signed, because it can also be interpreted as just a random number. According to the RFC, the OCSP responder signs its response which in SK's case, contains the original Nonce (document hash), response providing/signing time and ID of the certificate used to give the signature, binding the three pieces of data together and providing the validity confirmation for the digital signature.

The main features of the above concept are:

- OCSP unites time-stamping, certificate validity and electronic notary services
- it is based on standard protocols and standards
- verification process is lightweight and the document is self-contained – no additional verification services are needed

SK has implemented all of the above, including both client and server parts, in its DigiDoc digital signature architecture.

4 Long-time Validity of Digital Signatures

SK runs secure logging system which logs all changes in certificate status (activation, suspension, termination of suspension and revocation) and all validity confirmations given by OCSP responder. In case logging procedure fails, then given transaction will not be completed. This principle ensures existence of log record in the system.

Log records are cryptographically linked to prevent insider attacks and forging log records (for example backdating the log record). Once a month, cryptographic hash is printed in newspaper. Log record database is backed up in timely basis with three copies stored in different locations.

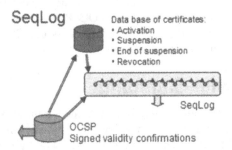

This kind of secure log system provides for dual purposes:

- auditability – in case of disputes there are means to prove that some validity confirmation was (not) issued, was issued before/after some other event, etc.

- long term validity preservation of digital signatures – even after complete breakdown of all keys and RSA algorithm one can prove that document signed at past is valid – by matching confirmation data with log data.

Secure log is completely invisible to end-users with one exception – every ID-card holder can check their personal records (certificate history and issued validity confirmations).

5 Document Format and DigiDoc

In order to bring digital signatures into everyday life, common understanding and signature handling practices are required. In addition, software and technology must be available for anyone interested, in order to create compatible applications. After all, the key to unleashing potential digital signature benefits lies in communication between organizations, not within one organization. Therefore, it is vital that all organizations in a given community interpret and understand digital signatures the same way. In case of Estonia, the community is the whole country.

A number of digital signature implementations and applications are available on the market, all claiming to be suitable for specific purposes. However, no known application or implementation of the latest standards was found which would suit the needs of the Estonian project, and reliance on foreign software providers guaranteeing the functioning of a country's everyday life relying on digital signatures can also be seen as a strategic risk. Therefore, a whole new approach – and a whole new software architecture – was needed.

In 2002, SK together with its partners created an all-around digital signature architecture called DigiDoc. As the name suggests, DigiDoc aims to meet all the needs users might have about digital signature creation, handling and verification.

On the server side, DigiDoc provides an RFC2560-compliant OCSP server, operating directly off the CA master certificate database and providing validity confirmations to certificates and signatures. On the client side, it provides a number of components.

The most important component is digital document format, which is a key to common digital signature implementation and practice. As of 2002, a number of standards have been adopted or are in preparation. SK based the DigiDoc document format on XML-DSIG [XML-DSIG] standard. In February 2002, ETSI published its extensions to XML-DSIG as ETSI TS 101 903 [XAdES], also known as XAdES. DigiDoc document format is a profile of XAdES, containing a subset of its proposed extensions. The DigiDoc format is described in a specification document.

Based on the document format, a library was developed in C and Java languages that binds together the following:

- DigiDoc document format
- SK's OCSP service
- Interfacing with the user's ID card using Windows' native CSP interface or cross-platform PKCS#11

The DigiDoc library provides easy-to-use interfaces to all of the above and there is no need for application developers to know OCSP protocol specifics or DigiDoc (XAdES, XML-DSIG) format internals. It can be embedded in any application and on top of it, a COM interface has been implemented, making it easy to add DigiDoc support to any Windows application supporting COM technology. A Java implementation is also provided.

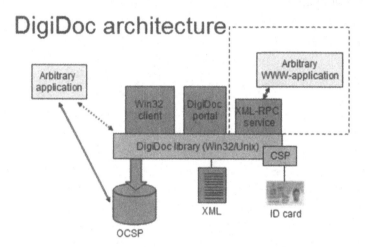

However, providing the libraries and formats was not enough because these do not add value to end users without real applications. Although it is expected that DigiDoc support will eventually be present in most Estonian document management systems, web sites dealing with documents etc, a number of example or "reference" applications are also provided. DigiDoc Client is a Windows application that lets users simply sign and verify documents, and DigiDoc portal is an application that lets users do the same online without the need to install any stand-alone software. Naturally, both are based on the same DigiDoc library and thus fully compatible – signatures given in Client can be verified in portal and vice versa.

The libraries, specifications and applications are provided to Estonian public free of charge, and it is expected that digital signature usage in common life and everyday business and government practices will grow significantly already in 2003. The first official digital signatures in Estonia were given using DigiDoc Client on October 7, 2002, and implementing digital signature on a national scale naturally takes a while.

6 Conclusion

DigiDoc is proven and standards-based technology for implementing nation-wide digital signatures. It does not require anything very specific from infrastructure part – except real-time OCSP server. DigiDoc client and portal can handle different smartcards today. This all makes it feasible to consider DigiDoc as a good basis platform for European-wide interoperability of digital signatures today. Follow the address www.openxades.org for more information,

References

RFC 2560   Myers, M., Ankney, R., Malpani, A., Galperin, S., Adams, C., X.509 Internet Public Key Infrastructure: Online Certificate Status Protocol - OCSP. June 1999.

RFC3275   Eastlake 3rd D., Reagle J., Solo D., (Extensible Markup Language) XML-Signature Syntax and Processing. (XML-DSIG) March 2002.

XAdES   ETSI TS 101 903   XML Advanced Electronic Signatures (XAdES). February 2002.

WWW sites   www.openxades.org
              www.id.ee

Pragmatic Solutions to Make E-Mail Security Work

Henning Seemann

Utimaco Safeware AG
Germanusstraße 4
DE-52080 Aachen
Germany
henning.seemann@aachen.utimaco.de

Abstract

The concepts for secure e-mail are available for quite some time. Nevertheless only few users have adopted them.

The classical concept of end-to-end e-mail security provides maximum theoretical security. But the effort to implement and enforce it at every client has limited the spreading of security and therefore the overall benefit.

Centralized e-mail security overcomes this problem. A gateway between internal and public network provides security where it is needed – in the internet.

This presentation reflects aspects like standards, integration, security policy, central virus detection, implementation efforts, and key-recovery as well as business requirements like reduced administration costs and optimized workflow.

1 History

E-mail security has been developed for quite some time and went through a long and deep analysis of security concepts including cryptography, key management, digital signature, and public key infrastructure.

Two standards evolved from this development: PGP and S/MIME. Both provide essentially the same functionality: encryption, digital signature, and a key management based on asymmetric algorithms. The only significant difference is the key infrastructure, which is hierarchical for S/MIME (i.e. X.509 certificates) [Rams99] or unstructured for PGP (i.e. web of trust) [CND+98].

Both standards are designed to provide end-to-end security. I.e. the sender signs and encrypts the e-mail in his local e-mail client before sending it. The recipient decrypts it and verifies the signature in his local e-mail client. This concept provides maximum security, because the e-mail is protected on the full transport path. The e-mail is only endangered in client computer of the sender and the recipient (e.g. Trojan horses, unsecure storage). Both standards spend significant effort to ensure that the protection is not interrupted between the sender and the recipient in order to prevent man-in-the-middle attacks.

From the technical point of view e-mail security is a solved problem except for technical details like enhancing the used cryptographic algorithms from time to time.

S. Paulus, N. Pohlmann, H. Reimer (Editors): Securing Electronic Business Processes, Vieweg (2004), 169-175

2 The Problem

Nevertheless e-mail security has not been implemented by a larger number of users. Still most e-mails are sent over the internet in plain text. The best security technology can not provide benefit, if it is ignored by the users. Therefore significant improvement for the security of e-mail come from increasing acceptance of e-mail security by the users.

The following actions can improve the acceptance of e-mail security:

Regulation: Governmental or non-governmental (e.g. business-to-business (B2B)) regulations can force users to implement e-mail security. Otherwise they will be excluded from certain fields of business or communication. Regulation forces the user but does not convince him. Furthermore it is limited to the applications where the regulations applies.

New Applications: E-mail security allows to use e-mail for new applications like B2B or business-to-customer business. This provides benefits for the user. Nevertheless this argument has shown limited power to convince the user in the past.

Less Obstacles: Implementing e-mail security for larger organizations or customers has proven to be a challenging task. This is caused by financial and non-financial obstacles. Financial obstacles include costs for:

- **The software:** If client software has to be acquired for a large number of clients, the total cost can be significant. Upgrades for the used client operating system or the general mail client can require an upgrade of the e-mail security software. Although the technology for e-mail security is quit mature, the software vendors provide frequent upgrades with new functions, improved interoperability or improved security.

- **The roll-out of the software:** Installing, upgrading or maintaining software in a large number of clients creates a lot or work and therefore a lot of costs. OS vendors provide mechanisms for an automatic rollout of client software in large organizations. Nevertheless they require quite some preparation and testing. A heterogeneous client infrastructure may increase the effort.

- **End user training:** This includes two issues convincing the end user to use e-mail security and to tell them how to do it. Most users are very busy to do their job. E-Mail security sees to be just another duty from there point of view. Therefore they are often very reluctant to use e-mail, if there is only the smallest obstacle. When end users have understood that e-mail security is necessary, they still have to learn how to do it. If they do not use e-mail security frequently they will easily forget how to use it. This requires periodical training.

- **Certificates obtained from an official trustcenter:** Certificates from an official trustcenter cost between 8 and 200 Euros. For large organizations with thousands of users this is a significant cost factor.

- **Support and maintenance:** Support and maintenance effort scales with the number of installed client systems. This includes the reinstallation of broken clients, resetting forgotten passwords etc.

Non-financial obstacles include:

- **Legal implications:** If every user has a key valid for a qualified signature, he may issue legally relevant signature although he is not entitled to sign legal documents. In most organizations only a very small fraction of employees is entitled to do legally relevant signatures.

- **Uncooperative end users:** Every organization has unsatisfied and lazy employees. Employees are sometime unwilling to learn new technologies. They sometimes feel that their normal workload is too high to care about new requirements like e-mail security. Sometimes they just do not understand the issue.

- **Stiffness of grown IT infrastructures:** The IT infrastructure in many organizations has grown for a long time. Different client versions are in use. Due to mergers and acquisitions different technologies may be in use (e.g. Lotus Notes and Exchange) in the same organization. Outdated systems may be incompatible to current technologies and standards.

- **Technical risks in the software roll-out to a large number of end user client systems:** A flaw in the automatic rollout of client software may affect many users. Even wit extensive testing it can not be guaranteed that all potential problems can found prior to the rollout.

- **Incompatibility with other IT technologies like central virus scanning:** E-Mails can only be scanned for unwanted content (e.g. viruses, worms, spam, adult content) as long as they are in plain. Outgoing e-mails must be scanned before they are encrypted. Incoming e-mails must be decrypted before they are scanned. If a client based software is used for e-mail encryption, the scanning has to be done in the client, as well. This can cause the following problems: (1) Plugins for scanning and encryption may be incompatible with each other even, if each plugin alone is compatible with the mail application. (2) Malicious content may affect the client after leaving the encryption plugin but before entering the scanning application. (3) If the mail application calls the scanning and the encryption plugin in the wrong order, the scanning may be useless. This problem may be hard to detect.

- **variance and incompatibility in end user client systems:** Client software vendors provide their clients for a number of client operation systems and operation system versions. Nevertheless it may happen that the desired client software is not available for all clients in the organization. In this case it may be necessary to move to a less attractive software vendor, to use client software from different vendors or to exclude some clients from e-mail security.

"Regulation" and "New Applications" are well known aspects and have been used as arguments for pushing e-mail security for quite some time. "Less Obstacles" is an aspect which is receiving more attention recently.

Due to the mature technology for e-mail security there is no significant improvement for be expected from technical development of existing the e-mail security products.

3 The Solution

Using central gateways instead of distributed clients is a new technical concept for providing e-mail security [PhPW02] [Pohl03]. It can overcome the dead lock, in which classical client-based e-mail security solutions are caught. The difference between gateway and client concepts are not primarily technical but organizational.

A central gateway is placed at the border of a secure e-mail domain (e.g. the internal network of a company) and an insecure e-mail domain (e.g. the internet). It provides e-mail security by signing end encrypting (or decrypting and verifying) e-mails at a single, central place. A gateway is for e-mail security what a central firewall is for network security. It handles security at a central point, because it is very difficult to handle it at each client.

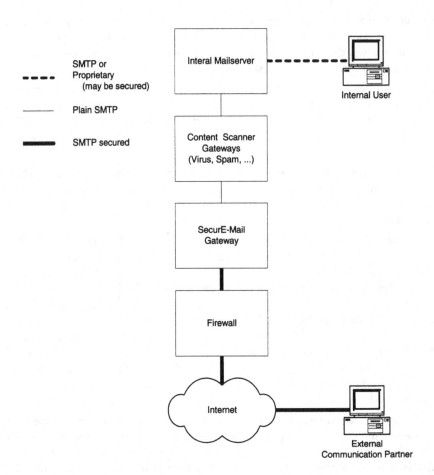

Installing IT security at a central point is a common procedure in order to overcome the problem of ensuring security at each host. Other applications of this general concept include firewalls for central network access control, central virus scanners for email, FTP and HTTP traffic, RAS and VPN gateways for central authentication and encryption, and intrusion detection scanners for central network monitoring.

A central gateway provides the following advantages compared to a client based end-to-end security solution:

- The security policy can be enforced at a central point. End users can not bypass security regulations by chance or by intention.

- All secure e-mail operations (e.g. verification reports) can be reported at a central place. This includes archival of all e-mails and timestamping.

- All e-mails can be checked for unwanted content (e.g. spam, viruses) centrally before they are encrypted or after they are decrypted.

- Key recovery is much simpler if all keys are used centrally and not distributed. Key backup is just a part of the general server backup for the gateway. Server backup is a well established process in nearly all organization. So, it is easily extended to the gateway.

- The rollout, and later the maintenance, for a single gateway is much simpler than for a large number of client systems.
- The end users need not be trained because they are not actively involved in the security processing of their e-mails. I.e. they need not worry about handling own and foreign keys. They need not select encryption and signing in their e-mail application.

A gateway solution has disadvantages, as well. They include:

- A qualified signature according to local legal regulations usually requires that the end user is the physical owner of the private key used for the signature. This is in contraction to the idea that keys are stored and used centrally on a gateway.
- A central gateway in the usual application does not protect the e-mail on the internal network. E-mails can be read, altered or spoofed in the internal network.
- A central gateway is an oversized solution for small companies an individual end users (e.g. home office, mobile users).

A full-fledged e-mail security solution for an end customer usually includes gateway and client based components. They can be combined in order to add the strengths and to eliminate the disadvantages of both components.

Such a solution can be designed in the following way:

A central gateway handles the following tasks:

- Incoming e-mails are decrypted.
- The signatures of incoming e-mails are verified and may be removed.
- Outgoing e-mails are encrypted.
- Outgoing e-mails are signed. This signature proves that the e-mail comes from this domain. It indicates the individual user.

The e-mail security client application handles the following tasks:

- The signatures of incoming e-mails are verified, if the verification must be done by the end user instead of the gateway.
- Outgoing e-mails are signed, if a qualified signature is required. This signature proves that the e-mail comes from this user
- Outgoing e-mails are encrypted, if the content is so confidential, that they must be encrypted in the internal network, as well.

These tasks are usually only required for a small number of clients. The majority of the users do not need client based e-mail security. This fact preserves the advantage of the central gateway solution.

Qualified signatures is one major argument against a central gateway. A deeper analysis of the business processes which require a qualified signature usually show that the qualified signatures are rather used for documents than for e-mail. It is the same situation as with traditional mail.

Example: When you send your annual tax declaration to your local tax authority, you sign it, because it is a legal document. But you sign it on the tax declaration form and not on the mail envelope. When the tax authority receives your letter, it takes the form out of the envelope and throws the envelope away. The tax declaration is processed further and finally archived. Therefore your signature is required to be on the form and not on the envelope.

If you implement this process using e-mail, you have to sign the tax declaration as a document (e.g. as a PDF file). This has to be done using a client based software and probably using a smart card. When you send this document to your tax authority, the e-mail need not be signed at all, because the authenticity of the tax declaration is verified with the document signature. The e-mail signature is rather comparable with the printed address and logo on the official envelopes of a company. It is an indication for authenticity.

Content scanners are placed between the central gateway and the internal clients. They handle the following tasks:

- Removing unwanted content from e-mails (e.g. viruses)
- Eliminating spam e-mails. End-to-end encryption could be used in future by spammers to bypass central spam filtering!

Internal e-mail infrastructures (i.e. servers and clients) (e.g. Lotus Notes or Microsoft Exchange) handle the following tasks:

- Storing and forwarding e-mails
- Managing e-mail accounts including address translation and mailing lists
- Authenticating end users at their clients before using an e-mail address / account.

E-mails can not be signed at a central gateway with a legally valid signature. Nevertheless the internal e-mail infrastructure can be combined gateway in order to sign e-mails with a reasonable level of confidence. This requires a properly configured e-mail infrastructure with a good end user authentication. Usually the gateway and the e-mail server are placed at the same location. In this case no special protection for the communication between them is necessary. If they are separated by an unsecure network, the connection can easily be secure with a point-to-point VPN or with SMTP over SSL. This is sufficient for many real world applications.

This general concept can be modified for individual customers with individual requirements. Some examples are discussed here:

An industrial user needs an e-mail security solution for the communication with customers and suppliers. Such a B2B environment requires encryption in a first place. Most e-mails contain confidential information but no legal contract.

A government customer needs an e-mail security solution for the communication with the citizens. Legal aspects play an important rule. Signatures of incoming e-mails must be verified including their legal status. The receipt must be confirmed and archived (timestamp). Outgoing e-mails must be encrypted to ensure the protection of individual and confidential data.

4 Conclusion

E-mail security is a mature technology today. All major technical issues were solved. Nevertheless e-mail security is not in wide use. This is the major limitation to e-mail security in real life.

The pure client based approach to e-mail security has not lead to the expected success i.e. wide implementation of e-mail security. Central gateways are an important extension to the existing e-mail security concepts. They can lead to an improved acceptance for e-mail security by the majority of users.

In real world scenarios hybrid solutions with a central but usually small number of secure e-mail clients will dominate. This approach combines the advantages of client and gateway based e-mail security.

References

[CND+98]   Callas, J. et al.: OpenPGP Message Format, (RFC 2440), Then Internet Society, 1998

[PhPW02]   Philipp, Andreas, Pohlmann, Norbert, Weiss Bernhard: Security Gateway – Plattform zur Absicherung von Unternehmensnetzen. In "Enterprise Security", Editor: Patrick Horster, IT Verlag, 2002

[Pohl03]   Pohlmann, Norbert: Die virtuelle Poststelle. In IT-Sicherheit im verteilten Chaos, Editor: Bundesamt für Sicherheit in der Informationstechnik, SecuMedia Verlag, 2003

[Rams99]   Ramsdell, B.: S/MIME Version 3 Certificate Handling, (RFC 2632), The Internet Society, 1999

ArchiSig in Health Care

Thomas Gitter[1] · Tobias Gondrom[2]

[1]T-Systems, Vienna, Austria,
Thomas.Gitter@t-systems.at

[2]IXOS Software AG, Grasbrunn/Munich, Germany,
Tobias.Gondrom@ixos.de

ArchiSig in Health Care – workflow with electronically signed documents and long-term provability of the legality of the signatures – a case study

Within the scope of the project "ArchiSig" (www.archisig.de, supported by the German Federal Ministry of Economics and Technology (VERNET program) under the number 01MS121) a solution for the handling of digitally signed documents in a workflow in health care is implemented as an example to proof the feasibility of the concept for secure and long-term storage of high volumes of digitally signed documents for scenarios in the public sector generally.

The documents are produced in a SAP environment, signed by various persons and stored securely in a Document Management System for long-term (30 years +) storage and retrieval. The signing of the documents and the workflow are implemented as well as the support of a cost-efficient way to preserve the legality of the signatures of the documents for an unlimited amount of time for high document volumes.

1 Problems and Objectives / Situation

Day by day in the health care business thousands of signed documents are produced, sent from doctor to doctor, from doctor to GP, or are just signed to document the approval of various persons in some kind of workflow. In most cases these signatures convert some paper into a document with significant relevancy in law-cases. To build a bridge from the today mostly manually signed documents in health-care to digitally signed documents various problems have to be overcome. ArchiSig is especially addressing the problem that many of these documents have a relevancy for law-cases for an unlimited amount of time (in some cases even for durations equal to the life-span of the medical treated patient).

Normal paper documents are quite easily to be stored for long terms and even after 50 years the validity of the manual signature can be proofed with an acceptable amount of effort. With digital documents this differs in multiple ways. The storage of a huge amount of valuable documents makes it necessary to use a high quality archive (with intelligent mechanisms to support the storage of the documents for such long periods of time. With the knowledge how to migrate the documents, let's say once per decade from one media to the next and the necessary expertise to guarantee stability and availability for an unlimited time span). In addition, if no further steps are taken one can not expect that it is possible to proof that the signature was really applied by the person named in the certificate after 30+ years. E.g. the key length might no longer be sufficient to guarantee that the signature is genuine. Or new algorithms, new mathematical concepts might arise that cause one or more of the algorithms used in the digital

S. Paulus, N. Pohlmann, H. Reimer (Editors): Securing Electronic Business Processes, Vieweg (2004), 176-181

signature loose their security suitability. In these cases the German Signature Law states that the signatures have to be renewed before this happens by applying a new signature with adequate hash-algorithms and PK-algorithms according to the publications of the Regulatory Authority for Telecommunications and Post (RegTP). (In some countries the specific signature laws state that a renewal must even be done before the user certificate expires. This more often needed renewal can also be realized in an efficient way with the ArchiSig concept.)

So unlike the manually signed paper document the digitally signed document cannot remain uncared once it is created and signed. On the contrary an electronic archive has to constantly watch over the various algorithms and apply new signatures from time to time to conserve the reliability of the documents.

Summarizing the following requirements derive from the use of digital signed documents in the health-care business:

- Conformance with the German Signature Law (SigG)
- Conservation of provability for an unlimited time
- Economic aspects (not one timestamp for every single renewal of each document)
- Performance (access documents as seldom as possible, huge volumes, on different media, etc.).

2 Scenario:

The overall scenario consists of a workflow modeled in SAP (ISH and IS-H*Med) and the high performance archive from IXOS. The SAP workflow uses the documented Interface SSF and an enhanced library from Secude Informationssysteme GmbH for the mechanisms to sign and verify the documents and enrich them with various verification data (e.g. OCSP responses, certificate chains, etc.).

Within the pilot department at the University Clinic of Heidelberg, Germany, dismissal letters are matter to digital signature and secure long-term archiving. The documents are created partly by physicians themselves, partly by transcriptionists following analogues dictation. By standard means of the HIS (Hospital Information System) IS-H*MED a dedicated document-cycle is customized covering the complete cycle of the documents from their initiation to archiving. By using a status network workloads are generated for the different groups of employees and the chief of the department, respectively.

The transition between several statuses requires the application of a digital signature. The dismissal letter to be signed is being transformed into pdf – Format and displayed for verification. Digital signature is applied using a SAP – function-pool for communication with the client-based library from Secude Informationssysteme GmbH. Standard formats as PKCS7 are used for attached signature – integration and hash algorithms, respectively. The user is not forced into a second application, all functions are integrated in the HIS user-interface.

Similarly the validity of signatures can be proofed with the signer(s) being displayed within the application.

Later changes or additions require the initiation of a document version.

After the intended signature-chain has been applied, documents are released for archiving. On retrieval the IXOS-eCONserver returns the signed documents in the originally archived format using the SAP-certified interface http content-server. On request, the IXOS-eCONserver provides the Archive Time Stamps for validation.

After the workflow is completed the signed documents are stored in the IXOS eCONserver. The eCONserver guarantees the easy availability and handling of the documents for an unlimited time span and the conservation of the provability of the signatures on these documents strictly conform with the German Signature Law (SigG) by applying ArchiveTimeStamps.

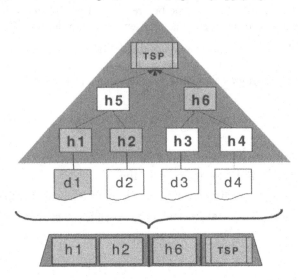

Fig.1: Hashtree and reduced hastree

From an economic view the renewal of signatures of documents using one timestamp for each document is quite expensive. For this ArchiSig introduces the ArchiSig-ArchiveTimeStamp that signs the mother knot of a tree of hash values of documents.

By using this construct we can reduce the need for timestamps extremely to e.g. one per day.

3 Renewal

We have to consider two cases of renewal:

3.1 Renewal of Timestamps

If one of the algorithms used in the timestamps can no longer provide the needed security (e.g. if the PK-algorithm can be broken by new mathematical concepts) it is necessary to renew all timestamps at the mother knot of the hashtrees in the archive. For this it is not necessary to load the documents themselves from the media and to calculate new has-values from them. You can simply build a hashvalue from the timestamp at the mother knot and put this in a new hashtree that can be signed.

3.2 Renewal of Hashtrees

If the hash algorithm with which the hashtree is built (the hashvalues of the leaves of the tree and the next level of the knots of the tree) is no longer reliable, one has to renew the complete hashtrees. This can be a quite expensive task but we expect it will happen much more seldom than the "Timestamp-renewal", if at all.

From the point of view of a document the hashtrees have to be reduced to provide the current ArchiSig-ArchiveTimeStamp and the document has to be accessed and a new hashvalue (with a new hash algorithm) has to be calculated consisting of the document and this current ArchiSig-ArchiveTimeStamp.

4 Format

The ArchiSig-ArchiveTimeStamp will be provided at first as an additional file in ASN.1.

In the future other formats e.g, XML can also easily be implemented.

The ArchiSig-ArchiveTimeStamp is retrieved by an extra ArchiveLink call from the archive and can be sent together with the document e.g. to an library for verification or to lawyers and judges for verification by external reviewers.

5 Solution

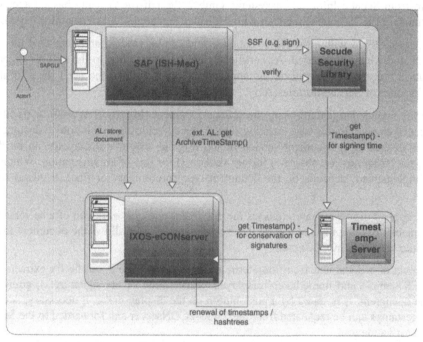

Fig.2: Application architecture:
SAP(IS-H*MED), IXOS-eCONserver, Secude Security Library, Timestamp server

In the solution as implemented at ArchiSig the various components of SAP (IS-H*Med, the Security Library of Secude, an Timestamp-Server and the IXOS-eCONserver play together.

Integrity of medical documents in common is provided by the means of the HIS application even without secure digital signatures. For long term archiving and conformity with legal issues, however, these documents had to be printed, manually signed and archived either as paper or by microfilming or scanning. To get rid of the media-breaks secure digital signatures have to be applied and long term archiving becomes crucial not only with the goal of reduction of on-line data-volume but for legal reasons.

A dismissal letter for an inpatient on a medical ward contains information on the diagnoses and therapy of the patient and usually interactively selected summaries of important reports on diagnostic or therapeutic procedures. For generating these letters, IS-H*MED offers a structured reporting tool and the in-place integration of Word®, Microsoft corp., respectively. At the pilot – department the latter method is in use.

A single document usually undergoes several steps of dictation, transcription and correction. Multiple persons may be involved. Following the default-process a dismissal letter has to be signed by the so-called assistant doctor, is then being read and signed by the "Oberarzt" and finally is seen by the chief of the department. Only letters with 3 signatures are supposed to leave the department. Both the "Oberarzt" and the chief may apply changes and additions to the letter. This requires a complex status-network that is dedicated to a special type of documentation. Some transitions from one status to the next are linked to the mandatory need for a digital signature. In attempting to move along the status network, the document is being displayed as a pdf-file by the means of in-place AcrobatReader® and the user is prompted to insert his/her personal signature-card and enter the PIN.

Using a RFC – communication between the client-server-based HIS and the locally installed software from Secude Informationssysteme GmbH, the pdf-file is being hashed and packed into a standard PKCS7 object together with dedicated signature- and signer-information.

This object is stored within the HIS – database and can be verified and displayed for review wherever and whenever needed. As certificates are being attached to the PKCS7 object, the verification process can be run on the application server without the need for a locally installed instance of Secude-libraries, too.

During the intended signature-chain the source document (Microsoft Word® or rtf-file) can be matter of change. In this case, existing signed objects referring to this source document can either be deleted or a document-version of the original source – document can be drawn, keeping the (from now on obsolete) former version(s) for line of argumentation. Which process is implemented, depends on the document-type (preliminary or final dismissal reports, e.g.).

The last applied digital signature pushes the document onto the workload of a secretary, who is responsible for shipping and setting the "release-status", that allows the document to be archived into the IXOS-eCONserver.

On retrieval of a document from long-term archive, the pdf-file is on the fly extracted from the PKCS7 object and immediately displayed. Verification of the signature(s), going along with the document, is initiated by a push-button on the display-mask. If necessary, additional hash-timestamps can be requested from the IXOS-eCONserver and forwarded to the Secude – libraries for validation.

Documents (containing their signatures and verification data like e.g. certificates) are stored in the IXOS-eCONserver. After a customizable time (e.g. daily) a first initial ArchiveTimeStamp is applied to all freshly archived documents. This initial ArchiveTimeStamp makes it possible to unify the handling of the various used signatures from documents from unlimited (and maybe even unknown) sources with possibly different algorithms and variations.

With that uniform anchor all documents stored can be handled and their signatures conserved based on the known parameters without inspecting every individual signature at the document for it parameters.

Thus the verification of the signatures within the documents runs in 2 sequences. First the point in time is evaluated up to which the signatures in the document were valid (you could rely on their algorithms). Secondly using the ArchiveTimeStamp it can be proofed that the document and all applied signatures existed before that point in time and were not changed from then on. As the archive has a unified view and mechanism for all signed documents the

ArchiveTimeStamps have of course to fulfill the highest security requirements to not lower the value of signatures at some of the archived documents. For this reason we chose to use qualified signatures from an accredited Supplier for the ArchiSig-ArchiveTimeStamps. As the archive does not need to inspect the documents to conserve their signatures, the documents can of course also be stored encrypted so that high levels of confidentiality can be achieved.

6 Outlook

With this project the feasibility and usefulness of the concept for the conservation of electronically signed documents could be proven and demonstrated in a realistic workflow environment.

Meanwhile, the use of electronic workflows and archives is quite widespread for documents that are not electronically signed. For electronically signed documents it is important, if not critical, that we can store them for an unlimited amount of time without loosing the provability of the applied digital signatures. As long as this could not be guaranteed and demonstrated, many scenarios could not fully move from the normal paper workflow to an electronic workflow. The results now open the door for the use of electronically signed documents instead of paper documents in many new cases.

These can be scenarios from nearly any eGovernment, health care, and other processes that are dependent on electronically signed documents.

References

Brandner, R. / Fischer-Dieskau, S. / Lauer, S. / Pordesch, U. / Tielemann, M.: Integration notwendiger Verifikationsdaten in signierte Dokumente, Anforderungen und konzeptioneller Ansatz. In: ArchiSig-Arbeitspapier.

Brandner, R. / Pordesch, U. / Rossnagel, A. / Schachermaier: Langzeitsicherung qualifizierter elektronischer Signaturen. In DuD 2/2002.

RFC 3369: Cryptographic Message Syntax (CMS). In: Network Working, RFC 3369, 2002.

Frye, C. / Pordesch, U.: Berücksichtigung der Sicherheitseignung von Algorithmen qualifizierter Signaturen. In: DuD 2/2003, 73-78.

Brandner, R. / Pordesch, U.: Longterm conservation of provability of electronically signed documents. In: ISSE 2002

Rossnagel, A. / Hammer, V.: Kommentierung des § 18 SigV 1997. Roßnagel: Recht der Multimediadienste, 1999 ff.

Roßnagel, A.: Kommentierung des § 5 SigG: Roßnagel: Recht der Multimediadienste, 1999 ff.

Rossnagel, A.: Das neue Recht elektronischer Signaturen - Neufassung des Signaturgesetzes und Änderungen des BGB und der ZPO. In: Neue Juristische Wochenzeitschrift 2001; 25/2001: 1817-88.

SigG: Gesetz über Rahmenbedingungen für elektronische Signaturen und zur Änderung weiterer Vorschriften. Bundesgesetzblatt Teil I 22: 876-84.

SigI: Bundesamt für die Sicherheit in der Informationstechnik (BSI): Signaturinteroperabilitätsspezifikationen, Abschnitt B5 Mehrfachsignaturen / Erneute Signatur, Version 1.2, 30.8.1999.

SigV: Verordnung zur elektronischen Signatur Entwurfs-Fassung zur Notifizierung aufgrund der Richtlinie 98/34/EG, August 2001

Practice

ChamberSign Bridge CA

Maike Bielfeldt

ChamberSign aisbl
Bielfeldt@chambersign.com

Abstract

ChamberSign a.i.s.b.l. (international non Profit Association) is an initiative set up by Chambers of Commerce with the aim to create a comprehensive architecture for secure business-to-business electronic commerce across international borders. The ChamberSign focus is to promote and enable the digital signature technology, making it widely available to the business community and achieving international recognition and interoperability.

With Certificate Authority's in nine different countries throughout Europe issuing digital certificates to its members, ChamberSign. has implemented a Bridge CA. The solution is an initiative set up by Chambers of Commerce with the aim to create a comprehensive architecture for secure business-to-business electronic commerce across international borders. The ChamberSign focus is to promote and enable the digital signature technology, making it widely available to the business community and achieving international recognition and interoperability. Today with various CA infrastructures available in each member country, the ChamberSign Bridge CA is the approach to meet the objectives.

1 Background

The European Chambers of Commerce and Industry, EuroChambres[1], founded the association "Chambersign"[2] in July of 1999 to promote and support the distribution of the digital signature and the development of applications within an international context. Its current member countries are *Austria, Belgium, France, Germany, Italy, Luxembourg, the Netherlands, Spain, Sweden and the United Kingdom*[3]. Thus, ChamberSign´s main focus is international with a main emphasis on European projects regarding the acceptance and usage of the qualified digital signature application.

ChamberSign is currently the political framework and organisation to support the Study on legal and market aspects of the application of Directive laying down a Community framework for electronic signatures and on the practical applications of the electronic signature. ChamberSign's approach is by setting up an international network of registration authorities in all membership countries to allow for easy access to the qualified digital signature according to the EU Directive 1999/93/EC based on common standards.

---

[1] http://www.eurochambres.be

[2] http://www.chambersign.com

[3] Represented by the Wirtschaftskammer Österreich, the Federation Nationale des Chambres de Comerce et D'Industrie de Belgique/Nationale Federatie der Kamers voor Handel en Nijverheid van Belgie, the Assemblee des Chambres Françaises de Commerce et D'Industrie, the Deutscher Industrie- und Handelskammertag (DIHK), the Unione Italiana delle Camere di Commercio, Industria Artigianato e Agricoltura, the Chambre de Commerce du Grand-Duché de Luxembourg, the Consejo Superior de Camaras de Comercio, Industria y Navigacion de España, the Svenska Handelskammarförbundet, and the British Chambers of Commerce.

S. Paulus, N. Pohlmann, H. Reimer (Editors): Securing Electronic Business Processes, Vieweg (2004), 185-190

At this point, the Eurochambres organisation represents 36 national Chamber Organisations, 1,500 regional and local Chambers of Commerce and Industry, thus 15 million enterprises, most of which are SMEs. Thus, the impact ChamberSign has both on a European, but also on a global level will allow for standard-setting regarding the digital signature application. Since interoperability is one of the key for the acceptance of the digital signature in the future, ChamberSign's approach by setting-up this project tackles the wide acceptance and diffusion of digital signature applications throughout various applications.

2 ChamberSign and the EU Directive 1999/93/EC on Electronic Signature

The EU Directive 1999/93/EC goes to great length demonstrating the benefits of the digital signature for European eBusiness and eCommerce. The Directive itself is meant to facilitate the use and acceptance of the digital signature within the EU and beyond national borders. It is particularly aimed at levelling the divergent rules and regulations of every EU member state. The EU Directive, thus, tries to establish international standards that eventually will be adopted into national law by each member state to avoid meeting obstacles in international online business. It is a measure to support the free flow of goods and services within Europe. Thus, interoperability is a major objective of the Directive. It is aimed at enabling every participant in the global market to act within just that market. Thus, the Directive supports any effort that is aimed at improving the online business relationship between international companies and calling for standardisation and common security standards. While the EU Directive was written with the European business partners in mind, it cannot stop right there but is reaching out to other nations as well. For all players, both in the EU and the member candidate countries, it is of utmost importance to work within a framework of common laws and practices.

ChamberSign, aims to put the ideas expressed in the Directive into practice by offering its members a digital signature application that ensures interoperability starting with its member states and meets the EU Directive's very high safety standards.

3 The ChamberSign a.i.s.b.l. Approach and Objective

With Certificate Authority's in nine different countries throughout Europe issuing digital certificates to its members, ChamberSign. has implemented a Bridge CA. The solution is an initiative set up by Chambers of Commerce with the aim to create a comprehensive architecture for secure business-to-business electronic commerce across international borders. The ChamberSign focus is to promote and enable the digital signature technology, making it widely available to the business community and achieving international recognition and interoperability. Today with various CA infrastructures available in each member country, the ChamberSign Bridge CA is the approach to meet the objectives.

The Bridge CA project has been running since 2002, assessing solutions appropriate for ChamberSign to meet the defined aim. As the last phase of the project, ScandTrust AB was assigned the responsibility to be the supplier of the technical solution in the beginning of 2003.

3.1 PKI Concepts

Today most countries around the world have adopted the PKI concept both legally and in practice. As for Europe the European parliament presented a directive to implement a community framework for electronic signatures 1999 that now has been adopted by each country within the European Union.

Public Key Infrastructure (PKI) is a solution based on the innovation of public key encryption that makes it s possible to sign and encrypt without a shared secret. In the PKI environment certificate authorities (CA) are the trusted entities that issue certificates and provide status information about the certificates the CA has issued. To implement a PKI environment, three models are used:

The basic implementation of PKI is a single CA responsible for all PKI services; including issuing and revoking certificates, providing certificate status information, etc. This implementation results in a single user trust point, the CA's public key.

The hierarchical PKI configuration involves a superior-subordinate CA relationship, where all users trust the same "root" CA. In this configuration the "root" CA does not issue certificates to users, instead certificates are issued to subordinate CAs. These CAs issue certificates to users or another level of subordinate CAs.

Another configuration of PKI is to connect single CAs with a peer-to-peer relationship, defined as a mesh PKI. This require that each CA goes through a cross certification, where a cross certificate is issued by one CA which contains a CA signature key used for issuing certificates. The result is a certificate trusted within one CA in the mesh, also is trusted in another CA within the same mesh.

The implementation of PKI and the configuration used is dependent on the community it is supposed to operate in. As the single CA is the easiest, it may be used in a closed environment. The hierarchical CA provides scalability where several subordinate CAs can manage end users. With a mesh configuration the bi-directional trust relationship is established between each CA in the mesh.

3.2 Bridge CA Concept

The basic question that needs an answer for all PKI configurations is: "What is the easiest way for me to trust a message signed or encrypted by a user". As you move from an internal environment to a global, all configurations mentioned above turn out to be too isolated or too complicated. With this experience in mind, the development of the Bridge CA concept has turned out as a new dimension of PKI.

The implementation of a Bridge CA can be described as a mesh configuration with a hub or a hierarchical configuration with an established external relationship. One difference is that a Bridge CA does not issue certificates directly to users, neither is it intended to be used as a trust point by the users of the PKI. Instead the trust relationship is configured as a star to be a "bridge of trust", where the Bridge CA is the centre of trust in the community.

3.3 Technical Features

A Bridge CA can be implemented based on two different approaches:

- A Bridge CA that actually issues certificates for other CAs.

- A Bridge CA that doesn't issue any certificates at all. Instead it provides a list of trusted CAs.

The ChamberSign Bridge CA is built around the first approach, where each CA approved by the Bridge is known as the "Principle CA". After approval the Principle CA certificate is signed by the Bridge CA public key and is available at the ChamberSign Bridge CA website.

The main limitation of a Bridge CA is that users of the Bridge CA must perform active steps in terms of configuration and software set-up in order to make use of Bridge certificates. This is the case for organisations that will use the Bridge CA for the services offered, because the ChambersSign Bridge CA root is not a trusted root in any application. For end users no configuration is needed or required, as the origin certificate chain will maintain valid as long as it has not been revoked.

4 Who can Become an Authorized Issuer?

Only Chambers of Commerce organizations may act in the role of authorized issuer. Only after being authorized by the ChamberSign Policy Authority, following successful completion of a compliance audit, certificates may be issued. Additionally, the issuer needs to enter into an agreement with the ChamberSign Policy Authority. The authorized issuer may subcontract services and obligations to certificate manufacturers (CM) and registration authorities (RA).

Since the issuer remains finally responsible, the RA and CM must be bound to all obligations concerning registration, identifications, and authentication functions policy as well as certification manufacturing and repository functions through a suitable contract with the issuer.

ChamberSign Qualified Certificates are only issued together with a Secure Signature Creation Device (e.g. a smart card or other secure storage conforming to Annex III of the EU Directive). The certificate issued shall only be used to support "qualified electronic signatures". Such signatures will then "satisfy the requirements of a signature in relation to data in electronic form in the same manner as a hand-written signature satisfies those requirements in relation to paper based data", as specified in article 5.1 of the EU directive or other international laws.

The chosen CA who serves as one of many, or the only issuer of certificates needs to respond to the following legal requirements as spelled out in the European directive. This regards data protection, the technical and organizational measures taken to protect the data from unauthorized access, from accidental loss and destruction. All information needs to be completely protected from illegal and unintended disclosure.

4.1 Rules and Regulations

The CA is required to operate under non-discriminatory policies and procedures, has to be a legal entity, has implemented a system(s) for quality and information security management, and has made adequate arrangements to cover liabilities, that is to bear the risk of liability for damages. It needs to prove financial stability and has to have the resources to guarantee due processes. It has to employ enough sufficiently trained personnel, has policies and procedures implemented for the resolution of complaints and disputes and it properly has documented agreements and contractual relationship in place where services involve subcontracting, outsourcing and other third party arrangements and, finally, it must have no known record of prior intentional wrongdoing or legal problems.

The CA must have a management system in place for certificate generation and revocation management. The members of this system need to be independent of other organizations. In particular, its senior executive, as well as senior staff in trusted roles, must be independent and free from commercial, financial and other pressures and should set up impartial structures.

4.2 Liability

In regard to liability, issuers can limit their liability by providing a liability cap per transaction. This limitation of liability must be clearly mentioned in all certificates issued by the issuer, but it cannot under any circumstance be an amount smaller than € 37.000. Thus, issuers – in co-operation with RAs – must take out an insurance policy to cover the liability risk throughout the entire registration and certification period. It is recommended to cover liability of RA and CA in one policy. The issuer shall obtain and maintain insurance coverage of at least €1 million for this purpose.

The CA must make available to subscribers terms and conditions of use of the certificate, limitations on its use, subscribers' obligations, information on how to validate the certificate, including requirements to check the revocation status of the certificate, so that the relying party can reasonably rely on the certificate, limitations of liability, the period of time which registration information is retained, etc.

The CA shall ensure that certificates are made available as necessary to subscribers and relying parties. All information regarding that and other aspects has to be promptly published in the repository which shall be available at no cost for reading access to subscribers and relying parties.

4.3 The Mandatory Audit

Before initial approval, an authorized issuer, the CA, shall submit to a compliance audit. The audit needs to be performed by an independent recognized security auditor which needs to be approved by the ChamberSign Policy Authority and has to ensure the quality of the issuer services, compliance with the policy and all the requirements.

The application is based on personal presence of the subscriber to be identified by the RA officers. Identification and authentication rely on those data, regarding personal information. A procedure for renewal, re-key, revocations and updates needs to be in place.

4.4 Operational Requirements

The CA together with the local Chamber of Commerce registration authorities shall ensure that subscribers are properly identified and authenticated; and that subscriber certificate requests are complete, accurate and duly authorized. The data submitted for identification needs to be accompanied by proper evidence such as passports or other proper national IDs. Such records need to be archived for a period of time for the purpose of providing evidence of certification in legal proceedings.

The security audit procedures need to be in place and properly described.

An archival system needs to be established which has to be protected and accompanied by an archive backup system. Rules and regulation regarding disaster management as well as CA termination must be established. Physical, procedural and personnel security controls must be in place before the mandatory audit.

5 The Future

The Bridge CA model is today a very interesting approach that has been given a lot of attention lately. Several projects at different places around the world are in progress, where some of them are still in a test phase while others are ready for operational use. The next critical step to ensure the success is incorporation of the bridge functionality into products, especially the use of Commercial-off-the-shelf products. Then the Bridge CA functionality is likely to be both efficient and effective, providing a means of working across borders in a global enterprise environment.

The ChamberSign Bridge CA has accomplished a proof of the Bridge CA concept, where both the organizational network and the technical infrastructure is in place. There is already software available that provides the use of Bridge functionality, like Microsoft Explorer. We now need business processes to adopt the use of digital certificates as a competitive advantage and to teach users to be aware of the strength that digital certificates provide.

With ChamberSign as an organisation represented throughout Europe with a focus to promote and enable the digital signature technology, a critical success factor is now in place.

References

Directive 1999/93/EC of the European Parliament and of the Council, of 13 December 1999, On a Community framework for electronic signatures.

Request for Comments: 2459, Internet X.509 Public Key Infrastructure, Certificate and CRL Profile, January 1999.

Bridge Certification Authorities: Connecting B2B Public Key Infrastructures, William T. Polk and Nelson E. Hastings, National Institute of Standards and Technology.

Public Key Infrastructure Interoperability: Tools and Concepts, Kenneth D. Stillson.

Another dimension of PKI – ChamberSign Bridge CA, John Wallhoff (CISA, CISSP), September 2, 2003 (www.scillani.se)

Secure Collaboration Platform for Notaries

Dr. Erwin Haller

GFT Technologies AG
erwin.haller@gft.com

Summary

Confidentiality and authenticity are key requirements in many eGovernment scenarios. GFT Iberia has developed a secure collaboration platform for the General Notaries Council of Spain (GNCS) based on a Public Key Infrastructure (PKI). Based on 2-factor authentication with chip cards and an intuitive webmail, client notaries may encrypt and sign documents and transactions in full compliance with the legal requirements. This contribution covers both technological and business aspects.

1 Context

Information exchange is a basic pattern in every business scenario. Unauthorized or fraudulent access to such information by internal or external intruders constitutes an inherent risk. Such risks are assessed and rated in the usual way according to their potential impact and their probability to occur.

Table 1: Risk mitigation services

Confidentiality	ensures that the information is accessible only by intended parties
Authentication	ensures that all intended parties can be properly identified
Integrity	ensures that no one can modify the message without all parties being aware of change or destruction.
Non Repudiation	ensures that neither the sender nor the receiver of the information be able to deny the sending or receiving of the message

While this has already been a challenge in classical scenarios with paper based documents, electronic information exchange based on the Internet (e-Mail) allows a much more systematic and reliable handling of these issues. Due to its ubiquity, effectiveness, and ease-of-use e-Mail has established itself as a mission-critical core service in most businesses.

E-Mail interchange in its basic incarnation is, however, not a secure transport mechanism. All flaws known from classical mail traffic can also occur. There are mechanisms available to avoid these flaws but they are often cumbersome and difficult to use. They require a certain level of understanding and awareness and also discipline and diligence when using them. A key requirement in this project was to offer an e-Mail platform that supports a high level of security by default and in a very intuitive and comfortable way.

S. Paulus, N. Pohlmann, H. Reimer (Editors): Securing Electronic Business Processes, Vieweg (2004), 191-196

2 Legal and Political Environment

Several national and European-wide laws and directions address the issue of secure e-Mail and digital signatures. Compliance with them is non-trivial due to the fact that they leave more room for (conflicting) interpretation than we would have liked:

- Electronic Signatures Directive 1999/93/CE of the European Parliament defining an European framework for digital signatures
- Spanish Real Decreto-Ley 14/1999, 17 September, on digital signatures
- Spanish Orden Ministerial 21 February, 2000, approving the regulations of certification services providers accreditation and some digital signature products certification
- Spanish Law 24/2001, 27 September, section 8.a, on advanced digital signatures use by Notaries

It is important to note that the last guideline directly addresses the community of Notaries and is mandatory for them. Based on this, GNCS defined a set of certification practices to address some specific certificate requirements which run under the label FEAN (Firma Electrónica Avanzada Notarial).

3 Specific Requirements

The customer GNCS has declared this project as mission critical and has added a list of specific requirements and constraints:

1. A corporate e-Mail platform already exists
2. Current investments must be protected
3. e-Mail users work from various changing workplaces at different geographies
4. Internet access is available at all locations
5. Information exchange with other communities using digital signature is required
6. The existing e-Mail platform currently supports 3,000 users, all of them with digital signing capabilities
7. The solution must be easy to use for non-technical users like notaries

As a consequence of requirements 3) and 4) the usage of smartcards seemed to be an obvious option. This implies the availability of specific hardware on all workstations in order to digitally sign the message. As the cost of desktop card reader software is decreasing and is available from many computer stores for the users to purchase themselves, this would not affect the overall budget of the implementation. To go beyond the current e-mail accessibility, it had been decided to go with native web clients as the e-Mail client platform.

4 Solution

4.1 Functionalities

Secure information exchange is accomplished based on asymmetrical encryption and a Public Key Infrastructure (PKI). A PKI is a framework to develop and manage secure applications on an insecure platform like, e.g., the Internet. Core elements of a PKI are public and private keys which are issued by a Certification Authority (CA) to individuals and organizations. The distribution follows established patterns. Mail exchange is based on the S/MIME (Secure/Multipurpose Internet Mail Extensions) standard. With the availability of public keys and private keys of both sender and receiver the above mentioned services are realized as follows.

Table 2: Realization of risk mitigation services

Confidentiality	The message is encrypted by the sender with the public key of the receiver and decrypted by the receiver with his own private key.
Authentication	The message is encrypted with the private key of the sender and decrypted by the receiver with the sender's public key.
Integrity	Server-side access logging as well as the generation of a hash value from the original message and transmitting it as part of the message allows for validating the integrity.
Non Repudiation	Verification of the identity of the author ("signer") of a message and server-side logging of all participants in a communication.

4.2 Solution for GNCS: S-WebMail

Secure WebMail or S-WebMail is a complete electronic web mail system with components to support confidentiality and reliable accessibility on the Internet.

Functionalities included in S-WebMail solution are the same that are usually provided by any other WebMail solution plus some added values such as digital signature and privacy. Each one provides interesting business value per se, but their combination (digital signature and privacy) is mandatory for guaranteeing a fully legal compliant secure e-Mail solution. Use of the value added features is an option for the user, as not all usage scenarios require signing or encryption. Another relevant feature is platform independence as explained below.

The solution presented here has been integrated into the e-not@rio framework of GNCS. e-not@rio is the standard IT platform for all notaries in Spain. Access to S-WebMail is only allowed within the e-not@rio platform. Its deployment and rapid acceptance corroborate the relevance and importance of secure applications in governmental institutions.

4.2.1 S-WebMail Digital Signature

Signing e-mails is the first and basic PKI functionality accessible with S-WebMail. With this feature, GNCS public governmental organizations are able to legally and formally sign the contents which they send to third parties.

From a legal perspective, the signature has the same value and implications as an ordinary paper-based signature. The private key of the GNCS member is used. To guarantee secure access, this private key is stored on a smartcard which is issued to every GNCS member. Smartcards are personal and cannot be transferred. They obey the same policies like credit cards or personal identification documents. Digital signatures included in mails can be checked using the public key of the sender. GNCS uses certificates which are issued by a governmental CA. Digitally signed documents can also be sent to external receivers as they don't require a smartcard to decrypt it.

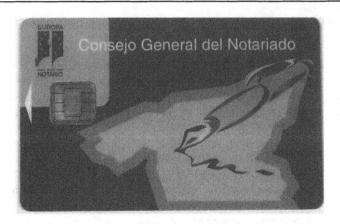

Fig. 1: e-Not@rio Smart-card

4.2.2 S-WebMail Privacy

Privacy required by GNCS is obtained applying PKI encryption to the messages sent using S-WebMail. For this purpose the public key of the receiver is used. Decryption is only possible by the receiver with his private key.

4.2.3 S-WebMail Client Security Assurance

Knowingly, the client machine is always the weak link in such a system. S-Webmail allows the Notarios to have more control over the client as it is a standard browser and the standard for all modern browsers is not to save encrypted pages to disk which would allow that mail messages are not saved to the client machine unless the user specifically requests that it be. This is true for most uses without regard for forensic applications which can search for retained information and the possibility of disk caching of memory.

4.2.4 S-WebMail Server Security Assurance

The server side of S-Webmail has been established in a secure perimeter network with only the required network access of the HTTPS protocol port 443. Security is tested quarterly by professional security testers and all operating system and application patches are managed by a full-time administrator. While white-listing of particular IP addresses is not possible here because of the required ubiquitous access, in other implementations it would lend an additional security layer to authentication and authorization.

4.2.5 S-WebMail Architecture

An important characteristic of this solution is its platform independence. This feature applies to every element of the architecture. The core components of the solution are based on Java and J2EE. Extensions and supporting components are leveraging established standards like LDAP, SMTP or IMAP which are also platform independent.

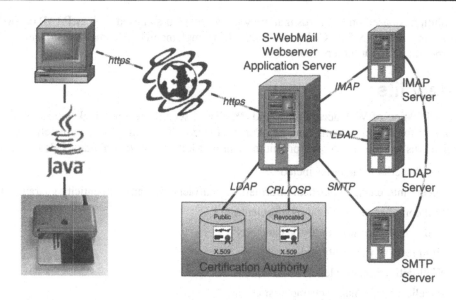

Fig. 2: Basic architecture

The basic architecture of the S-WebMail solution is depicted in figure 2. A particular focus has been put to the usability of the solution. Therefore, all functions can be accessed by standard web browsers. The server code is implemented according to the J2EE standard.

HTTPS has been chosen as the protocol for communication with the servers. On each client workstation a Smartcard adapter is available. In order to access the Smartcard information via the Smartcard adapter, a signed applet is used. A Java Runtime Environment (JRE) is required to be available as plug-in for the web browser to access Smartcard private key of the user if required.

The S-WebMail server logic has been implemented in a Unix architecture taking advantage of Apache as web server and Tomcat as application server. Any other server architecture that guarantees J2EE compliance could also be used.

An LDAP server is available in the S-WebMail architecture as a repository for X.509 certificates of the system users. Additionally, access to a CRL / OCSP server is needed to check during run-time potential revocation of the stored certificates (2-factor authentication). This information is provided by a trusted CA.

An IMAP and an SMTP server are used to send and receive the e-mail messages.

Confidentiality of information is assured since no visible or decrypted e-mail is transmitted at any point in the network. Only final clients have local access to the decrypted or plain electronic message. Authenticity is provided by the smartcard device. Smartcards are created, certified and delivered by a trusted certification authority. In this case FNMT[1], a special CA related with country-specific governmental certifications, was chosen.

Tasks like certification revocation control and digital signature verification are done on the S-WebMail server side. This solution provides a centralized and controllable solution.

---

[1] FNMT: Fabrica Nacional de Moneda y Timbre

The solution is based on standards that are widely accepted and used such as IMAP or SMTP for mailing systems, X.509, CRL and PKCS #7 for implementing PKI mechanism and LDAP for corporate information repository.

5 Benefits

The combination of Web accessibility and PKI based security features makes this solution a true option for e-mail systems running over the Internet. The initial focus on enterprises and organizations was shifted to offer premium secure e-Mail support to individuals also.

The major benefits for notaries include:

- Secure interchange of critical information: confidentiality and authenticity guaranteed
- Full compliance with legal requirements
- Full compliance with industry standards
- High level of flexibility and versatility
- Well-defined service levels
- Excellent performance characteristics
- Role-based access method to authenticate copies
- Availability of document building blocks for pre-defined scenarios
- Scalable architecture that allows for straightforward functional enhancements

The Czech Social Security Smart Card

Jiri Hybl

OKsystem
Prague, Czech Republic
hybl@oksystem.cz

Abstract

The smart card project has been developed as part of the Czech social security IS. It is the first project of its kind to be used by the Czech government. The main aim of this project was to create a security framework within which all the social security offices could use their information systems. 10,000 professional cards and 1,000 client cards have already been issued. The system consists of the card issuing and management centre and the PKI infrastructure, which is made up of the certification authority and the 200 remote registration authorities. The Internet application has been developed to retrieve, complete and sign the social security forms.

Experience gained as well as current situation and plans regarding PKI and smart cards in the social and health sectors in the Czech Republic will be discussed.

1 Social Security IS

The Czech social security information system is based on a partially distributed database system with one central server at the Ministry of Labour and Social Affairs (MoLSA) and about 200 remote databases in local offices. All these systems are connected through a dedicated WAN. The third level is created by smaller remote offices connected with ISDN lines. The purpose of this system is to receive the claims for social benefits from citizens, decide their rightfulness and distribute the financial benefits.

There are six social benefits currently established by the Czech law. Three of them depend on the total family income, thus the checking of other documents is necessary to approve claims. To avoid fraud the social security IS exchanges data with the other ministries' information systems, currently with finance, defense, and interior ministries. The actual sum paid to the client depends on the current value of the living minimum, periodically set by the government. The total volume of benefits distributed yearly exceeds 30 billions CZK (1 billion Euros).

Due to the complexity in the social security system the MoLSA had to overcome many obstacles to fulfil the requirements of the law. The logical outcome was an intensive exploitation of information technology, which had led to the current state. This state can be described as a stable and reliable IT platform with a good growth potential. In comparison with other government's information systems MoLSA holds a position amongst the top performers, for years, with several IT projects of much wider importance and acceptance than only in the social area.

To mention just one, the address registry project (UIR-ADR) created a database comprising all addresses in the Czech Republic. The data is continuously being updated to incorporate all changes. The registry is available for free on CD and accessible on-line as a form-based ap-

S. Paulus, N. Pohlmann, H. Reimer (Editors): Securing Electronic Business Processes, Vieweg (2004), 197-203

plication or as a web service. It has been integrated into many commercial and non-commercial products.

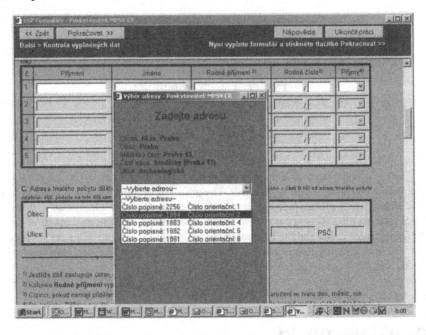

Fig. 1: Populating a web form using data from the address registry (UIR-ADR).

2 Aim of the Project

MoLSA's leadership in adopting state-of-the-art technologies as well as their commitment to data protection led to the decision of building the complete security infrastructure based on PKI and smart cards. The main aim was to fulfil and in some aspects to exceed the requirements of the Czech Personal Data Protection Act [ActP00]. The other important legal document is the Czech Electronic Signature Act [ActS00], which creates a base for using digital signatures in legal relationships.

The first project, which started in 2001, included building the certification authorities of the MoLSA and equipping the clerks with the professional cards and card readers. The aims were two-fold, one to provide a more secure two-factor authentication to the operating system and applications and the second, to involve the non-repudiation principle into the decision process. Securing the e-mail communication between different decision levels and to the other ministries was of great importance.

The second pilot project was aimed at client cards. The primary target was to test the option of using smart cards as an identification tool for social security clients and to provide them with the option to submit claims electronically using the Internet or public kiosks.

The number of client cards was limited to 1,000 and no plans for further deployments of social cards are in place at present. The project was meant as a test bed for technology and logistics; however there are no plans to deploy a social card on a nation-wide scale. Rather its functionality will probably be integrated into some multi-application card. A different situation exists with the professional cards. After the successful completion of the pilot project in 2002 the deployment of cards for all the ministry's employees followed. With 10,000 smart cards issued, the project of professional cards is one of the most important smart card projects in the Czech Republic to date. There are plans to issue next 10,000 cards in 2003.

3 The Infrastructure

The smart cart infrastructure consists of a PKI, a card management system and registration authorities. The in-house certification authority (CA) was established at the ministry. The CA issues authentication/encryption certificates and non-qualified signature certificates. The CA hierarchy includes an off-line root CA and 3 subordinate CAs issuing certificates for users. For the qualified signature certificates the agreement exists with a third-party trust provider. The purpose of the agreement is to include a unique ID number into the qualified certificate, which allows identifying certificate holders in the social security database. The certification servers are based on Microsoft's Certificate Services with some enhancements. The certificates are stored in a database and published via a web interface. The certification service is now being replaced by a more robust and flexible solution (Java engine and a secure cryptographic module).

The card issuing centre uses a thermotransfer card printer and four PC workstations equipped with PC/SC readers to print and personalize smart cards. A database application controls the process and manages information about issued cards. All systems are placed in a secured environment at MoLSA. The capacity of this simple "production line" is about 60 cards per hour, which was sufficient for the initial phase of the project. For the long run however, MoLSA plans to outsource the card personalization.

Registration authorities (RA) were built at 200 offices throughout the country. There are two options: the on-line RA, which checks the data immediately against the central database; and the off-line RA, which only creates the request which is then validated centrally. In both cases the request is sent to the centre by a secure email.

4 The Logistics

At a registration authority the requests for smart cards are created. The registration workplace is equipped by a scanner and a digital camera. The requests from the RAs include applicant's personal data, a photograph and a scanned image of its personal ID card. This data is transformed into the XML format, signed, encrypted and sent to the card management centre. The card management application validates and archives all requests and allows creating production batches based on arbitrary criteria. The personalization begins with printing; the second phase generates two key pairs (on-card key generation), creates certificate requests and finally stores two certificates on the card (authentication/encryption + signature). In the same step other applications can be downloaded. The keys are secured by a randomly generated PIN numbers. These PINs are printed on secure PIN mailers and sent to the users. Cards are then sent to the RAs, where the users collect them.

For the qualified certificates a PC application exists, which allows the card holder to create the certificate request. The request is then delivered to the CA using a diskette. An XML interface between the certification authority and the MoLSA database was designed to enable the CA sending a secure XML query to the MoLSA's database for the unique ID number which is then included into the certificate. The certificate is then downloaded to the card using the application. This process is too complicated for most users, thus improving the integration with the trust provider is one of the issues to be addressed in the future.

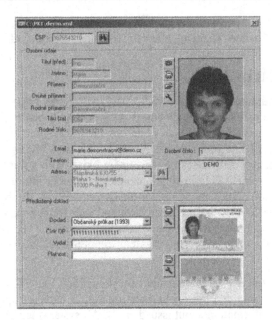

Fig. 2: The registration authority creates a request

5 The Card

The Java Card technology was selected because of its flexibility and portability. Two applets are used in this phase, one for the IAS functionality and the second serving as a data container. The IAS applet works together with a middleware which offers both PKCS#11 and CAPI interfaces for cryptographic functions. The data applet was created to provide a secure data storage with several supported authentication methods including the card verifiable certificates. It allows to authenticate the professional to access (and/or modify) the client card data using the professional card.

Both client and professional cards exploit the same technology and data structure, the difference is only in the stored data (certificates). It allows using the professional card for the same purposes as the client card.

Some of the professional cards are dual-mode cards with a second chip operating in contactless mode (Mifare interface).

To support adding and modifying applets, a card management application was developed to download new applets remotely through a secure channel between the card management database and the user's workstation.

Fig. 3: The card

6 The Applications

The main aim – increased security – has been reached via full use of PKI and smart cards for authentication and data security. The clerk starts his or her work with the authentication to the operating system. MoLSA exploits Windows 2000 and Windows NT. Windows 2000 supports smart card logon by default. For NT systems a special logon module (GINA) was developed to support professional cards. The principle application systems (OKdavky for social security and OKprace for employment offices) were modified to accept professional cards for the strong, two-factor authentication. Administrator can decide if the card or the name-password combination is allowed for the authentication.

The professional and client cards can also be used for authentication at public kiosks and for access to the client's private data held by MoLSA. The card allows to digitally sign electronic forms in the social security applications. The electronic forms are published on the Internet and users (equipped with client card and reader) can create digital signatures on their home computers.

Digital signatures are also used for non-repudiation evidence of the data exchange; the first usage of the professional card is the signed and encrypted request from the RA to the card management centre. Other applications are being modified to use cards for non-repudiation in the social security decision process.

The e-mail communication is secured by digital signatures and encryption using two different certificates and private keys in Microsoft Outlook.

7 Lessons Learnt and Problems to be Solved

The project produced wealth of experience in many aspects. It includes the experience in developing and supporting Java Card applications, personalizing cards, educating IT specialists, coordinating the deployment and managing all other complex processes during the project run. Some problems require changes in the legal and standardization framework to be solved in a proper way.

- The need for a unique identifier of a person is one of the most important issues. The birth number used in most databases is not suitable, because it includes personal data (date of birth and gender). The ID number used in MoLSA's databases solves this problem; however it is not accepted in other information systems. Of course the introducing a new ID for all citizens would evoke many discussions regarding privacy issues.

- Similar questions arise about the content of certificates and dealing with them (publishing). Neither current Czech legal documents nor IT standards specify these issues in detail. Both personal data protection and interoperability are concerned here.

- A national standard is needed for the professional smart card used by all government offices. It would allow wider deployments and ensure interoperability. The discussion about this standard has started already, the first draft was proposed by the Czech Ministry of Informatics (IT). The standard must be based on existing European standards and recommendations.

- As the main obstacle we identified the price of qualified certificates issued by an accredited provider (required for the public administration by the Czech Electronic Signature Act). The certificates from the first Czech accredited provider are unacceptable expensive for large scale deployments (€ 20/1year).

- Defining and enforcing a strong security policy for the Social Security IS is necessary. Public administration reform moved the social security offices to local authorities (municipalities), so the ministry can only "recommend" solutions at present.

- Training and help desk were identified as crucial factors especially during the initial phase of the card deployment.

- The actual number of operations with the issued client cards is very low. Integrating the social application into a multi-application card helps to better use the investments into the technology.

- The Cyberflex Java Card performs excellent, but there are some limits too, especially regarding the available space. 32K is not much memory, if it stores both code and data. The reliability is high, only 2 cards failed (10,000 issued).

8 The Future – Czech Health Insurance Card?

The Project "Implementation of Electronic Identifier as a Health Insurance Client Card" is a two-phase project. It was launched by the Czech General Healthcare Insurance Company at the end of 2002.

The objective of the first (current) phase is the analysis of the potential benefits and risks of the implementation of the electronic identifier with the intention of using it not only in exchange for the current paper card, but also to build an open modern solution based on smart card technology.

The analysis also serves another purpose, which is the design of a solution that could go beyond the health insurance sector and towards fulfilling other governmental department needs, for example social services.

The idea is to design an open solution in both technological and organisational aspects. The smart card infrastructure will be based on published standards for card interface and application interface. This model will enable competition between different hardware and software providers. The organisation structure enables all insurance companies to share the card and cooperate in developing and managing the system.

The basic function will be the identification, but the solution will provide value-added functions aiming at improving quality of healthcare.

This analytical phase will be completed by September 2003 and the Czech General Healthcare Insurance Company will evaluate the results and decide whether or not to continue with the second phase, the implementation.

It is very important for the project to properly position itself within the emerging European smart card system, in order to be compatible with the main European initiatives like eEurope, eEurope Smart Card Charter, and the European Union health insurance card.

It is equally important to analyze similar projects, mainly in Europe, and to utilize the experiences from those projects.

References

[ActP00]   Act No.101/2000 Coll. on Protection of the Personal Data and on Amendments to Some Related Acts, http://www.uoou.cz/eng/101_2000.php3

[ActS00]   Act No.227/2000 Coll. on Electronic Signature, http://mvcr.iol.cz/sbirka/2000/sb068-00.pdf (in Czech)

[OrdS01]   Ordinance of the Government No.304/2001 Coll. Implementing the Act No. 227/2000 Coll. on Electronic Signature, http://mvcr.iol.cz/sbirka/2001/sb117-01.pdf (in Czech)

[OrdP01]   Ordinance of the Personal Data Protection Office No.366/2001 Coll. specifying conditions appointed by §6 and §17 of the Electronic Signature Act and specifying requirements for the electronic signature devices, http://mvcr.iol.cz/sbirka/2001/sb138-01.pdf (in Czech)

The Siemens PKI –
Implementation of PKI Self Services

Dr. Guido von der Heidt

Siemens AG
CIO IS
Suedalle 1
D-85356 Munich, Germany
guido.von_der_heidt@siemens.com

Abstract

The Siemens PKI, a global enterprise PKI with more than 200.000 users and 100.000 smart cards issued world-wide, was started in 1998/99. Deploying a PKI well-organized processes are a key success factor. Entering the second 3 years certificates life cycle in Siemens in 2002 managed re-keying via de-central Local Registration Authorities (LRAs) turned out to be very difficult and cost intensive.

"PKI Self Services" provide web-based smart card and certificate life cycle functions allowing a user to manage the certificates on his/her smart card securely from the desktop without going to an LRA. The paper describes first the challenge, the solution and the business case. The last chapter covers the security and technical architecture of the implementation.

1 Introduction

Siemens is a multi-national electrical engineering corporation with about 400.000 employees in more than 190 countries world-wide. In 1998/1999, Siemens was among the first large corporations to develop and deploy a Public Key Infrastructure (PKI) (see [Glae99]). The Siemens PKI realizes a corporate wide security infrastructure securing internal and external communications and business transactions. With more than 200.000 users today it ranks with the largest enterprise PKIs world-wide. Since 2000 a multi-functional smart card, the "New Corporate ID Card", has been introduced. And currently more than 100.000 Corporate ID Cards with PKI key material have been issued.

Deploying a PKI and Corporate ID Card well-organized processes for rollout and managing the PKI are a key success factor. Having rolled out the PKI and Corporate ID Cards the smart card and certificate life cycle management via de-central Local Registration Authorities (LRAs) turned out to be logistically difficult.

The "PKI Self Services" simplify these PKI processes significantly by providing web-based smart card and certificate life cycle management functions which allow a user to manage the smart card and certificates securely from his/her workplace without going to an LRA.

The paper describes the Siemens PKI, the "Post Issuance Problem", the PKI Self Services solution and the business case. The last chapter covers the architecture and the security of the PKI Self Services implementation.

S. Paulus, N. Pohlmann, H. Reimer (Editors): Securing Electronic Business Processes, Vieweg (2004), 204-209

2 The Siemens PKI

The Siemens PKI started its operation in November 1998 and provides services for employees, business partners and legal entities. The PKI consists of an internal Trust Center for key generation and issuing digital certificates, a world-wide network of Local Registration Authorities (LRAs) and the Siemens Corporate Directory (SCD) publishing the certificates in the Siemens Intranet. The LRAs are responsible for registration and personal identification of the users, issuing the key material on the New Corporate ID Card (smart card) or on floppy disk (soft-key) and certificate management like re-keying and revocation. They are connected with the Trust Center via a secure channel.

The PKI provides multipurpose X.509 certificates and PGP encryption certificates (PGP only soft-keys). By September 2003 205.000 X.509 and 133.000 PGP certificates have been issued through 126 LRAs in 45 countries.

The New Corporate ID Card is a multi-functional smart card covering a cryptographic chip for PKI, a contact less chip for physical access and a magnetic stripe for older access systems, canteen payment etc. By September 2003 more than 100.000 Corporate ID Cards with PKI key material have been issued.

In order to secure electronic business transactions within Siemens and with business partners the Siemens PKI is currently being extended in the project "PKI 2" (see [vdH01]). The major activities of the PKI 2 project are, s. figure 1:

- Introducing dedicated X.509 certificate types for encryption and authentication/signing with the Corporate ID Card as single key bearing medium

- Publishing Siemens certificates and certification revocation lists in an "External Repository" in the Internet

- Development of "PKI Self Services"

In addition to the described PKI for persons and legal entities certification services for web-servers and IPSec gateways have been implemented.

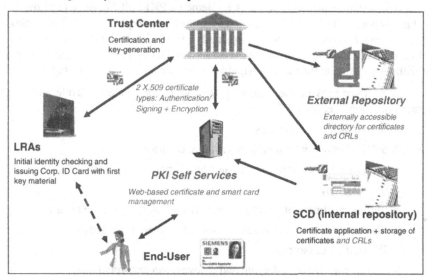

Fig. 1: The Siemens PKI

3 Post Issuance Problem

During the PKI rollout 126 LRAs in 45 countries have been set-up. But, in a highly distributed environment like Siemens with about 650 Production and Research & Development sites and an multitude of additional smaller offices it is not possible to operate an LRA at each site.

Issuing Corporate ID Cards at sites without LRA is handled via courier services or temporary LRAs. These are usually one-time logistic efforts organized by the local IT department.

But, how to manage regular certificate life cycle functions after issuance of a Corporate ID Card? I.e. how to manage

- re-keying of expiring certificates,
- revocation and
- recovery of encryption certificates

at sites without LRA?

Especially, for re-keying when a certificate expires a user has either to visit an LRA at another site or the card has to be sent to the LRA and back to write a new key and certificate on it. This means a high effort for the user or that the card can not be used during the transport to the LRA and back.

Siemens chose a 3-years certificate validity and most business units carried out the PKI rollout between 2000 and 2002. Therefore, a large number of certificates will expire within the next 2 years and an innovative solution providing simplified smart card and certificate life cycle management functions outside an LRA was required.

4 PKI Self Services

4.1 Functionality

Facing the post issuance problem Siemens implements PKI Self Services to allow a user to manage his Corporate ID Card and certificates from his workplace. A PKI user obtains the Corporate ID Card from an LRA being personally identified. Afterwards he/she can manage his/her Corporate ID Card and certificates securely via PKI Self Services based on an authentication with the existing authentication/signing certificate and "Secure Messaging".

The PKI Self Services provide the following web-based certificate life cycle and smart card management functions, see figure 2:

- Certificate management functions
  - X.509 authentication/signing, encryption certificates
    - Re-keying of expiring certificates on Corporate ID Card
    - Revocation
    - Initial enrolment of encryption certificates on Corporate ID Card
    - Recovery of encryption keys as soft-key via encrypted mail
  - PGP certificates (soft-key)
    - Initial enrolment, re-keying and recovery via encrypted mail
    - Invalidation
- Corporate ID Card administration

- Displaying smart card information (version, operating system, certificates)
- PIN changing and unblocking
- Migration from the current PKI to "PKI 2"
  - Update of smart card file structure and enrolment of new certificates

Since most users are not experienced with PKI processes and terminology these functions are provided via typical user scenarios guiding the user to the required functionality, e. g.:

- "My certificate is due to expire (I got an expiry notification)"
- "My keys are misused"
- "I want to change my PIN"

For experts these functions are also provided in an "Expert Mode" as generic PKI functions: New, Re-keying, Revocation, Recovery, Change PIN etc.

The PKI Self Services provide also problem support when e.g. a user lost the Corporate ID Card and has to receive a new one via an LRA or a Corporate ID Card is not properly functioning.

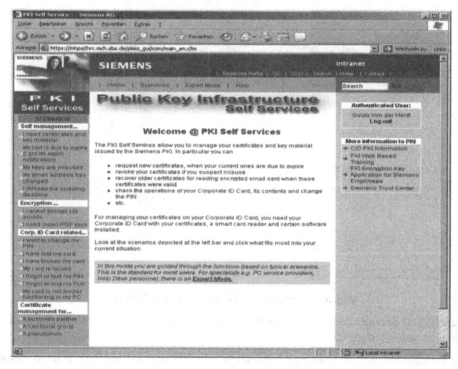

Fig. 2: PKI Self Services

4.2 Business Case

The PKI Self Services provide two main cost saving factors. The PKI Self Services reduce LRA service costs by avoiding certificate life cycle management in an LRA and they increase productivity since the users do not have to go to an LRA anymore. In addition costs for organizing local certificate management processes and user support by the local IT department are reduced.

The following simplified calculation considers only regular re-keying: Based on the assumptions

- 3 years certificate validity and 200.000 deployed Corporate ID Cards, i. e. 66.000 re-keying processes per year on average (different validity periods for encryption, authentication/signing and PGP certificates are not considered),
- costs of € 10 per managed re-keying in an LRA and
- time-savings of 30 minutes per user and re-keying process on average which is equivalent to € 25.

PKI Self Services already give cost savings for Siemens of € 2.3 mln per year.

5 Architecture and Security

The basic architecture of the PKI Self Services is outlined in Figure 3.

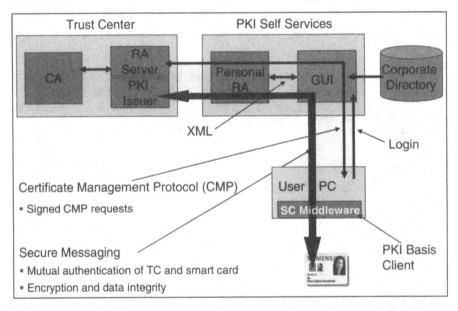

Fig. 3: PKI Self Services – Architecture and Security

The PKI Self Services consists of 2 main components, the Personal RA and the Siemens specific user web-interface (GUI).

The Personal RA acts as additional registration authority next to the LRAs. It interfaces with the RA Server in the Trust Center over CMP (Certificate Management Protocol) and provides generic certificate life cycle management functions. The RA server manages and validates the certificate management requests whereas the PKI Issuer ensures secure end-to-end communication between the Trust Center and the Corporate ID Card.

The Siemens specific GUI addresses the specific requirements of the company. It realizes:

- The implementation of the generic certificate life cycle management functions as user scenarios and expert mode as described
- The integration of the PKI Self Services as web-application in an Enterprise Portal

- Siemens look and feel
- Flexibility with respect to changes

The user interface communicates with the Personal RA based on XML structures. The Siemens Corporate Directory is the data source for all certificate management requests.

Personal RA and RA server are products of the Trust Center's CA (Certification Authority) software vendor. PKI Issuer, GUI and Corporate Directory are Siemens products.

The security of the PKI Self Services is implemented in two different layers:

The authentication of a user requesting a certificate management function takes place by signing the corresponding CMP request which is validated in the Trust Center by the RA server and a separate user login to the PKI Self Services web-application.

If keys or certificates are read from or written to the smart card a mutual authentication of smart card and Trust Center as well as confidentiality and integrity of the exchanged data are ensured by "Secure Messaging". The Secure Messaging protocol is part of the ISO 7816 standard. Secure Messaging takes place between the smart card and the PKI Issuer component in the Trust Center based on pre-shared symmetric keys. Thereby the encrypted data are transmitted over the CMP protocol and the smart card middleware.

Applications access the Corporate ID Card via the Microsoft-CAPI or PKCS#11 interface which are also provided by the smart card middleware.

References

[Glae98]   Glaeser, Martin: Strategy and Implementation of a PKI Rollout in an International Company, ISSE 1999.

[vdH01]   von der Heidt, Guido; Marhoefer, Michael; Oeser, Thomas: The Siemens PKI - Implementation and Evolution of a Large Scale Enterprise PKI, ISSE 2003.

Development of Secure Web Financial Services in Serbia

Mr Zoran Savić[1] · Dr Milan Marković[2,3]

[1]National Bank of Serbia, Information Security Department
Pop Lukina 7-9, 11000 Belgrade, Serbia and Montenegro
zsavic@nbjzop.co.yu

[2]NetSeT
Karadjordjeva 65, 11000 Belgrade, Serbia and Montenegro
[3]Mathematical Institute SANU
Kneza Mihaila 35, p.f. 367, 11001 Belgrade, Serbia and Montenegro
milan@netset.co.yu, mmarkov@beotel.yu

Abstract

Abstract Text – Recently, a boom of trusted electronic banking services has happened in Serbia. A lot of broker companies, and other legal persons (approximately more than 20000 from the begining of this year), use a trusted electronic financial services through Serbian commercial banks and National Bank of Serbia. All of them perform the remote electronic payment service through the web banking service secured with digital signature and envelope technology based on PKI digital certificate and asymmetrical keys stored on PKI smart cards. Digital certificates are issued mostly by banks themselves or throuh some of the outsourcing Certification Authority schemes. As an example of the secure electronic banking system, a trusted web financial portal which is now dominant technical solution in Serbia is described in this paper. The system provides the highest level of security and large functional and cryptographic customization capabilities.

1 Introduction

This paper is dedicated to the case study about development of the secure web financial services in Serbia that has been happened this year. These services are developed now mostly for electronic banking services of the companies/legal persons through their commercial banks, as well as for some independent services offered by the National bank of Serbia. These services are mostly based on web technology and include completely establishing of the PKI systems.

As an example of the secure electronic banking system, a trusted web financial portal which is now dominant technical solution in Serbia is described in this paper. The system is based on application level security mechanisms consisting of asymmetrical and symmetrical cryptographic algorithms and smart cards for digital signature and certificates storage. The system includes SSL protocol or the proprietary transport level security solutions based on http crypto proxy. Client security module is based on ActiveX control cryptographic engine for Windows based clients or Java cryptographic mechanisms for Unix/Linux based clients. Besides the many Serbian commercial banks, the similar trusted web security engine with

S. Paulus, N. Pohlmann, H. Reimer (Editors): Securing Electronic Business Processes, Vieweg (2004), 210-219

stronger crypto is implemented in Central Register and Depositary of Securities and Register of Solvency Information for legal entities operated by National Bank of Serbia.

The paper is organized as follows. The Serbian trusted web financial portal model is described in Chapter 2. Chapter 3 is dedicated to the secure web transaction system – a core crypto engine system that is the basis of the trusted web portal. Additional security level with securing financial databases based on cryptographic proxy gateways as application level proxy firewalls is described in Chapter 4. Successful case studies based on the considered web security model including electronic banking and registers operated by the National Bank of Serbia are elaborated in Chapter 5. Conclusions and future directions of Serbian financial e-business systems are given in Chapter 6.

2 Trusted Web Security Model

Recently, as the generally accepted model in Internet application development, three-tier or multi-tier applications are used. Moreover, new trends show that most of these applications are web-based applications [Oppl00]. In this sense, a typical three-tier web Internet application, see Fig. 2.1, consists of clients, web server and database server. In this model, client is always an Internet browser program and web server could be web server only or a combination of the web and application server.

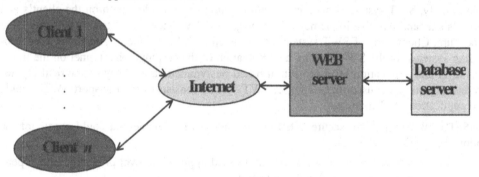

Figure 2.1: A simplified block diagram of the typical web Internet three-tier application architecture

Security mechanisms in this architecture consist of two segments:

- Security segment for communication security between client and web server,
- Security segment for communication and access protection between web/application server and database server.

Security part between client and server is realized by implementing security mechanisms on application and transport layers in the Secure Web Transaction (SWT) environment, described in the Chapter 3.

Security solution for communication security between web/application server and database server is realized by using cryptographic proxy gateways (CPG) as a proprietary application level security gateway firewall with two Ethernet interfaces. CPG should be used as the last defense in front of data sensitive financial database server. If the system uses both WEB and application servers, CPG should be placed between the application and database server. Modern security trends request the application of the proprietary firewalls that offer greater level of security, instead of standard commercial ones, for this purpose.

3 Secure Web Transactions (SWT) Systems

Secure WEB transaction system (SWT) is designed to cryptographically enhance any WEB server to browser communication by implementing originally developed cryptographic functions. SWT is a NetSeT's proprietary system which is, in the transport level part, similar to the standardized and widely used SSL protocol. However, SWT system has four main advantages compared to SSL protocol:

- SWT system includes data protection on the application level based on asymmetric cryptographic algorithms (e.g. RSA [RiSA78] with ≥1024 bits key length),

- SWT includes a proprietary server-browser authentication procedure, "stronger" than one applied in SSL, for establishing cryptographic tunneling,

- SWT includes originally developed symmetric cryptographic algorithms for data protection on transport level with encryption key length (≥256 bits) larger than the keys used in SSL protocol (40 or 128 bits key length). SWT system also offers three possible options for symmetric cryptographic algorithms: public algorithms (DES, 3DES, RC2, RC4, IDEA, AES), proprietary SCA-13 NetSeT's algorithm with very long non-linear pseudo-random noise sequence ($>>10^{100}$), and user's defined symmetric algorithm,

- SWT system is fully verifiable on the source code level.

Additionally, SWT system is associated with the smart card readers both on the client's and server's side and has also implemented the originally developed user "strong" authentication procedure. Client parts of SWT system are designed both for Windows and Linux-based operating systems. In the SWT system, a combination of the cryptographic tunnel on the transport level and application level protection based on symmetrical and asymmmetrical cryptographic algorithms is used. In this sense, SWT system consists of the transport SWT module and application SWT module.

NetSeT's SWT system for secure WEB communication is scalable and could consist of the following solution categories:

- A system based on the SWT smart card based application level protection and "open" (unsecured) transport level communication,

- A system based on the SWT smart card based application level protection and SSL security protocol on transport level based on digital certificates generated by NetSeT's Certification Authority system,

- A system based on the SWT application and transport level protection on the basis of smart cards completely provided by NetSeT – the complete SWT system.

3.1 Transport SWT Module

This module is based on proprietary cryptographic proxy components for both on the client and server side. By applying these components, a protected communication channel – cryptographic tunnel based on symmetrical cryptographic algorithm is established. This tunnel is established only if the proprietary bilateral strong authentication procedure between client and server is successfully realized. This challenge-response authentication procedure is cryptographically stronger than the one used in SSL protocol and it is based on symmetrical and asymmetrical cryptographic algorithms, two session keys and X.509 digital certificates for both client and server.

3.2 Application SWT Module

This module realizes fuctions for digital signature of the application data (providing authenticity, integrity protection and non-repudiation) and encryption (providing confidentiality protection). Namely, NetSeT's cryptographic application programming interface (API) is a set of the asymmetric and symmetric cryptographic functions which could be implemented in any of the user's applications, designed for Windows 98/NT/2000/XP and Linux platforms. This set consists of the following main functions:

- Digital signature (RSA algorithm with a key ≥1024 bits),
- Verification of the digital signature,
- Encryption (use of standard, NetSeT's proprietary or user's defined symmetric algorithms),
- Decryption,
- Communication with smart card reader with implemented authentication functionality,
- User's authentication.

These API functions are fully compatible with existing de facto standards – PKCS (Public Key Cryptographic Standards), such as: PKCS#1 [RSAL99], PKCS#7 [RSAL93] and PKCS#11 [RSAD99].

Besides transport level security module, application level security mechanisms enable "end-to-end" security between the client and application server that is mostly located in a domain behind the web server (it is often located directly on the database server). On the other side, SSL protocol provides security only between the client and web server, and all the data running over the internal network (behind the WEB server) is in clear. This module is realized as an ActiveX component or JAVA applet. These components are installed on the client side; they are integrated into the html pages and activated through client's Internet browser program.

Two working modes are possible, regarding the type of the application. Namely, it is possible to protect data in the interactive communication between client and server (on-line) or protection of data or files could be done in advance (prepared signed and encrypted files) through some off-line cryptographic procedure. Both on-line and off-line procedure use the same ActiveX (or JAVA applet), but in the different environment (on-line is used through Internet browser program and off-line is used through some specialized off-line cryptographic application).

The components of the SWT system are based on a modular structure, see Fig. 3.1, and both of them have application and transport SWT module. The main difference between the two SWT components is in the server and client's local application interface (SWAL – Secure Web Application Link) that has a purpose of integration of these components into the WEB application. SWAL module enables WEB applications the use of the set of cryptographic API functions, necessary for the application level protection.

In order to additionally improve the functionality and overall security of the server side of the SWT system, a PCI card-based crypotgraphic coprocessor solution, called NST2000 [MSON01], is to be implemented. The hardware security modules, realized as coprocessors, represent strong points of the modern security solutions for the computer networks. The existence of hardware security modules is ultimate for design of the computer network system with high performance and high level of the security. In that case, the encryption algorithms and the other security related functions (e.g. access control functions) are securely executed on the hardware element and sensitive data are never loaded on the user's computer memory. Without these modules, it would be not possible to achieve the trusted aplication concept with a full control of the system access and resistant to the Trojan Horse attacks [AbJo95]. It is proven that PC operating systems and other system software components have some security drawbacks, and this is especially critical for the software-only cryptographic tools.

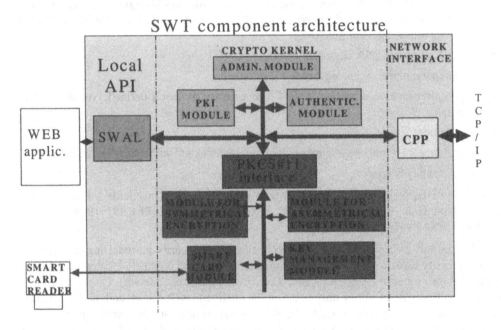

Figure 3.1: SWT system component modular architecture

3.3 WebWatch Module

WebWatch module, a simplified block diagram is given on Fig. 3.2, represents a mean for sophisticated integrity protection of WEB server sensitive data. Applying the NetSeT's WEB watch module, WEB server security applications are immune to attacks of "Trojan horse" type. Before the starting the NetSeT's designed security application, WEB watch module checks the application integrity and this could not be started if the integrity is not verified. NetSeT's WEB watch module is based on asymmetric and symmetric cryptographic techniques and smart cards technology. A function of automating recovering after the detected intrussion attempts could be included in this module.

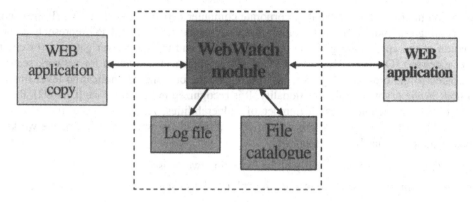

Figure 3.2: A simplified block-diagram of the WebWatch module

4 Cryptographic Proxy Gateways

Cryptographic proxy gateways (CPG) are security crypto-communication gateways for securing data in financial and corporate networks based on TCP/IP. CPGs offer combined data protection on the application and transport level.

Main features of CPGs are:

- Application level protection by using RSA algorithm with ≥ 1024 bit key and MD5 hashing algorthm. Possible options of including DH, DSA and SHA-1 algorithms.

- Transport level protection by using symmetric cryptographic algorithms. There are three possible implementation options for symmetric algorithms:

- Using of public "de facto" standardized algorithms, such as: DES, 3DES, RC2, RC4, IDEA, AES,

- Proprietary algorithm SCA-12 with encryption key ≥ 256 bits designed by NetSeT Co. with very long non-linear pseudo random sequence ($>> 10^{100}$),

- Users are free to implement their own symmetric cryptographic solution into the Net-SeT's CPG crypto environment.

- "Strong" authentication (five phases) procedure for establishing cryptographic tunnel between two CPG's based on digital certificates, asymmetric algorithms and session keys.

- "Strong" user authentication procedure based on smart cards.

- Additional data protection by using a proprietary protocol for communication between CPG's.

- CPG has two Ethernet cards, one in a domain of particular LAN segment and other in the omain of the secured networks (connected to the communication devices, e.g. routers).

CPG represents a type of application level proxy gateway and can be used for data protection in any of the financial and corporate computer networks based on TCP/IP for securing communication between remote LAN segments. The main characteristics of CPG are presented in the paper published at the ISSE 2001 Conference (Information security Solution Europe) [SaNM01]. CPG represents a type of application level proxy gateway and can be used for data protection in any of the financial or corporate computer networks based on TCP/IP protocols for securing communication between remote LAN segments. In fact, CPG represents a combination of the application gateway (or proxy server) and transport layer gateway (or circuit level gateway) [Oppl98]. This way, CPG is more sophisticated solution for network security compared to the ordinary IP packet filtering technique or standard application level firewall without strong cryptographic functionality. It is recognized in literature, see [Chap92], that IP packet filtering technique has a number of vulnerabilities. Additional protection could be achieved by establishing an original proprietary protocol for communication of the workstations inside particular LAN and its CPG.

The CPG operation consist globally of the following two phases:

- establishing the secure connection by aplying the strong authentication procedure,
- transmitting messages through established cryptographic tunnel.

Namely, each of the standardized message or commercial transaction, as well as a particular file, is digitally signed, encrypted and sent through cryptographic tunnel, pre-established between two CPGs. The cryptographic tunnel is established by using the abovementioned original strong authentication procedure. Secure message interchanging module of CPG is particularly suitable to exchange message in an automated, interactive way, and provides access to mission and time-critical applications, such as real-time gross setlement systems (RTGS). On the other hand, secure file interchanging module is interactive communication service supporting the exchange of files between parties, and it is particularly suitable for the exchange of large volumes of data. These modules are conceptually similar to S.W.I.F.T InterAct and FileAct services, respectively.

Also, CPGs could be used for secure separating of the network segments. Namely, based on the fact that CPGs have two network interface cards (dual-homed firewall), they could be used for secure separation of the internal network parts from the public parts, see Fig. 4.1.

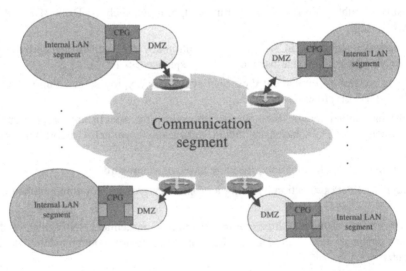

Figure 4.1: CPG application for secure separating the internal LAN segments from the DMZ network parts (DMZ – Demilitarized Zone) and public communication segment

In the trusted WEB security model, described in the Chapter 2, CPG is used for protection of the second model segment – namely, for communication protection between the WEB/application server and database server. In this configuration, a simplified block-diagram is given on Fig. 4.2, it is necessary to implement a special cryptographic component on the WEB/application server, named CPG gateway, which is used for establishing secure communication (strong user authentication and cryptographic tunnel) between WEB/application server and databases server. In this way, all communication between WEB/application server and database server is encrypted and only servers with CPG gateway could have access to the database server.

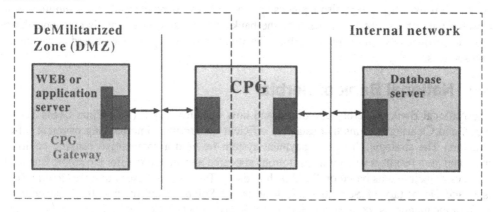

Figure 4.2: Security protection between WEB/application server and database server.

5 Case Studies – Financial Web Implementations

Starting from last year we have been faced with a number of secure financial web services established in Serbia. Almost all of them feature smart cards, digital certificates and digital signature technology. Most of them use the trusted WEB security model described in this paper. Particularly, security services offered by commercial banks, as well as by the National bank of Serbia has been applied for Serbian legal persons, mostly in the electronic payment applications.

5.1 Commercial Banks

The reason for such a fast development of security electronic banking services for Serbian legal persons, offered by the commercial banks, has been a structural change in payment system that happened last year. Instead of centralized Payment Bureau that was responsible for all payments in a country during last 40 years, starting from this year, Serbian banks are found themselves in position that they are responsible for payment transactions for their clients, both legal and physical persons. As a response to the new payment environment, the number of local banks started to offer Web based electronic payment services to their clients. These services have been assumed as a competitive advantage they use to attract the new customers. Now, practically all of the Serbian commercial banks that offer the secure web-based electronic banking service implement them on the basis of the PKI smart cards for their legal persons (legal persons that have account in this bank). In this way, legal person receives the e-banking packet from the bank consisting of the CD with client software (both application and security part), smart card reader and personalized smart card with X.509 digital certificate and asymmetrical private key. With this smart card and the software, legal persons are enabled to make financial transactions using Internet browser program and web site of the bank with a full set of secure functionalities (asymmetrical and symmetrical cryptographic algorithms, single-sign-on based on smart cards, etc.). Most of the Serbian commercial banks use secure web services based on the trusted web security solution, described in this paper. Also, there are several certification authority schemes (in-house and out-source) that banks use for issuing the digital certificates for their users. Besides, several banks joined their efforts and built Electronic Payment Bureau companies – Service centers. They act as a service provider to interconnect banks and their clients using open networks such as Internet. Usually, banks outsource complete web communication and legal persons connect directly to the service centers, not to the bank. The system also includes special security adapters to protect communication between the Service center and each of the banks. These companies are also responsible to provide adequate security support such as Certification authority and smart card personalization services.

5.2 National Bank of Serbia

The National Bank of Serbia introduced and now operates RTGS (Real Time Gross Settlement) and Clearing systems that establish efficient countrywide interbanking payment infrastructure. The strategic change in payment system fostered a competitive banking environment and, as a result, several new institutions appeared and started to offer electronic financial services to their clients based on WEB technologies. The most representative are Central Register and Depositary of Securities and Register of Solvency Information for legal entities. Both of the mentioned registers use the secure WEB services based on PKI smart cards for establishing secure communication channels between the users and the system. Also, both of the registers use the trusted web security model described in this paper. For the systems that are part of the National Bank of Serbia, the Information Security Department is responsible for overall PKI support. This is a special part of the National Bank of Serbia that provides Certification Authority service, key management and smart card personalization and management.

6 Conclusion

In this paper, we give the brief description of a trusted web financial portal for secure electronic banking system, which is now dominant technical solution in Serbia. The system is based on application level security mechanisms consisting of asymmetrical and symmetrical cryptographic algorithms and smart cards for digital signature and certificates storage. The system includes SSL protocol or the proprietary based http crypto proxy protocol in order to implement transport level security functions. Client security module is based on ActiveX control cryptographic mechanisms for Windows based clients or Java cryptographic mechanisms for Unix/Linux based clients. Besides the many Serbian commercial banks, the similar trusted web security engine with stronger crypto is implemented in Central Register and Depositary of Securities and Register of Solvency Information for legal entities operated by National Bank of Serbia. A several other electronic business systems are in preparation and most of them are also based on the trusted web security portal principles based on smart cards for users. These systems includes e-government applications based on citizens' smart ID cards, e-healthcare applications based on citizens' patient cards and healthcare professionals' PKI smart cards, etc.

References

[Oppl00]   Oppliger, R.: Security Technologies for the World Wide Web, Artech House, ISBN 1-58053-045-1, 2000.

[RiSA78]   Rivest, R., Shamir, A., Adleman, L.: A Method for Obtaining Digital Signatures and Public-Key Cryptosystems, Commun. of the ACM, Vol. 21, No. 2, pp. 120-126, Feb. 1978.

[RSAL99]   RSA Laboratories, PKCS#1: RSA Encryption Standard, Version 2, 1999.

[RSAL93]   RSA Laboratories, PKCS#7: Cryptographic Message Syntax Standard, Version 1.5, November 1993.

[RSAD99]   RSA Laboratories, PKCS#11: Cryptographic Token Interface Standard, Version 2.10, December 1999.

[MSON01]   Marković, M., Savić, Z., Obrenović, Ž., Nikolić, A.: A PC Cryptographic Co-processor Based on TI Signal Processor and Smart Card System, Communications and Multimedia Security Issues of the New Century, R. Steinmetz, J. Dittman, M. Steinebach, Eds., Kluwer Academic Publishers, 2001, pp. 383-393.

[AbJo95]   Abrams, M.D., Joyce, M.V.: Trusted system concepts, Computers and Security, VOL. 14, No. 1, Elsevier Science Ltd., 1995.

[SaNM01]   Savić, Z., Nikolić, A., Marković, M.: Cryptographic Proxy Gateways in Securing TCP/IP Computer Networks, in Proc. of Information Security Solution Europe Conference, ISSE 2001, London, September 26-28, 2001.

[Oppl98]   Oppliger, R.: Internet and Intranet Security, Artech House, ISBN 0-89006-829, 1998.

[Chap92]   Chapman, D.B.: Network Insecurity Through IP Packet Filtering. Proc. of USENIX III, Sept. 1992.

A Pragmatic Vulnerability Management Approach

Thomas Obert, CISSP

Information Security Manager
SAP AG
thomas.obert@sap.com

Abstract

An increasing number of reported software vulnerabilities concerning security issues leads to the need for a systematic approach. This paper enumerates and explains the success factors for vulnerability management of security weaknesses. Further it provides an introduction to a pragmatic approach and the main constraints that must be considered. An outlook then closes the article.

1 What is Vulnerability?

Vulnerability exists, when quality requirements of a good have not been met 100%. In generally, vulnerability is named as one when the time of detection is later then the general release date. Under this consideration warranty issues rises and a vendor or producer of a good is asked to provide a solution to circumvent or remove the vulnerability in a way, that the main function of the good is not affected. This is a substantial right of the consumer.

In a mainly IT controlled environment, supported by operational data centres, vulnerabilities can occur both on hardware and software components. Hardware vulnerabilities lead normally directly to reduced functionality or to failure. Operators will then identify this kind of weaknesses immediately. Calling the pre-defined service staff then is the one and only solution for that. In most cases the service staff then changes the defect hardware and installs new one, e.g. mainboards, processors, hard disks, etc. And in general these costs are covered in a general maintenance contract the data centre owner has signed together with the hardware vendor or reseller. The precautions to cover these issues are proper contracts, reliable hardware vendors or resellers, on-site operators and a general hardware monitoring. The process of identifying hardware problems is quite easy: a central computer-monitoring console raises an alert. A first check done by the onsite-operator will uncover in a short time, if the alert is software or hardware based. The next step is then to call the service staff and wait until the central monitor tool removes the alert. Quite simple and does not require sophisticated processes or tools.

Much more difficult is the management of vulnerabilities in software. First, today's software is getting more and more complex. It is a rule of thumb, that the complexity of software at least linearly increases number of vulnerabilities in a software product. The software developers are interested in bug-free solutions. After general release of a software product the developers would like to focus on innovation and improvement. Fact is, that more complex software requires strong efforts in so called software maintenance. In hard times, each company is looking for cost saving opportunities. The emerging costs of maintaining vulnerable software solutions are overwhelming. Within a software solution life cycle, vulnerabilities can occur in many stages. The earlier a vulnerability is built in and the later a vulnerability will be identified, the higher the costs to close the vulnerability are. Investigations have shown, that an uncovered weakness within the design stage is about 10 times more costly to remove against a weakness within the implementation phase. Why is it like that?

A example from real world will make this clearer: Think what would have happened, if Henry Ford would have decided to build cars with 3 wheels only (e.g. to reduce the costs and so the price of a car). He would then decide to produce 1.000 of these cars before selling it to consumers. The general functionality tests all ended with a green status, and, in these early years of automobile manufacturing, security was not a big issue (software manufacturing seems to be in the same stage). So nobody would have found out, that this car might overturn under special circumstances. After releasing the car, and all 1.000 pieces have been sold, the first accidents happen because of instability when driving in curves while climbing a hill. This is a kind of warranty issue, because nobody has told the customers, that climbing a hill with a car may be dangerous. So the Henry would have performed an investigation and found out, that a car with four wheels is much more stable than a car with 3 wheels. But, there is no chance to install a fourth wheel on each released car. In the same way it is not possible to re-implement a software solution that's based on millions of lines of source code. A In general, the solution provider (in our case Henry) designs a workaround, e.g. two pieces of carrying wheels that have to be installed on the right and left rear side. Sure, the car will vary unlikely overturn in future. But the car now looks very strange. And the maximum velocity is now reduced for about 20 %. A workaround like this is typical for design flaws.

The workarounds offered by software vendors to reduce the impacts of design flaws are in best cases complicated and expensive. Good luck, popular and successful software, which is also used in critical business scenarios have been proved many times in advance, so that the existence of design flaws can be excluded. Or the existing workarounds are in a way that the complexity of implementation and operation does not increase significantly.

In the world of automobiles, it may be happened, that some rear wheels have been broken while driving backwards. An investigation of these claims leaded to the conclusion, that some of the screws used did not fulfil the required material stability. Well, the solution is easy, but cost consuming. Automobile vendors generally try to contact all their customers and ask them to visit a garage near to them so that the insufficient screws can be changed. If they would act like software vendors, they would send packets including the screws to all customers and ask them to exchange by themselves. Of course, a manual would be included and may be a phone number, if problems would rise. And if a customer would then really call this service number, the hotline staff would help the customer to identify the nearest garage according customers' home.

Very special vulnerabilities do not only lead to malfunction, but would also uncover threats to life. If the screws would also break while drive on a motor way with about 80 miles per hour, many people would be injured dangerously or die. This fact is unacceptable. Automobile vendors generally ask the customer strongly to visit the nearest garage cost-free to let the service staff resolve this perilous vulnerability. What do software vendors do? First, perilous vulnerabilities are very seldom in daily business. But the sustainable interruption of business critical processes could lead to bankruptcy. In case of so-called "high risk" of "critical" software vulnerabilities, the costumer will receive not only one mail and a link to a proper patch that should be installed. No, she receives an additional mail focusing on the urgency and importance of this issue. But still the consumer has to act the resolve the vulnerability. Sure, the direct comparison of real world and virtual world is not valid in any case, but it helps to identify areas of improvement.

Back in a virtual world, the next question to clarify is: What is security vulnerability? Easy to answer: A vulnerability that can lead to a break of confidentiality (i.e. unauthorized access), integrity (i.e. unauthorized and unrecognised modification) and availability (e.g. non-existence of backups). Breaching software using well-know security vulnerabilities is not longer a sophisticated method governed only by very skilled hackers. Easy-to-use virus- or hacking-toolkits are available for download and can be exhausted (?) by school kids (so called script kiddies). Scary, isn't it? You invest millions in software and maintenance to improve your business and safeguard business critical processes and some kids playing around create millions of loss to you within minutes or hours. Alone this fact increases the risk, especially the probability that security vulnerability is used to break your security policy.

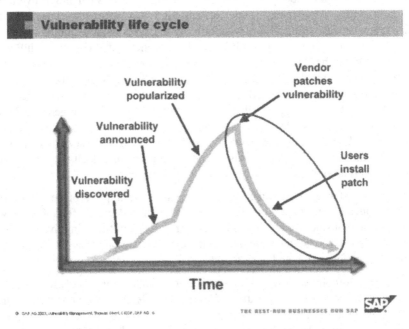

Fig. 1: Vulnerability life cycle and the focus area of this article

Hold on a moment: Vulnerabilities exist and there is no way to avoid vulnerabilities at all. Workarounds and solutions to manage vulnerabilities inn general are available. Not address-ing existing vulnerabilities endanger your daily business. Security vulnerabilities especially protect your assets. Exploiting existing security vulnerabilities is easy and often performed by so called script kiddies. There is now way out! A special security vulnerability management approach is required. In times of decreasing IT budgets, a pragmatic approach is necessary to solve this issue on a permanent basis.

2 Success Factors

What are the key factors of a successful, pragmatic vulnerability management approach?

1. **Time-to-system**
   Derived from the well-known principle to reduce time-to-market when designing new products, the time-to-system describes the time between general notice about a new (se-curity) vulnerability and the implementation. The time-to-system depends on available

staff, number of systems affected, level of automation, and existence of a solution, e.g. a patch.

2. **Solution**

   A vulnerability can be uncovered and disclosed to the customers (and possible intruders) before a proper solution is available. Ongoing disclosure discussions are aimed to increase to pressure to software vendors to reduce the time-to-system by immediately investigate the problem and provide a solution, e.g. a patch. The most respected disclosure procedure is to give the software vendor a pre-defined time, e.g. 45 days to investigate the problem and provide a solution to all customers before releasing details about the vulnerability. In the hacker community non-disclosed vulnerabilities are very popular. This fact leads to an increasing risk to be attacked by a very skilled hacker and reduces the risk of automated viruses and worms and script kiddies.

3. **Functionality**

   The main objective of a security patch is to reduce the risk of exploitation. But too often it happens, that the implementation of a security patch leads to malfunction within the software. Too bad, because the main tasks of the software are subject of interruption, self-explaining that this is unplanned.

4. **Reliability**

   Maybe the system is running well after a security patch has been implemented. But, how can I be sure, that the vulnerability does not exist any longer? Well, the installation popup told me that the patch has been installed successfully. Is this sufficient? Certainly not! Like testing functionality after a change, security weaknesses need to be checked also.

A pragmatic approach to reduce risks based on software vulnerabilities addresses all key factors described above.

3 What is a Pragmatic Approach?

Pragmatic in general is not sophisticated and uses existing resources to solve a "new" problem. The problem of implementing patches is not new and normally part of a well-defined change management process within IT departments. But all the issues described above have proven, that security vulnerabilities are a bit different to functional patches and so require special treatment. The pragmatic approach is based on existing change management procedures and rules and enlarges the change steps to address the key factors time-to-system, solution, functionality and reliability.

The change management process for security vulnerabilities can be divided in 5 phases:

1. *Information collection and evaluation*

   Security vulnerability notices can be retrieved via several security related mailing lists, e.g. BugTraq or by vendor mailing lists. Due to the general respect of non-disclosure agreements, security vulnerabilities sent via these mailing lists already provide a solution normally based on an installable patch provided by the software vendor. In special cases, workarounds are necessary for a first protection approach, e.g. to block special ports on your firewall.

   One important question is about reliability of the notice. Is this notice real? Or is it a fake to make me installing a Trojan horse? The main software vendors use digital signatures based on PGP to achieve trust in published advisories.

Further, the receiving party has to evaluate, how critical the vulnerability is for his environment. This depends on the architecture, infrastructure and implementation details. The more these factors match the description of the vendors' advisory, the nearer the vendor provides your risk.

Larger companies have already installed Computer Emergency Response Teams who focus on the preventive task to gather information from public lists, evaluate the content, provide a company specific risk assessment and publish a company-oriented security advisory to internal administrators with an recommendation, what to do. At this point, the change management processes of the IT department starts, with special handling according to the security needs.

2. **Decision**

The first important step within the IT change management process is to make a decision about the information received. An individual evaluation of the general risk assessment focusing on risks for the whole company have now to be done for the IT area of each responsibility, e.g. network, different operating systems, different business systems etc.

The decision is based on:

a. Should we implement the patch at all or is it easier / sufficient to implement a workaround?

b. What's the risk for my environment (e.g. an MS Internet Explorer security patch may not be of special risk for the networking team)?

c. How quick do we have to implement to patch?

d. Do we have to violate existing service level agreements with our customer, especially for unforeseeable additional downtimes?

e. Who is responsible for?

f. How do we check success?

All these questions are general change management practice.

3. **Testing and Preparation**

After the decision to implement that patch has been taken, the preparation period follows. Within this area, some test and pilot installations have to be performed. After successful tests the mass rollout can be prepared. In this phase, generally change management checks, if the functionality is still guaranteed. In security cases, additionally the success of the patch implementation must be checked. This can be done by using a vulnerability scanner / checker. Such tools try to exploit the well-known vulnerability like a hacker / virus / worm would do. The results of a successful preparation phase leads immediately to the mass rollout.

4. **Implementation**

For mass installation a lot of tools are available either by vendors, e.g. MS Software Update Service (SUS) or specialized software companies providing patch management tools, e.g. UpdateExpert from ST. Bernhard Software.

After packaging the security patch to a format support by the patch management tool used, may be some scripting will be added for actions to take in advance or after the patch has been installed, e.g. reboot.

It is very helpful, if security patch implementation tools provide a central status monitoring, how many patches have successfully been installed.

5. *Success checks*
   Though the installation monitors may show you an implementation rate of 100 % (means all servers have been patched), a check by a vulnerability scanner is highly recommended. In some cases, the software or operating system tells you about successful installation of the patch, but under special circumstances the vulnerability still exists. If you are not able to identify these vulnerabilities all the efforts taken so far are for nothing.

4 Summary, Conclusion and Outlook

Mastering this 5-step process for a successful vulnerability management is vital in a software steered world with increasing complexity. Today, this seems the only way to get one step in front of the information attackers. But it's time consuming and cost intensive. Both aspects do not amuse CFOs. In times, where ROI and TCO are the main factors a CIO is controlled by an CFO, software vendors will have to think about the security patch strategy they offer to their customers. The most important approach software vendors must follow in future is to avoid (security) vulnerabilities already in all phases during software development life cycle. This requires strong quality management processes, which attend the whole solution development process. Sure, this increases the time-to-market of new products. But successful software of the future needs to prove a certain level of security to win in strong markets. And this level is far higher than offered by most leading software vendors today. The latest example is the Asian approach to develop an open source based alternative to Microsoft software.

Markus Korschen
Efficient SAP® R/3®-Data Archiving
How to Handle Large Data Volumes
2002. x, 156 pp. with 15 figs. Hardc. € 49,90   ISBN 3-528-05799-8

Contents: Introduction - Important Archiving Terminology (Concept, Procedure and Necessity of Data Archiving) - Data Archiving and Business Processes in SAP R/3 - Database Analysis - Customizing-Settings for SAP R/3-Data Archiving - Practical Archiving Management - Selection-Criteria for Archive Systems

This book is a practical guide for managing archiving projects with SAP R/3 efficiently. Hereby it is addressing both R/3 consultants, system administrators and key-users. Detailed solutions for optimal archiving strategies as well as the manual for a comprehensive database analysis are provided in this book. But thereby not only the technical side, but also the business side of data archiving is taken into account. Thus the reader will be able to implement an archiving project.

vieweg

Abraham-Lincoln-Straße 46
65189 Wiesbaden
Fax 0611.7878-400
www.vieweg.de

Prices and other details are subject to change
without notice. Please order at your bookstore.